Rooftop Societies: The Middle East Paradox

Fereydoon Rahmani, Ph.D

de Sitter Publications

Library and Archives Canada Cataloguing in Publication

Rahmani, Fereydoon
　　Rooftop Societies: The Middle East Paradox

ISBN 978-1-897160-95-4

Copyright © 2020 Fereydoon Rahmani

All rights are reserved. No part of this publication may be reproduced, translated, stored in a retrieval system or transmitted in any form or by any means, electronic, mechanical, photocopying, recording or otherwise, without prior written permission from the publisher.

de Sitter Publications
111 Bell Dr., Whitby, ON,
L1N 2T1, Canada

deSitterPublications.com
289-987-0656

Contents

FOREWORD

INTRODUCTION   1

CHAPTER 1: The Middle East: A Rooftop Society   11
  I. Rooftop Societies: Paradoxical Components   11
  II. A "Rooftop Revolution"   16
  III. Roots of the Middle Eastern
     Socio-political Paradoxes   21
  IV. State and Society Antagonism   25
  V. Modernity Versus Tradition: Modernism Collapsed
     in Religion, Tradition and Militarism   33
  VI. Intellectuals' Antagonistic Stances on Modernity   40
  VII. The Dilemma of Double Standards and
     Dualistic Journalism   46

CHAPTER 2: The Middle Eastern Militarism   59
  I. The Middle East Perpetual Longing Towards
     Militarization   59
  II. Militarism and Regimes' Legitimacy and
     Democratization Process   67

CHAPTER 3: The Middle Eastern Genocide   73
  I. Genocide: A Multilayer Concept   73
  II. Devastating Centuries of Ethno-religious
     Massacre and Genocide   83
  III. Political Discrimination and Violence Suppression   88

CHAPTER 4: Sharia Law, Human Rights & Democracy   95
  I. Sharia Law and Human Rights   95
  II. Compatibility of Islam and Democracy   131
  III. Human Rights Violation Against Indigenous
     Minorities: Kurds   137

CHAPTER 5: Rudiments of Quality of Life Research
  for the Middle East & Sensitive Communities   153
  I. Introduction   153
  II. Definitions, Conceptualization and Theories of
    Social Indicators of Quality of Life   154

III. Historical Background of Social
   Indicators Movement   157
IV. Doxography and Philosophical Origins of Quality
   of Life Studies   160
V. Modern Developments and Approaches in
   Quality of Life Research   162
VI. Limitations of Quality of Life Research in
   the Middle East and Sensitive Societies   170
VII. Suggestions for Implementing QOL Research
   in the Middle East and Developing Societies   174
VIII. Conclusion   177

LITERATURE   181

Acknowledgement

I would like to dedicate this book to the members of my family, who suffered or perished by atrocities of both brutal regimes of Ayatollahs and Saddam Hussein; including my oldest brother Nader who lost his life. To the people of the Middle East, including my siblings and their children, who have been struggling for centuries to inaugurate human rights and a dignified life. To my wife Parisa, and my both sons Midya and Puya, who carried the burdens and the hardship of my absence due to my extended academic work in the Middle East.

Foreword

"Rooftop societies" is a ground-breaking investigation into Middle Eastern communities and socio-political constructs of the region. The theories and ideas behind "Rooftop societies" are meant for resistance and paint a picture of perpetual antagonism and dualism within these societies. Deep rifts between the state and society, the elites and regular citizens, and modernist forces and religious traditionalism are still vehemently manifested in the socio-political and cultural fibers of the region. Here, Dr. Rahmani understands the rooftop to be a shared cultural and physical space in which many socio-political and religious events take place. The people, state, and diverse groups within society have been using this space for centuries either to hide their furtive measures or resist oppression and practice their identities. Dr. Rahmani takes the Middle East's long and abundant history of conquest and invasion and situates it within despotic systems of political tyranny and extensive patriarchal structures in order to understand the key sources of today's paradoxical contexts.

While rulers in the Middle East benefit from using the flat rooftops to further limit citizens' fundamental rights, citizens conversely utilize such structures for resistance, the reinforcement of their identities, the preservation of their rights, and escaping the sad experiences of authorities' broken promises and forgotten assurances. In addition to state apparatuses, many fundamentalist terrorist groups have also become greatly interested in using such arenas for showcasing their cruelty and inflicting fear and destruction on the populace.

The author calls the Iranian revolution a "Rooftop Revolution," as protesters and Ayatollah Khomeini's followers in major cities had initially started with playing recorded speeches of anti-government elites above public buildings' or mosques' rooftops to invite people to take to the streets in protest. The book outlines some of the historical reasons for and instances of undying resentment between the state and the public, as well as the infidelity and hypocrisy that have become defining characteristics of many Middle Eastern elites, political leaders, and intellectuals. Specifically, this book takes note of incoherent and opportunistic attempts by Iranian and Middle Eastern leftist intellectuals to marry Marxist ideology with Islamic principles and guidelines. The role of the King, Shah, Sheikh, and Sultan as a universal and omnipresent power of God on earth has always exacerbated the widening rift between the state and diverse layers of society. As such, this book devotes special attention to the role of the inner circle of the court as a furtive apparatus, which has always been a major determining factor in the fates of Middle Eastern nations.

Dr. Rahmani pays special attention to the characteristics of Middle Eastern societies that have brought (and continue to keep) the entire region into hostile cycles of violence, genocide, forced migration, displacement, and social exclusion. The countries' immense desire for further militarisation and ongoing arms races has especially harmed the regions' Indigenous and ethnoreligious minorities. In addition, a special chapter discusses the issues of Human Rights, democracy, Islam and Sharia regulations, and how Islamic countries diverge in respect to their distinctive definitions of Sharia law. Rahmani explains how liberalistic interpretations of Islamic traditions remain the most appropriate avenue through which Muslim communities can benefit from modern democracy and human rights principles.

In the book's final chapter, Dr. Rahmani proposes an experimental model for Quality of Life research, which has evaluated indicators of well-being and quality of life within war-torn societies and the Middle East for over two decades. He sees quality of life as the irrefutable foundation for people's human rights. Furthermore, the preservation of human rights is fundamental to people's dignity, as while people are unable to sustain an acceptable quality of life, any discussion of their human rights will prove futile. Human rights violations not only deprive people of their fundamental freedoms, but also prevent them from reaching acceptable levels of satisfaction and happiness throughout all aspects of their lives.

Almas Heshmati
Professor of Economics
Jönköping International Business School (JIBS)
Jönköping University, Sweden
2019

Introduction

The Middle East of today endures tumultuous events of perpetual change, with minimal discernible progress. The scope and speed of the region's transformations are immense, but the environmental and human costs are cataclysmic, and the citizens' gains are marginal. Both human rights and quality of life are fundamental indicators of human dignity and are completely disregarded by many political authorities and elites across the Middle East. Oppression and subjugation along with traditional as well as newer forms of enslavement, militarism, state sponsored terrorism, and genocide or near genocidal conducts are still prevalent here more than anywhere else on the planet. As has been the case for millennia, the state owns almost everything, and dictates the outcome of national decisions. Quite often, links between the situations faced by modern states and their historical counterparts are too complex and intricate to readily understand. Nevertheless, the region's history and the political structure play an immense role in the daily lives of Middle Eastern communities and shape their sociocultural postures, attitude, and worldview.

Regardless of whether political regimes are overthrown by a Marxist or quasi-Marxist revolutionary mode, or by a revolving door of military coupes, fear, coercion, tyranny, injustice, exclusion and corruption continue as permanent and ongoing factors in daily life. At time, it almost seems as if the people of the Middle East are doomed to having the sword of Damocles hung over their heads. Each time one empire falls, they somehow find themselves reincarnated once more into an even more sophisticated and well-equipped regime of brutalism. The Young Turks reign of fear within the Ottoman dynasty was succeeded by new Militarist regimes, and later on by Erdogan's new Sultanism; Vicious Shiite Safavids were replaced by Velayat-e faghih despotism, while the Sunni Umayyad Caliphate revived itself within the Saudi fundamentalist regime of Wahhabism. Russian Tsarism has also returned as Putin's megalomaniacal interventionism, while British imperialism has been replaced by American hegemonic politics. While centuries have passed, it almost looks as if everything has remained intact. The masses and minorities in the Middle East are still greatly deprived of their rights, privileges, and resources, while most opportunities are determined by ruling powers' provisions. Tensions between the predominantly Sunni Saudi state and the predominantly Shi'a Muslim Islamic Republic of Iran have flared extremely over the past few decades, while disputes and proxy wars continue to dominate the entire region.

    The masses and the state in the Middle East are growing further and further apart from each other, and religion, ethnicity, and sectarian politics have played a hideous role. Franz Fanon (1925-1961) saw Middle Eastern countries' national cultures as at the mercy of colonial domination and interrogation, which sought to systematically destroy them or condemn them to clandestinity (F. Fanon, 2004, p. 171). Two centuries of intense colonial influence in the Middle East should not be mistaken for being unconnected to earlier historical conquests and unremitting raids, which had overburdened the entire region and its inhabitants. At the Frankfurt School of Social Science, Max Horkheimer criticized bourgeois societies for being torn apart by social injustices, political and economic contradictions, and ideological paradoxes. Such account can easily be extended to Middle Eastern societies as well it seems where religious and political despotism along with perpetual systems of absolute obedience, fear, self-censorship, and an exhausting history of invasion-evasion is widespread. This has been a major source of uncertainty and permanent fear within the public, which has contributed to a state of distrust and duplicity.

    For millennia, the Middle Eastern masses have felt detached from their political power apparatus and have often considered their sovereign a tyrant who views his subjects as a provisionary source for his authoritarian system. Therefore a cycle of lies, double standards, and *Taqiyah* (religious dissimulation) have become part of daily life and embedded within greater culture. In his famous work on sociological analysis of the Iraqi people, the secularist Iraqi sociologist Ali al-Wardi (1913-1995) describes the difficulties faced by Iraqis in adapting to their environment and bridging the emerging gap between their historically tribal-nomadic values and rural-urban living conditions. Here, he labels the Iraqis as having a dualistic and split personality and demonstrates how psychological and social pressures have lead Iraqis toward personality conflicts. For example, while an Iraqi man values being able freely choose his own wife and, like westerners, would enjoy meeting with his female partner or exchange love letters, he would never approve of his sister having a similar relationship.

With one of the longest histories of civilization, the Middle East is still a space rife with permanent antagonism between the state and society, as the "unaccountability of the state and un-governability of the society" have enjoyed a precarious marriage for millennia. Historically, the sovereign and his court's inner circle tended to endorse or sanction major national affairs without their formal ceremonial executive or legislative organs even being approached for advice.

Researchers and academics have labelled the Middle Eastern societies differently: "Third world" or "developing countries"; "Short-term societies" compared to western "long-term societies" (Catouzian, 2004); "Sectarian society" or "dual economies" (Stiglitz, 2003), "Khalijee Capitalism" (Hanieh, 2010)*, "patrimonial state", or "unstable oil regimes". Even Marxist theories of Asiatic modes of production warrant special designations within Asian societies in general and the Middle East specifically, which have been "held in thrall by a despotic ruling clique". A century after Marx voiced skeptical views toward Asian regimes, Karl August Wittfogel in his monumental work referred to oriental *societies* rather than "oriental despotism," which instead accentuates a bureaucratic system of irrigation and water control. In this, Wittfogel coined the term "hydraulic empire" for such political system. In an ideological amalgam of pan-Arabic nationalism and Marxist-Leninist concepts, Anouar Abdel-Malek (1962) labels post-WWII Egyptian society a "société militaire" whereby a new middle class has viciously seized political power.

The present writing calls the Middle East a "Rooftop Society" where people throughout history have been forced to live a paradoxical life where their true identities remain hidden out of fear, and they struggle to resist repressive regimes, injustice, exclusion, and human rights abuses. As both a spatial and physical structure, the Middle Eastern flat-roof architectural design has been of different benefits to citizens and state authorities alike. The state and its agents have used and still use these arenas to safeguard their political power, employ their secret service, and spy on their citizens. Indeed, most Middle Eastern despotic systems have used such spaces to shoot anti-government protesters and kill their own young demonstrators, who do not have any other mechanisms by which to convey frustration or dissent. Additionally, fundamentalist organizations like ISIS and Al Qaida in Iraq, Syria, and Yemen have used the rooftop to showcase their brutality by executing their dissidents, non-Muslim community members, or members of LGBTQ communities. On the other hand, regular civilians, ethnic and religious groups, and members of younger generations have been using the rooftops as sanctuaries, where they can flee (or at least seek temporary relief) from state-led atrocities and oppression. In notable examples, such rooftops have been regularly used for mounting banned satellite dishes, celebrating outlawed socio-cultural, religious, and ceremonial, activities, or even for leisure and recreation.

This paradox within the Middle Eastern societies has become part of the daily culture and is broadly spread over society, its institutions, and intellectual fragments. Numerous authors, academics, and intellectuals inconsistently and opportunistically play with people's conscience and manipulate their consciousnesses. From awkwardly and unprofessionally mixing religious creeds—such as Islamic traditions with Marxist-Leninist ideologies—to becoming the agitators or instigators of brutal systems and corrupt media outlets, those who have access to knowledge and power are responsible for paradoxical stances easily recognizable within the Middle East. While benefiting from western education, Jalal Al-e Ahmad (1923-69) the Iranian leftist intellectual, Sayed Qotb (1906-1966) the Egyptian educator and author, Sayyid Jamal al-Din al-Afghani (1838-1897) the Afghan-Iranian reformist and political activist, and many others have vehemently campaigned against western culture and lifestyles while inviting people to return to fundamental traditional Islamic ideologies. Similarly, while trying to distance himself from western cultural elements in work "Westoxification" (*gharbzadehgi*), Al-e Ahmad sees Shiite-Islamic characteristics as important and inseparable elements of the Iranian cultural identity. He never hid his frustration toward the pre-revolutionary Iranian government, which had facilitated modern western education and ways of life, as well as increased distance from Islamic Shiite traditions. In addition, though educated at western universities, The Malaysian Islamic scholar Syed Muhammad Naquib al-Attas, fervently called for "de-westernization of knowledge" or "Islamization of knowledge" while failing to make any connections with the real world. Personally, I remember when al-Attas was invited to the Faculty of Social Sciences at the University of Tehran in 1980s, where he preached emancipation to the masses at the same time that Iranian Ayatollahs were executing 20,000 political prisoners. Importantly, Al-Attas' concern was not the emancipation of the Iranian political prisoners, but rather how to hold the Palestinian leader Yasser Arafat out of peace negotiations with Israel.

Following the Second World War, the most horrific political systems in the 20th century Middle East have been supported by communist and Marxist-Leninist political parties. The brutal Baathist National-Socialist regimes in Iraq, Syria, and Egypt or absolutist *Velayat-e Faghih* regime of the Iranian Islamic republic gained profound levels of support from even those who count as the most liberal Islamic nations. Turkey has fed ISIS, Pakistan has been supporting Taliban, and Iran and Syria support Hamas and Hezbollah.

The founders of the oldest communist parties in the Middle East have been honest enough in their political proclamations. Instead of being critical agents of their societies who enlighten and educate the masses on their rights and social responsibilities, many party leaders have fallen into the trap of opportunism, selfishness, and ambition. There are countless cases that illustrate how Iranian and Arab communist leaders have become factual facilitators of despotic systems and have paved the way towards establishing the world's most brutal regimes, all while intellectuals and philosophers have closed their eyes to the brutality and rights violations.

After four decades, Iranians have not forgotten Noureddin Kianouri—the Tudeh Political party leader—who preached the "Imam Lines" (velayat-e Faghih) in order to facilitate an anti-Imperialistic, anti-American movement that guaranteed fundamental rights and freedoms, and essential economic changes. In the same way, Michel Aflaq, Salah al-Din al-Bitar, or Zaki al-Arsuzi, who facilitated the most brutal Baathist regimes, are still remembered by Arab nations and oppressed minorities of the region. Such claims can also be extended to much more academic and professional intellectuals such Edward Said who initiated Orientalism, one of the most influential theories on the Middle East. He extensively criticized western nations and their intellectuals for being intruders and facilitators of a colonial system of oppression and enslavement, while he himself had closed his eyes to local despotic systems and their atrocities. For many years he could not accept that the Iraqi dictator, Saddam Hussein, had committed genocides against its own Kurdish and Shiite compatriots during the 1980s. Additionally, this concept of orientalism did not prove useful in assisting Arab nation's combat decades of national development and emancipation struggles. Importantly however, Said's theory did end up being of great interest to the rising fundamental Islamic ideologues in Iraq, Lebanon, Syria, Egypt, Turkey, and Iraq. Such a paradox and set of double standards is still readily noticeable within Middle Eastern intellectual circles, and there are few activists and academicians who risk their own lives to speak the truth (Ali al-Wardi in Iraq, Ismael Bishekci and Salahattin Demirtas in Turkey, or Narges Mohammadi in Iran are notable exceptions). As the Lebanese political scientist Fouad Ajami accurately described of the Arab world today, intellectuals are either beaten down by the stick or seduced by the carrot. As if to illustrate this point, in 2001, the Egyptian Ministry of Culture burned 6,000 volumes of the classical Arabic poet, Abu Nuwas, who lived in the 8th century. Similarly, Jihad al-Khazen, the Lebanese journalist, admits that he and his colleagues have committed extensively self-censorship in their writings, and instead covering news, they have been covering up the news; an event which has become a daily routine in all Middle Eastern societies.

While populations within the majority of Middle Eastern countries are suffering from poverty, inequity, injustice, and marginalization, militarism and arms races have comprised an immense share of national production and expenditure. Every corner in this region has suffered from all forms of state violence and discrimination, while many of their citizens are threatened with genocide, mass-killings, forced migration, exoduses, and dislocation. As recently lamented by Joseph Stiglitz and many other economists, the world and especially the Middle East have become extremely divided realms of unequal development. The underlying explanations for such unjust and uneven developments are nothing except persistent exploitation, inequality, and ethno-racial injustice, while welfare, luxurious life conditions, and inclusiveness are enjoyed by elites persists everywhere.

The Middle East can be understood to suffer from three major inimical phenomena: a long history of tribal conquests, the patrimonial despotic rule, and the use of religion, territory and sovereignty over the common people. This has made citizens become the last thing that states tend to worry about, though ethnic and religious minorities typically assume a worse position and are often excluded or disregarded when accessing any state-run opportunities.

Militarism has become a chronic issue in the Middle East: Of the 10 countries with the highest military expenditures in the world in 2017, seven are in the Middle East. An extraordinary share of the GDP in the Middle East is given to further militarizing the region, which instead of helping to stabilize the region makes it more vulnerable to war and violence. As Florence Gaub (2014) claims, due to increased military spending the Arab nations continue to remain prone to conflict. In her opinion, a higher spending in military means a higher probability of conflict. Furthermore, diverse studies indicate that military procurement goes hand in hand with civil war, socio-economic deterioration, and injustice, and today's Middle Eastern nations are plain examples; at least 15 percent of the defence budget in these countries in involved in some way with corruption.

Since the Akkad ruler Sargon the Great invaded the Sumer civilization in Mesopotamia and erected the Akkadian empire five thousand years ago, the Middle East and especially the Mesopotamian region has become the epicenter for ongoing wars and ethnic conflicts. There is no doubt that colonial and imperialist forces had played an immense role in irritating and exacerbating regional conflicts from the 18th century onward, but one must not forget that many such civil wars and disputes are also inborn and majorly rooted or facilitated by internal political or socio-cultural forces. Historical and diplomatic documents indicate that the local leaders and authorities are the ones knocking on the doors of foreign agents and politicians and begging for the highest military and anti-protesters' technologies to further weaponize of their country, while large swathes of the population still lack fundamental life requirements. In an example, Erdogan has purchased some of the most sophisticated missile systems for billions of dollars from the Russians and Americans, while over 10 percent of his population live under the poverty line and unemployment had risen to over 15 percent in 2019. Similarly, the Egyptian military owned over 40 percent of the entire nation's wealth for many years, while Iran's Islamic Revolutionary Guard Corps control over 50 percent of the country's economy. Here, a major problem in the Middle East arises when the military corps do business, leading businesspeople to take over politics, while at the same time religious communities that are unfamiliar with the nation's socio-economic structures dictate and control society.

The millennia-old tribal invasions and conquests of rival empires cannot really be accounted as simple power transfers. Historically, the Middle East had been the epicenter of mass-killings, genocide, exoduses, and forced migrations. Like many other newly established countries of the 20th century, the modern Turkish state grew on basis of such an appalling legacy and continues the same policy of extermination and apartheid into the 21st century. Erdogan's recent territorial expansionist plans linked to demographic change and ethnic cleansing in the northern Syrian Kurdish region are reminiscent of the infamous Nazis' ideological principle of "Lebensraum". Following the Nazi regime's brutality against the Jews, the Ottomans' and Yong Turks' atrocities have ranked as some of the worst acts of genocide, and within the Middle East, have possibly claimed the most lives. Such a density of genocides and brutality in the Ottoman realm as inspired Levene to refer to Eastern Anatolia as a "zone of genocide", where Armenians, Assyrians, Kurds, Alevites, and many others have become continuous targets of mass-killings or deportations. In addition, it is believed that the Kurdish Yazidis had endured 72 cases of genocide campaigns during Ottoman and Arab-Islamic Caliphate rule. As a result, such campaigns of genocide are referred to as "Farman" or royal decree in Kurdish vernacular. Saddam Hussein, the Assad regime, and ISIS have also committed numerous acts of genocides against diverse communities in the region. The majority of Middle Eastern regimes including Turkey, Syria, Iran, Saudi Arabia, and Iraq have been equally responsible for the modern incidences of massacre, terrorism and forced displacements.

There are numerous events in Middle Easter countries' history which exemplify grave state sponsored violence and systematic abuses against followers of diverse religious or ethno-cultural minorities. The controversial and schismatic Islamic Sharia law has further fueled the Middle Eastern divide, pattern of exclusion, and human rights disputes. A veiled apartheid appears to exist within Sharia dominated nations, whereby adherents of diverse religious or ethnic minorities (Muslim and non-Muslim both) face systemic discrimination. Individual Islamic countries' domestic laws as well as the paradoxical Cairo Declaration on Human Rights in Islam (CDHRI) have never regarded religious minorities and members of other faiths as normal citizens or equal human beings, who are instead seen as second class members of their society who fall outside of the "Ummah" definition. According to the CDHRI, citizens of the Islamic countries or "Ummah" deserve governments' and authorities' special attention, while non-Muslim members are completely overlooked. Such Islamic laws view Muslims beyond their national political borders as integrated parts of their legislative or legal framework, but their own non-Muslim citizens, who for millennia have lived within the same geographical or political spheres, are completely excluded.

The CDHRI is rather paradoxical in its major articles, as followers of other religions are technically free to exercise their faith and perform their religious rites, but are very much limited to act within the provisions of the states' laws, which is usually Sharia law. In all the Islamic countries, paucity clauses state that no law can be contrary to the tenets of Islam. Even within the diverse Islamic school of jurisprudence, there are sometimes considerable legal differences of opinion on Muslim community's socio-economic and political matters, which leads to legal and legislative inconsistencies. Depending on the Islamic jurist, an offense or action could be interpreted leniently by one country and strictly by other. Unfortunately, Sharia laws have not benefited Muslim communities, and have instead further fuelled the paradoxical culture of separation, fear, and exclusion. In this, human rights violations in countries with stricter Sharia laws, such as Iran and Saudi Arabia, have often been ranked as some of the most atrocious. Such events have led to further speculation as to the possibility for compatibility between democracy and Islamic ideology, and many see immense contradictions between the people's sovereignty in modern democratic systems and the Islamic theocracy based on God's sovereignty. Though there are also some scholars who believe that Islamic traditions are compatible with the modern democratic notion, no actual breakthroughs in real life have occurred yet. After two centuries of democratic revolutions around the globe, and sixty years following the introduction of the Universal Declaration and Human Rights to the world community, there are still grave deteriorations of freedom, democracy, and human rights in the entire Middle East.

One fundamental aspect of human dignity in respecting democratic rights for every single human being is the preservation of some acceptable level of quality of life. The recent events of war, violence, and forced migration in the Middle East require a more comprehensive and human-based model of quality of life, in which human dignity, human rights and elements of social justice are of central importance. This book promises to introduce a universally more agreed upon and applicable model of analysis of both subjective and objective quality of life, which could be used easily in further evaluations of the region's living conditions. Finally, this model hopes to help translate human rights into emancipation within the diverse Middle Eastern ethno-religious communities.

Chapter 1

The Middle East: A Rooftop Society

I. Rooftop Societies: Paradoxical Components

Listening gleefully to "Il conformista" has been another motivation to start a sociological analysis of the Middle Eastern societies including Iran. The song sarcastically uncovers the characteristics of those who adapt themselves to undesired situations without thinking critically about the circumstances. As a fundamental principle in biology, adaptation functions as a dynamic mechanism of survival and fitness, and on a personal level it also helps one break through the numerous competitive endeavors of modern life. In social, economic, or political realities however, it could have some rather deleterious effects. It seems common for citizens living under despotic systems to reluctantly accept measures set by the ruling authorities in their daily public life, while in private they relinquish and disregard them. In Iran, like many other countries of the Middle East, citizens and state follow such utterly divergent codes of conduct. Such unforeseen conditions, which have been molded through long historical processes and are sustained in the modern times, might appear at first irreconcilable but astonishingly have become a major socio-cultural characteristic of many Middle Eastern political regions in general. Many such communities have historically suffered from flawed political structures and hostile autocratic systems where either one person or a small elite of socially and economically aligned men control the entire country and its population. Throughout history, autocratic regimes in the region have been trying to manipulate, control, and dominate the public and bring people in line with their ideals, while also frequently portraying an image of benevolence. Common people have learnt how to deal with such contrasts and have occasionally been successful in overcoming associated threats. It is important to note that this situation promotes a twisted and dichotomous culture, which has involuntarily become a significant part of daily life and realizations of such a culture in interactions with the outside world often causes undesirable outcomes for citizens and statesmen alike. To survive the tension and rigidity of such permanent political and cultural aversion, both average people and the state have thus searched for a space of sanctuary. This physical structure or arena has played and still is playing a tremendous role in safeguarding people from permanent state intrusion and autocratic interference in people's private affairs. In this, the traditional architectural design and structure of Middle Eastern urban and rural settlements has provided common people with opportunities to escape the furious state control: Flat roof buildings historically found across Iran and the Middle East as common residential structures have proven important here, especially when many such buildings are interconnected as a series of attached structures. This chapter explores the conflictual elements of the Middle Eastern socio-cultural and political life, which determine people's existences and have led to a long-lasting hide-and-seek rehearsal.

For centuries rooftops have not only provided Iranian and Middle Eastern communities with a sanctuary away from inveterate states' punishments and tortures, but have also functioned as spaces for social, cultural, and even political interactions. For centuries rooftops provided refreshing cool bedrooms for the hot long summer season, and broad bedroom served as an immense opportunity for socialization between family and neighbors. Similarly, rooftops have also played a tremendous role in organizing religious functions or ceremonial events, especially regarding practices forbidden by state or ruling powers. Rooftops in urban settlements provided more secure performance arenas wherever citizens felt their rights had been curtailed and were prevented from practicing their collective habits and behaviors.

There are myriad instances in Iranian history where the rooftop has acted as an arena of socio-cultural, religious, or political reflection for citizens. Even the scenery of the comedy movie "tambourine"[1] (Dayereh-e Zangi, 2008) occurred on an apartment rooftop in Tehran, where a young boy tries to install government banned TV satellite antennas for a diverse group of residents with completely diverging views. Importantly, outlawed

Satellite TV was a major source of entertainment for the Iranian middle class and youth prior to the introduction of high capacity smartphones into Iranian markets. Furthermore, Satellite TV connected Iranians to the outside world, from prominent Hollywood films to broadcasting programs and activities by opposition groups. Such exposure was despised by Iranian clerics, who wanted to eliminate it from the Iranians' private lives by any means. In support of this, Steven Barraclough (2001) notes that "…the visible appearance of the medium publicly demonstrates the popularity of those very cultural products deemed to be anathema by the state" (Barraclough, 2001). In the case of Iran, an army of Islamic agents and police officers have been searching daily for satellite dishes installed on private rooftops. Their main job has been to dismantle and confiscate the dishes and report the owners to the Islamic court for prosecution. The hardline Iranian clerics see satellite programs as part of the "soft war" against the country by the United States and other enemies, while unofficial sources have confirmed that up to 65% of the people were using the banned satellite broadcasting programs in 2012 (Esfandiari, 2018). In neighbouring Iraq, the situation was not much different during Saddam Hussein's regime. There, people were more cautious and mounted banned satellite dishes in empty water tanks above their rooftops to escape authorities' attention. Here, Iraqi viewers have frequently testified using a state-ordered TV in their living room while hiding another TV equipped with foreign channels in a more private area.[2]

Simultaneously with many other Middle Eastern leaders, Reza Shah of Iran used his full force in modernizing the country and fought against all Islamic images, although it is not apparent that he had actually departed much from traditional religious mentalities or foundations. Ayatollah M. E. Hosseini Zanjani in an interview with the Institute for Iranian Contemporary Historical Studies explained how prior to taking full control as the monarch of Iran, Rezah Shah was taking part in rituals related to *Mourning of Muharram* and paying his tribute to the Shiite Imam Hussein's martyrdom with complete bare feet. In addition, Reza Shah has been observed standing in the front of the mourning parade while covering his head with mud out of respect to the Imam's death.[3] In January 1936, the Iranian Shah issued his famous Unveiling Decree (known as "*Kashf-e Hejab*"), which triggered controversy between the polarized and diverse social classes. The swift and forceful implementation of the policy along with door-to-door searches for women's traditional veils (*chador*) exposed society to new hostile scenarios: Many women were beaten, their headscarves and chadors torn off, and their homes forcibly searched. In a society where women had practiced veiling since the pre-Islamic era, such spontaneous law enforcement could have triggered series of social or clerical resistance. Until then, women part of the Iranian aristocracy as the courts had also participated in veiling. Much of the lower class who felt their rights and honour were oppressed by the autocratic system believed that the veil assured women's pride, honour, respect, and virtue, so they began searching passionately for an escape. Here again, the rooftop become an arena and sanctuary for veiled women who no longer viewed public places and streets as safe for their daily social practice.

This thesis defines "rooftop" as a physical or spatial concept of life realization, where factual and undisguised socio-political activism takes place; a major place that autocratic regimes and repressive state apparatuses alike try to take advantage of. Citizens have been using this space to remain out of the reach of state violence and carry out many forbidden duties or socio-cultural tasks, which have long been banned by the ruling power. In many cases state has also benefited from using the "rooftop" as a place to execute it's more controversial and infamous policies.

One may ask why this analysis has not employed existing terms such as "underground society" or "stealthy community" instead of "rooftop" society. Here, the term "rooftop" is seen to be more relevant in a socio-political system where the tyrannical regime implements its notorious practices and spreads fear over the entire population without being disturbed by its subjects. The ruling authorities use this space for further encroachments on individuals' liberties and take advantage of the space to demonstrate their aggressions and brutality for the purposes of intimidation. As an example, the prolific usage of sharpshooters on Tehran's rooftops in recent decades against urban protestors led by leaders of the Islamic regime is an intentional strategy to discourage protest against Mullahs' authoritarian power. Elsewhere, Barney Henderson (2011) notes that the Yemeni regime's snipers were deployed on rooftops around "Change Square", the epicenter of anti-regime protests in the Yemeni capital, in order to execute passers-by (Henderson, 2011). In these situations, the "rooftop" gives the regimes a suitable opportunity to not only exhibit their brutal power and ability to control, but also a trouble-free field of operation.

For ordinary people, rooftops also exemplify a safe arena for personal, socio-cultural, and spiritual life without being directly exposed to the authorities' aggression and give them the chance to promote or display their endurance despite formal threats and state coercion. Local authorities have used the rooftops in an attempt to fight terrorism and prevent violence, but also as a platform for instigating it. During the terror attack on Saudi oil installations in Al-Khobar which led to the massacre of 22 foreign workers, the Saudi security forces hopelessly landed on buildings' rooftops in the Oasis housing compound to prevent the massacre (Bakier, 2006). Similarly, ISIS militants executed dozens of people after accusing them of being homosexual by throwing them from rooftop structures in Syrian and Iraqi cities such as Mosul and Kirkuk. The group has additionally used this method to execute four people, including two of its own members, on charges of homosexuality and sodomy in the Dor al-Toub area in central Mosul. On numerous occasions, the ISIS-linked Sharia courts have executed many innocent Iraqis and Syrians by throwing them off the rooftops of buildings. Using the rooftops as space to execute brutal judiciary verdicts against civilians and minorities has given the extremist organizations and regimes within the region a better mechanism and an extended spectrum to showcase their savagery. The rooftops here become stages for displaying naked hostility and diffusing fear.

Following Chernobyl's nuclear meltdown, the German sociologist Ulrich Beck published *"Risikogesellschaft,"* (or Risk Society), which discusses the transition from industrial modernity to a new system of sociocultural transformation characterized by economic and environmental hazards, insecurity, and risks as well as struggles associated with production, and how the breakdown of risks reveal the political nature of technological choices. Indeed, Beck's concept of Risk Society could also be extended to Middle Eastern societies, which not only face daily technological and environmental peril, but also enduring systemic socio-political oppression, which was become commonplace. While Beck (1986) may not say it explicitly, it is reasonable to extend his concept to citizens of any despotic system, who deprived of their fundamental rights, suffer from abusive systems of oppression. While national mass media typically focuses on grandiose phenomena such as wars and dictatorships, citizens of "rooftop societies" are often ruthlessly targeted systematic course of oppressive violence, discrimination, and injustice. The citizens of these countries know very well that any open statement, action, or endeavor expressing objection toward state-run plans or policies could put their lives in jeopardy. For centuries many have been forced to hide their true identities or beliefs and present themselves or their family members as less threatening toward the government. For centuries, members of the ancient Kurdish religion known as *Yaresanis* were called Shiite *Ahle Haq* or *Ali-olahi* or even derogatorily as *Shaitanparast* (devil worshipers), as an example. Until recently, such terms did not concern the Yaresanis, since they protected them from being further abused by the authorities or hardline clergies. Aside from sociopolitical or religious contributors to fear, Beck also included environmental degradations or natural disasters as risk factors to industrial societies in the Middle East. When widespread flash flooding affected large parts of Iran in the spring of 2019 for example, citizens found sanctuary on their own and others' rooftops in the absence of governmental supports.

II. A Rooftop Revolution

During the 1979 Iranian Revolution, revolutionary pro-Islamic demonstrators and protesters used the rooftops of public buildings and mosques in Tehran and religious cities like Qom or Isfahan for their anti-regime activities. The followers of the Ayatollah Khomeini, the leader of the Islamic Revolution, left cassettes of his speeches against the Shah playing on speakers above the mosques' rooftops, inviting the masses to take part in the uprising against the regime; a form of passive public protest, which helped instigate the fall of Shah and rise of the Islamic Shiite tyranny, which has now lasted four vicious decades. The Persian web-logger named Saeed Saman calls the *'Allahu Akbar* (Allah is the greatest)' chanting in protest against Shah's regime the "Rooftop Allahu Akbar" (Saman, 2019).

Additionally, the rooftops of the Islamic schools of Alawai and Refah were used to execute the closest members of the Shah's administration and army during the dawn of the revolution. Similarly, Lieutenant General Mehdi Rahimi was sentenced to death by Iranian clergies on the midnight of February 26, 1979 on the rooftop of the Islamic Refah School, and many others were soon to join. "The first group of the Shah's high-ranking generals like Nasiri, Khosrodad, Rahimi and Naji were executed by Libyan-trained guards, right on rooftop of the Alavi Islamic high school in Tehran. Despite all the rumors, Ayatollah Khomeini and his son Ahmed were present at the whole execution process to make sure it was accomplished accordingly and even did his blessings or thanksgiving's prayer right on the school's rooftop" (Shafizadeh, 2000, p.192).

Hanna Arendt distinguished between total dominating regimes of totalitarianism and violence-based dictatorial systems, and described how the totalitarian rules established by a regime of terror start devouring the predecessor regime's agents, as well as its own children. "The decisive difference between totalitarian domination, based on terror, and tyrannies and dictatorships, established by violence, is that the former turns not only against its enemies but against its friends and supporters as well, being afraid of all power, even the power of friends. The climax of terror is reached when the police state begins to devour its own children, when yesterday's executioner becomes today's victim. And this is also the moment when power disappears entirely" (Arendt, 1970). It was not only the Ayatollah Khomeini climbing to the rooftop of a school supervising the horror sceneries of terror and execution. Hassan al Sabah, the eleventh-century Shiite Ismaili founder of the "Assassins" group had also climbed to the rooftop of his Alamut castle in northern Iran to oversee his people's acts and train and indoctrinate young clergies to carry out terrorist activities against people and authorities in today's entire Middle Eastern region (Lewis, 2002).

During the Iranian reformist mass demonstrations of 2009 known as "green Movement", the Iranian security forces along with foreign mercenaries were deployed and installed on the rooftops of the major buildings looking across the streets filled with protesters. Hundreds of young demonstrators were easily shot to death or injured right above such strongholds and many other thousands were identified and captured later. During the Iranian election protest against the fraudulent presidency of Mahmoud Ahmadinejad on June 20th, 2009, a young Iranian student, Neda Agha-Soltan was shot by a *Basij* (a paramilitary Islamic resistance force used to spread the extremist Shiite ideology) member hiding on the rooftop of a civilian house. Since the establishment of the Islamic Revolution, *Basij* has served as a "propaganda machine in political campaigns, [used to] justify clerical rule, protect politicians, and enforce Islamic morality and rules. They are part of the Islamic Republic of Iran's overall avowed plan to have millions of informers. The *Basij* also undermine dissent; for instance, they play a key role in suppressing uprisings and demonstrations" (Golkar, 2015). The Turkish President Recep Tayyip Erdogan had also ordered his coercive forces and his favored Syrian opposition fighters to stand on the rooftops of buildings in their controlled areas and hunt for any resistance, including Kurdish oppositional groups.

At the same time, many students were thrown off the rooftop of the Tehran University dorm by the Islamic security forces of the Iranian regime; something which was pursued and rehearsed few years later in 2014 by the pro-Morsi Islamic radical protesters in Alexandria's Sidi Gaber district, where two young boys were thrown off a residential rooftop. In August 2004 the Shiite extremist *Jaish Al Mehdi* of Muqtada al-Sadr's Mahdi militia used the rooftops of private homes to attack the US forces inside the city. Also, in the most recent deadly anti-government protests in Baghdad at the beginning of October 2019, Iran-backed militias reportedly deployed snipers on Baghdad rooftops targeting demonstrators (Georgy, 2019). This and the preceding instances of the use of rooftop spaces for socio-political interactions in the last four decades serve as sufficient evidence to justify calling the Islamic Revolution a "Rooftop Revolution". This is not simply because the rooftop acted as an important spatial element in the success of the revolution, but rather because it has the power to generate an "agonistic culture" of permanent fear, insecurity and intense divergence between all social, political, religious and ethnic factions of the country.

In the past four decades of the Islamic Revolution, the existing gap between different walks of life and all political factions has been widened further while distress and confusion has ruled the country. The Iranian opposition residing in the West has been unable to find sufficient common ground to create solidarity or action based on human rights and democracy, which the masses inside the country have been longing for and requesting for years. Much of the oppositions' activism and criticism has focused on blaming and disparaging each other rather focusing on the major issues related to the tyrannical regime.

During the Arab Spring, anti-government protesters and demonstrators in some cities benefited from volunteer security forces that were standing on the vicinity buildings' rooftops, protecting people from being attacked by authorities. At the same time, armed forces loyal to Bashar Assad barraged those residential buildings with artillery weapon and machine gun fire, killing many innocent people including women and children.

In related terms, Claudio Culagouri (2012) describes "agonistic culture" as "the lived system of meaning, the social text of values, rituals and practices that are based on the myth that conflict and competition are forms of positive productivity necessary to generate human social progress" (Colaguori, 2012). Here, Culagouri (2012) understands the philosophy of agonism to be a perspective that sees conflict as a positive force and a universal principle of life. The Islamic regime leaders in Iran see themselves in a state of permanent conflict and competition with Western countries such as the United States, which is referred to as the "Great Satan". They believe that the United States and Israel are the major enemies of the Islamic world and the Iranian clerical system, and as such the Iranians and the whole state should be alert and prepared for appropriate responses to their possible threats. While the state-ideological and religious settings fortify such competition with God's enemies in the mind of the ruling powers, many regular citizens and members of younger generations have showed a greater interest in the western culture, way of life, and materialism.

Four decades of formal dogmatism, fanatic ideological practices, and continuous enmity with Israel, the United States, and many other regional and international nations has caused an immense socio-cultural dichotomy within the broad spectrum of Iranians, and has created antagonism and double standards in many aspects of the formal governmental policies and decision-making processes. Many activities, sports, events, cultural rituals, open displays of music, and even Iranian Nowruz rituals such as Chaharshanbe Suri (a fire festival celebrated on the evening of the last Wednesday before the Iranian New Year's day), have been suppressed and banned since the establishment of the clerical regime. However, the Iranians have secretly continued in their activism and have often been successful in imposing their desires upon the Islamic authorities.

While private rooftops in many Middle Eastern societies were used for sleeping in the hot summer months, many rooftops have more recently become a low-cost accommodation option for travelers or external workers. For example, a European travel-blogger (Nina Travel) has noted Middle Eastern rooftop accommodations for as low as 1 Euro per night. In other regions, the economic downturn and extraordinary high level of living expenses has caused local and regional travelers as well as external workers in larger cities to look for more affordable overnight shelters and accommodations. Apart from many post-revolutionary forms of homelessness such as "grave-sleepers" (sleeping inside of empty graves to escape the cold) or "cardboard-dwellers", Iranians now face "rooftop dwellers" in some of its districts. A recent article published in Tehran reveals that low income workers and low budget travelers rent spaces on the rooftops of private and sometimes unfinished buildings for an overnight stay or even as a longer-term dwelling option.[4]

In the Palestinian Gaza Strip, security issues, land mines, and a lack of agricultural lands has forced people to use their houses' rooftops for agricultural purposes. A 2016 report by the CCTV follows the life of Um Mu'adh, a "housewife living in the Bureij refugee camp in the central Gaza Strip, whose family suffers from a low standard of living. […] [S]he participated in a training course on 'Rooftop/surface Agriculture' run by a local association called the Association for Rehabilitation and Development of the Palestinian Household, to use this technology to help her family."[5]

In the recent years in Iran, many young musical artists and groups consisting of both girls and boys have come together on the private residential buildings' rooftops. Even when deprived of any formal recognition or support, such artists have produced great musical pieces, and become referred to as Posht-e Bami (rooftop) bands. In an example, Marjan and Mahsa Vahdat, two forbidden Iranian singers on a rooftop in Tehran, performed "I have a dream," beautifully adapted from the Kurdish melody "Daya Daya", gaining international attention.

Ethnic and religious minorities as well as children in almost every corner of the Middle East have been using the rooftops of private or public buildings as a space for socio-cultural and collective exhibition of daily rituals and activism, and it can be said that there is a lot of life and engagements on Middle Eastern rooftops. People have come out for centuries to exhibit their daily lives, from hanging laundry or chatting with neighbors to escaping a world full of injustice, atrocity and oppression. Lebanese children escape social injustice and atrocities by accessing neighbouring rooftops to play soccer.

It is crucial that we understand how Iranian society—with a very long legacy of contribution to humankind's history—has been evolving in such a way, and how this long-lasting society has managed to survive despite numerous historical and authoritarian incursions. Many people and ethnic groups in the Middle East have been forced throughout history to hide their real identity in public life and lie to protect their very existence, while within their closer social sphere or kinship play their true role and characters. The primary drives for such a cultural phenomenon and socio-political construct of hide-and-seek (here they are placed together as characteristics of "rooftop society"), is firstly basic survival and physical protection, followed by the safeguarding of identity. The Kabyle people in the north and northeast of Algeria for example are not religiously affiliated, but often pretend to be pious Muslims to avoid violence or execution. They were seen majorly as "bad Muslims" (see Hugh Roberts, 2014).

Numerous different characteristics can be distinguished for "rooftop societies" which give a better insight into its analysis. A "rooftop society" is essentially based on socio-cultural and political contradictions and the historical rivalry and antagonism between existing components of society. In addition, antagonism between citizens and the state, political power struggles, the rivalry between modernism and traditional forces, and the presence of redundant parallel institutions and political power organizations are important characteristics that must be accounted for. The following section delves into greater detail in assessing the roots and characteristics of "rooftop societies".

III. Roots of the Middle Eastern Socio-political Paradoxes

With a diligent jaunt through the history of the Middle Eastern communities, one can easily encounter an in-exhaustive list of interethnic, religious, tribal and political warfare involving unremitting invasions, massacres, occupations, exoduses, and relocations. Almost all dynasties have who ruled over the entire Middle East in the last three millennia have come to power by use of violence and war. Armies of opposing nations have historically settled political disputes on the battlefield. The new ruling dynasty would increasingly dictate its own dogmatic ethno-religious ideas and start preaching against out-group communities, gradually creating socio-cultural and religious rifts between diverse community members dictated by its establishment. Mish Frederick C. (1985) notes that during the first ancient empire of Mesopotamia, the Akkadian empire in the 3rd millennium BC exercised influence across Mesopotamia, the Levant, and Anatolia, sending military expeditions as far south as Dilmun and Magan (today's Bahrain and Oman) in the Arabian Peninsula (Mish, 1985). Following conquests by Sargon (founder of the Akkadian Empire) and his successors, the Akkadian language was forcefully imposed on neighboring conquered states such as Elam and Gutium. Only after the fall of the Akkadian Empire in 2154 BC did the Mesopotamian people finally coalesce into two major nations: Assyria in the north and Babylonia in the south. The history of one of the earliest civilizations in the world and a major part of today's the Middle East, Mesopotamia, is a chronicle of near constant strife. Hostility and war in their tribal mentality, where outsiders are often viewed as dangerous, was considered normal (see Anglim et.al., 2013). The ruling empires and their armies came to grow in mass and size over time, which caused a deeper sense of brutality, oppression, and fear among the resident populations.

While many historians blame the fruitless wars between Iran and Rome as a key cause for the disastrous fall of the Sassanid Empire in 651, there are many other recorded events that have contributed to ongoing political tensions in Iran. From invasions by King Alexander III of Macedon and his successors' rivalry for control (known as the Wars of the Diadochi) to Persian, Ottoman and Arab invasions, the 13th century Mongolian conquest, Napoleon's eastern conquest, British and Russian interference in the Middle East, and many local and regional rivalries, the miseries, suppressions and cruelty that followed have instigated a permanent sense of terror and fear within the helpless masses. Such extensive accounts of brutality, harassment, and subjugation are a primary cause for inflicting anxiety and fear on a region's entire population, and the country as a whole. The fear of assimilation, culturicide, forced displacement, or losing one's life, loved ones, or property all are rational motives for ordinary citizens to hide their true identities and exercise caution.

A second cause of the dualistic and paradoxical way of life within the region can be observed within the despotic state system and political tyranny of ruling powers in the Middle Eastern countries. An intense and permanent feeling of fear and disgust from subjugation and oppressive conduct of despotic rulers is spread across the Middle East. Such intense fear of persecution has been and still is a major cause of precautionary dissimulation and denial of identity, religious beliefs, and practices within the masses of these countries. *Velayat-e faghih* in the 21st century as a fundamentalist, reactionary, religiously-based, relative race-based, and neo-colonial-like entity has controlled the entire lives of Iranian characters over the past four decades, in which the "*Vali-e Faqih*" (Islamic jurisprudence) "rules over the lives, property and honour of the people"[6] (*valiy-e faqih hakem bar jan o mal o namous-e mardom*). Jean-Baptiste Chardon (1643-1713) in his travel memoirs on Iran during the Safavid era talks about Iranians' views on their sovereign rights and power, in which he illustrates Iranians' disagreement on the issue of succession of the Hidden Imam (the prophesied redeemer of Islam, as per Shia religion). Chardon explains that many Iranians believed that a *Faqih*, who is familiar with Islam and Islamic Sharia and is a member of the Imam's bloodline, should hold political power in the country (Ferrier, 1996). Regardless of the degree to which Sheikh Safi, the head of the Safavids dynasty, actually possessed such key criteria is debatable, but his son still vehemently and brutally spread the Shiite ideology of "Hidden Imam" and called himself "*nayeb-e al-Imam*" or representative of the Imam.

A third and very important account for the spread of such distress within the masses could lie in religious institutions' and authorities' interference in the region's socio-political and personal or family affairs; not only historically but also in contemporary times. One's feelings, concealment of thoughts, character, or even religion, ethnic background, and identity have become the daily state of affairs of leading faces in addition to ordinary people. In other words, the Middle Eastern clergies have played a role in people's segregation, exclusion, and discrimination. The spread of hatred and calling non-members infidel, heretic, apostate, or even impure and *nijis* (dirty) has become a series of bitter repetitive experiments within minorities. The more traditional or religious the ruling ethnic or religious community is, the more it is influenced by their in-group clerics and religious authorities. Sometimes a widespread culture of suspicion, distrust, and terror rules over the entire society; from peasants to the members of the court.

When adherents are under threat of persecution or expulsion in Islam, martyrdom is regarded as honourable. Similarly, in many cases involving the Shiite theology, lying to protect one's life and property or even "gain the upper-hand over an enemy" is completely accepted. Of several forms of lying permitted under certain circumstances, the most eminent is called "*taqiyya*" derived from the Arabic root, denoting literally caution, fear, "precautionary dissimulation" or "prudent fear" (Encyclopaedia Britannica). Following the Islamic Revolution, when newly elected President Abolhassan Banisadr reminded Ayatollah Khomeini of his unkept promises to "establish a democratic system the same as French people's" as he was proclaiming earlier during exile in France, Khomeini responded that he had lied and committed *khodeh*. *Kitman* and *Khodeh* both mean nothing but lying, which are Shiite Islam's political tactics to defeat enemies or protect one from possible harm and suffering.

The Lebanese people are one rare example of a religious-based power-sharing political system that has been able to craft relative tranquility for some time. However, as a hodgepodge of many diverse religious communities, Lebanon has never been able to settle into a modern political system based on trust or acceptance. Six major religious communities of Maronites, Greek Orthodox, Roman Catholic Christians, Druze, Shia, and Sunni Muslims have repeatedly been at war, and at times have also turned to power-sharing arrangements with mixed success. Maintaining a political power-sharing system based on 1932 demographic data with no provision to update the census is an exceptionally tricky balancing act, especially where Saudi-Iranian interventions in the region and spillover from the Syrian war and Israeli-Palestinian conflict are possible. Following the American invasion in 2003, post-Saddam Iraq has taken similar strides in developing a federal power division based on ethno-religious identities. Since 2005, the position of president has been allocated to the Kurds from the north, while the majority Shiite-Arabs can be granted the position of Prime Minister, and Sunni-Arabs have the position of legislative power (Parliament). This has resulted in a fragile political power-sharing system based on mistrust which has ultimately failed to play its unifying role.

Ample research and academic findings indicate extraordinary resistance toward the democratization process within many Middle Eastern societies. In addition to a notable number of historical uprisings and protests, an extreme authoritarian robustness exists, hindering democratic influence. Overall, almost all countries in the region have failed to catch the wave of democratization that has swept nearly every other part of the world. "While the number of countries designated free by

Freedom House has doubled in the Americas and in the Asia-Pacific region, increased tenfold in Africa, and risen exponentially in Central and East Europe over the past thirty years, there has been no overall improvement in the Middle East and North Africa" (Bellin, 2004).

IV. State and Society Antagonism

Since the development of modern sociology and other social and political sciences in the 19th century, many scholars have devoted significant time and effort to investigating the interaction between the state institution and society. If many of these large-scale and mainly generalized theories—which tend to be ideological, doxographic, or philosophical—were disregarded, one could still confront the state-society dichotomy with numerous academic arguments. No matter how pervasive any assumption in both constructs is, academic analysis of the subject could be at a micro or macro level: It could evaluate the formation, rise-and-demise, or structure of the state in general or within a specific culture, or it could simply investigate the socio-cultural elements of state operation, peoples' mentality, and behaviors, as well as elites' level of patriotism or belief in citizens' rights. Sociopolitical analyses of interactions between state and society are still trying to better understand such interrelationships and explore how social structures and citizens' behaviors or attitudes could lead to a distinguished form of state, and conversely, how the state contributes to peoples' mentality. There is no doubt that the state and the populace vastly affect each other, while in many cases, one likely plays a greater role in leading, shaping, or reshaping the other.

Throughout the political history of Iran, regular people have rarely played a fundamental role in delineating the state and its policies. The arbitrary rule by the country's statesmen has typically denied its citizens a chance to have their voices heard. The leader has always acted as a lever of universal power with few restrictions and has often proclaimed to possess the eternal power of god or at least be the god's manifestation on Earth. With few exceptions, the country's despotic rulers have had full authority over the entire population, their lives, and their possessions. In this, property rights and agreements in Iran have not been valued as they ought to be to the point that even feudal landowners in medieval Europe had once fared significantly better. While many members of European aristocracies had full rights to their possessions and properties, even a Persian prince cannot be sure of his own life. During the 1980s the Iranian revolution leader, Ayatollah Khomeini, repeatedly proclaimed that the Islamic supreme leader or the *Vali-e Faqih* has the full authority or supremacy over the people's life, property and honour. Such proclamations referred to supremacy over everything, from a man's home to his wife! According to this account then, the rights of regular Iranians are negligible, even in the 21st century after 2500 years of sovereignty over a region larger than what is now known as the Middle East. Additionally, such pan-Islamic zealots do not feel the need to consent to the wishes and requirements of the country's younger generations.

While discussing the rights of individuals at the turn of the 19th century, the Iranian social reformer Talibov Tabrizi touched on the socio-political paradox which had spread throughout the entire country. For him, the rifts between the Iranian masses and the rulers as well as between Iranians and citizens of European nations were of special concern. He notes that while the entire country was collapsing, the Iranian Kings lived an extraordinarily luxurious life: "Other nations unite with a spirit of reform and talk at lengths to make their nation a better place while Iranians are silent about their problems, alienated from one another, and set in archaic, ancestral ways; the Qajar ministries are mere imitations without any institutional foundation and government officials are not appointed based on merit; education too is in a poor condition and no books are written for the advancement of sound pedagogy" (Tabrizi & Rahim, 1968).

Katouzian (2003) tries to understand the causes behind the dialectic of the state and Iranian society by performing a socio-political analysis of Iran's modern history. Katouzian (2003) believes this historical approach accounts for the continuing animosity between Iranian state and society, as well as the unaccountability of the state and un-governability of society, regardless of rulers, dynasties, regimes, religions and ideologies (Katouzian, 2003). For Katouzian (2003), even the most recent monarchs who reigned for nearly half a century between the First World War and the Islamic Revolution are "pseudo-modernist despots" (during Reza Shah's era) and "petrolic despots" (during his son Mohammad Reza's era).

The 1905 Constitutional Revolution which saw the establishment of the first legislative assembly (*Majlis*) did not ultimately empower Iranian citizens, as the constitution, which was ratified by most members, was seen by the King (and the Supreme Leader after the 1979 Islamic Revolution) as insignificant and null. The bombardment of the Iranian *Majlis* in June 1908 by the Shah of Iran (Mohammad Ali Shah Qajar) and incorporation an absolute clerical power into the Iranian post-revolutionary constitutional laws after 1979 are just two examples of many contributing patterns toward hostility between citizens and the state.

While countless uprisings and revolts in Iran's despotic systems have mostly involved peoples' struggles for survival or maintaining existing minimal standards, they occur in many democracies for the purposes of gaining human rights or increasing the standard of living. In the previous century alone, Iranians participated in approximately one hundred political revolts, uprisings, and social movements against political authorities in the hopes of bringing about changes to the totalitarian power structure and finding relief in their daily life. In most cases, the political pressure and socio-economic burdens returned with greater intensity, and any marginal advances gained were extirpated in a later time. Both the 1905 Constitutional Revolution and the 1979 Islamic Revolution were originally supposed to bring citizens political emancipation, equality, and justice. While both pivotal revolutions had originally been regarded as a source of liberation and political relief, they became some of the worst forms of tyranny.

For millennia the sovereign (Shah) had been supreme not only to all the lands and properties of Iran, but even considered the owner of all people working beneath him, including ministers, officers, servants, and even the Grand Vizier (Prime Minister), who had absolute power of attorney directly from the King. Practically every single position and formal appointment was directly arranged or influenced by the Shah and his own people. People were involved in such decisions only when the Shah wanted to give power to less turbulent authorities, such as those with little discordance with civilians. For example, the Shah's endorsement toward the people's appointment of their village headman was typically orchestrated to be of benefit to his own reign.

The inner circle of the court it a covert, informal, and private body with an extraordinarily long history in Iran and much of the Middle East. Major affairs of the country and its subjects are discussed, ratified, and sanctioned within the court, often without public endorsement or even proclamation. Visiting members of this inner circle lack a coherent agenda at times, as they are known to focus on their own personal interests instead of public welfare. In the grip of a crisis, a ruler will turn to his inner circle for advice rather than formal legislative or executive organs. In many of these inner circles, no-one is entirely trusted and the penalty for giving sound but unpalatable advice can be death. Beyond Saddam Hussein's family circle for instance, key figures can be counted on one hand: Deputy Prime Minister Tariq Aziz, Vice-president Taha Yassin Ramadan, Saddam's private secretary, Abed Hamid Mahmoud, and Izzat Ibrahim al-Douri, who was his deputy chairman of the revolutionary command council. In Iran, Hussein Ferdost, Asadollah Alam, Abdoul Karim, Ayadi Ashraf, Jamshid Alam, and Amir Houshang Dulo are people who have been members of the Shah's inner circle (Fard, n.d.). These inner circles often consist of "Many people with official or semi-official positions or even simply unemployed, or patrons and members of the court are those who surround the Shah. Within these people one can find talented and important people, intellectuals or even greedy and useless people".[7]

Such covert sources of political and economic decision making continued to influence the political climate of the country following the Islamic Revolution. With its continuously changing membership, the Islamic court has been running, planning, and manipulating Iran's affairs from business, politics, military, and national security to issues of ethnic or religious minorities and other countries' internal affairs. The current secretive inner circle was founded by Rafsanjani, Khamenei, and Rafighjdoost at the beginning of the Islamic Revolution. Since Ali Khamenei was appointed Supreme Leader and successor of Ayatollah Khomeini (the founder of the Islamic Republic) in 1989, everything began to change. Khamenei did not trust the old Privy Council members and so looked for a new inner circle for his court composed of those he knew who could satisfy his hardline political intentions. Ahmad Jannati (hardline member of the Islamic Guardian Council), Ali Akbar Velayati (the Supreme leader's adviser and a member of the council for foreign relations), Gholam-Ali Haddad-Adel (ex-speaker of the Iranian Parliament with family ties to the supreme leader), Mostafa Mir-Salim (previous hardline culture minister) and Mohseni Ejei (first deputy and the spokesman of Iran's judiciary system) could be named. These men are utterly submissive to the supreme leader's wishes and objectives.

The state's pressure on native Iranians such as Kurds and Zoroastrians and other minorities has often been intense, long-lasting, and hostile. Saravi in his historical narration on the country during 1790s explains how Zoroastrians from the Kerman region would hide their identity out of fear and introduce themselves as Jews (Saravi & Taghi, 1992). Similarly, Nazem Al-Islam Kermani in his famous diary (Kermani, 1982) describes how Zoroastrians and Hindus were labeled as infidels, abused, and tortured by the Islamic clergies and authorities. In addition, Isabella Bishop (1891) in her travel report of the Middle East discusses how Kurdish residents of Miandoab were expelled from the city following authorities' accusations that they had surrendered the city to the Ottomans during the war. She described how locals distrusted each other out of fear and how this phenomenon was caused by the oppressive system of power: "I do sincerely detest the cowardliness of the Oriental nature, which is probably the result of ages of oppression by superiors." (Bishop, 1891, p.174)

She shows in her writings how the society as a whole suffered from distrust, and people were forced to lie from the Shah downwards: "It is so vexing that the policy of trust which has served me so well on all former journeys has to be abandoned and that one of suspicion has to be substituted for it. I am told by all Europeans that from the Shah downwards no one trusts father, brother, wife, superior, or inferior. Everyone walks warily and suspiciously through a maze of fraud and falsehood. If one asks a question, or anyone expresses an opinion, or tells what passes for a fact, he looks over each shoulder to see that no one is listening." She continues: "A noble Persian said to me, "Lying is rotting this country. Persians tell lies before they can speak." Almost every day when one is wishing to be trustful, kind, and considerate, one encounters unmitigated lying, cowardly bluster, or dexterously-planned fraud, and the necessity of being always on guard is wearing and repulsive" (Bishop, 1891, p.174). In 19th century Urmia where many Christians and other Non-Muslim communities lived, a deputy-governor called "*Serperast*" existed whose duty was to manage Christian affairs. While this was instigated by the British Government, many Europeans simply regarded it as another means of oppression. Indeed, an increase in judges in the region meant nothing more than just a multiplication of injustice and an increased extortion of money.

It has been a routine policy of ruling powers in Iran to encourage regional tribes and ethnic groups to act against each other at times when the central government is unable to control the situation or solve existing problems. According to a court chronicler, when the 'ungrateful inhabitants' of Nishapur rebelled, the Shah of Qajar encouraged the local tribes to lay waste to the city (Abrahamian, 1982). Iran's history is full of rulers who lost their legitimacy and trustworthiness by deliberately devoting or surrender the whole country or entire regions to foreign powers. For example, Iranian medieval records indicate that elites and aristocrats of Khorasan in the tenth century AD requested help from Saljuk Turks against Sultan Masoud Ghaznavi. Additionally Yazgerd the III faced mass defection within his army at the time of the Arab invasion in the 650s. This event led to the execution of the last pre-Islamic ruler of Iran by his own people (Bosworth, 1999). According to Tabari's historical chronicles of the battle of Qadisiyah, 6000 Iranians stood up and watched the defeat of the Iranian Sassanid army by the Muslim forces, and many betrayed their own people by facilitating the Arab Muslims' triumph.[8] Just a century prior to this historical tragedy, an infamous revolt by Mazdak (Schmidinger, n.d.) plunged the whole Iranian (Sassanid) empire into chaos.

Throughout history, rulers have occasionally tried to relieve their subjects' burdens through tax relief, distribution of agrarian lands or water resources to the local peasants, or sharing the war spoils. Though such provisional economic transfer may be seen by historians or the state as generosity and clemency, these gestures often proved to be mere rehearsals and often served only to fortify the king's power and reinforce a system of absolute obedience and allegiance. This historical reality is one main reason for a hide-and-seek culture within society, causing a general state of distrust and duplicity. For centuries Iranian masses had felt completely detached from the power apparatus and considered the rulers to be tyrants who were just sucking their blood, controlling each and every aspect of their personal lives, and viewing them as resources to support the authoritarian system. The tyrants' lust to control every single citizen and simultaneous distrust of the entire population (including closest members of the court) has been a major cause for people to fear telling the truth.

Lying has thus inevitably become part of daily life for citizens and elites alike, including politicians and business people. Some researchers see this disposition toward hiding the truth as a "characteristic" of Persians which has grown out of history and religion. J. Niklos (1983) notes that "[s]ometimes for honorable or understandable reasons, sometimes for self-protection, and sometimes to advance one's own interests *Taqiyah*, or religious dissimulation, permits a person to hide his religion or disavow certain religious practices to escape probable or definite danger of death from those who are opposed to his beliefs". He further claims that although the "*Taqiyah*" has been continually reinforced by historical realities, the persecutions instigated frequently by the Shiite Imams have functioned as a weapon to protect the weak against the strong. But a major problem here is that such practices have become widely accepted by the entire population, socio-political groups, and ruling elites, which has rotten the entire post-revolutionary social and political structure. Even the Shah did not hide his disappointment surrounding Iranians' glorification of lying and mentions in his book that the "Persians lie" (Hutchinson, 1961).

The political acts of this seemingly permanent game of hide-and-seek, historical invasions, tribal wars, and a perpetual intrusion of the Iranian despotic political system into people's private and family affairs have shaped the trait of individualism manifested in virtually every aspect of Iranian behavior. Distrust and suspicion have overwhelmed Iranians from an individual level to inter-ethnic or interreligious relations. Research demonstrates that Iranians suffer from the lack or a relative absence of a meaningful group to belong to outside of the family (Miklos, 1983). While the frequently quoted advice of an elderly Iranian sage may at first glance appear exaggerative it hints at the personality structures and double standards within majority society: "Do not be afraid of abuse, humiliation or slander. When kicked out of one door enter with a smile from another. Be impudent, insolent and stupid for it is sometimes necessary to pretend stupidity–it helps. Try to establish connections with the holders of high office. Agree with everybody, no matter what his opinion is, so that you may attract his utmost favour" (Kamshad, 1966).

Another paradoxical condition within the Iranian socio-political structure was the centuries of yearly levies and compulsory contribution to state revenues. While no peasant could be relieved from their annual or seasonal duties and levies, Shiite clergies across the entire country enjoyed their share of followers' financial contributions, known as *"Khoms"* (the fifth of the family's income), which had to be levied directly to the local clergies. This made the Shiite clergies, unlike the Sunni Mullahs, independent of the state. Such financial privilege gave the Iranian Shiite Mullahs extraordinary power; something which could be considered one of the contributing elements to the Ayatollah's interventions in the state affairs, which culminated in the 1979 Islamic revolution. Such extraordinary financial situations were intentionally overlooked by the state authority, which had caused a permanent contradictory and discriminating taxation system.

A Perpetual Ambivalence: A Universally Oriented Political Islam Versus Locally Oriented Personal Practice of Islam

Apart from the impacts of despotic forms political power in the Middle East and an exhausting history of invasion-evasion, the spread of Islam and associated traditions has brought another kind of uncertainty within the public as well as clerics and elites. Islam's original purpose was to obtain political power, which has been demonstrated not only in Qur'an verses but also in the Islamic prophet's life. The prophet established the first Islamic society in Medina and through the use coercion, spread the religion across the entire Middle East (and beyond during the Islamic Kalifate of Omar and his successors). A legacy of war and invasion between diverse Islamic subdivisions convinced many Muslims to exercise their own way of religious practice rather than listen to opposing elucidations of local clergies and political leaders. After centuries of war and sectarian conflicts across the Middle East, the common people learned to either distance themselves from political Islam or tried to adapt some elements of the Islamic tradition into their daily lives.

Some scholars (Moaddel, 2002b) use crisis theory to explain the revival and growth of political Islam recent decades, and blame the economic deprivation and marginalization of Muslim communities along with the "failure of modernization" for economic decline. However, most of the uprisings and revolts that have recently occurred in Islamic nations like Egypt, Iran, Jordan, Syria, and Algeria involve protesters from the new urban middle class. The truth is that a series of international events along with the growth of modernist, pro-west, and despotic regimes and an unfair redistribution of oil revenues have triggered waves of Islamic fundamentalism in parts of the Middle East in recent decades. Events like the fall of communism in Central and Eastern Europe at the end of 1980s as well as the communist ideology fiasco around the globe and concomitant confusions, especially within the younger generations in Islamic countries, have played an enormous role. A series of military coupes, wars, and invasions[9] instigated and fed fundamentalist Islamist movements in the Middle East, which only strengthened and spread with regional and international interference.

In the 27 years following the Jungle Movement where Qazi Muhammed proclaimed a Kurdish democratic Republic in Mahabad region, Iranian nationalists have once again become hypocritical in their approach to rejecting minority (here Kurdish) nationalistic movements, while the same time praising the pro-soviet Gilan Republic in the northern part of the country. This is riddled with hypocrisy and double standards. The simultaneous respect toward the leaders of the Gilan Republic and hatred against the Kurdistan Republic movement grew worse after the 1979 Islamic Revolution. The culmination of such double standards could also be seen in the government's investment in the Kuchak Khan's Mausoleum in northern Iran and the abandoned tomb of Qazi in Kurdish town Mahabad: A clear sign of formal authorities' double standards and discrimination against ethnic minorities' desires and rights.

V. Modernity Versus Tradition: Modernism Collapsed in Religion, Tradition and Militarism

Almost every community within the Middle East is struggling to find a smooth path towards establishing a modern society acceptable to its diverse masses. If not with the turn of the 19th century then certainly with the end of the World War II, a multitude countries in this region have tried everything to become more progressive and modern. Through such an endeavor, the Middle East has become a huge laboratory for modernism; majorly invested in the militaristic, authoritarian, monolingual, and secularistic statehood of a one nation, one language, consumer society. The first and most readily observed step here has been the formation of national and rural military forces along with a national intelligence unit for further protection of a future authoritarian political system. Oil money financed more systematic military institutions as well as many internal and international wars. It made people like Saddam Hussein, Gaddafi, the Iranian Shah, and King Fahd greater players than they would have been otherwise, as they could buy weapons and materials that were ultimately used to harm their own citizens and neighbouring countries. Notable Middle Eastern intelligence units involved in these conflicts include *Stekhbarat* (the General Intelligence Presidency in Saudi Arabia), *Tukish İstihbarat* (National Intelligence Organization or *Millî İstihbarat Teşkilatı*, MİT), Iranian *Ettela'at va Amniyat* (SAVAK or VAJA), and Iraqi *al-Amn al-Amma* (General Security Directorate, GSD).

In an apt analogy to what has historically occurred, George Orwell in his 1949 novel referred to secret thought police (or "Thinkpol"), whose job it was to discover and penalize thought crimes. As a first step, through a system of total control and investigation, opposing ideologies or political groups considered to be threat to public order are identified and punished, as is the case in Iran. A second step might be to majorly delineate the country's borders in an intimidating way, without paying attention to possible comments, requests, or needs of the other party. An inquiry into the many Middle Eastern borders will show the Iran-Iraq as well as the Syrian–Iraqi borders to be characterized by ever-evolving tensions between resilience and degeneration within these countries. What this means, is that after decades of artificial and mandatory boundaries, local Kurdish families and tribes who dare to cross the fence to visit their kin are still targets of border guards or armed gendarmes.

A third step might be to have a cruel, rigid and, a violent nation-building strategy involving assimilation, culturicide, forced settlement, or displacement. Until the mid-20th century, most residents of Middle Eastern countries were living a pastoral nomadic, tribal, or semi-rural lifestyle. While many nomadic or Bedouin communities were self-contained, others played a central role in their regional or national affairs. The period following the Second World War was marked by extensive land reform and sedentarization and detribalization policies within many major Middle Eastern countries. However, many such policies evolved into brutal confrontation and hostilities. Overnight, a self-containing, independent, and productive way of life that had existed for millennia was changed due to new governmental perspectives that such a life was anachronistic and embarrassing to modernist-progressive nation-states.

A fourth common step would involve a move toward peripheral semi-capitalistic and hierarchical economic systems of dependency. In the time following the Second World War, the Middle East became marked as the geographic "center of gravity" of the world oil economy. Oil money had changed the balance of power between state and society further in oil exporting countries such as Iran, Iraq, and Saudi Arabia. By giving local rulers the ability to suppress the countries' popular institutions and ethnic minorities' societies and thwart traditional checks on their authority, they could enforce an authoritarian political model of postcolonial oppression. Furthermore, creating a regional hegemony under their own leadership was a major goal for the competing local rulers in Turkey, Iran, Iraq, and Saudi Arabia. "Before the second world war, Middle Eastern countries had to compete for oil company investment in much the same way as ranchers in Texas or Oklahoma. The large companies were more afraid of a glut of oil than oil shortages. Under the "Red Line Agreement" of 1928, the three largest, Exxon, Shell, and BP, along with a few smaller partners, agreed that none of them would explore for or develop new oil in the old Ottoman Empire unless all the partners consented" (Tétreault, 1983).

As in many other Islamic countries in the Middle East, Iranian society is stuck between modernity and tradition, and is rife with a culture torn apart by predominantly Islamic ideologies. While clerical forces have pulled the entire nation toward attachment to religious guidelines and constructs, they are resisting or avoiding any fundamental changes or reforms to its existence. The last century has become a major battleground for the conflicting forces trying to convince the public of their desired visions of social interaction and philosophy. The Iranian Shah, his court, and its administration have played a crucial role in the direction society is heading, and an immense regression towards Islamic Shiite traditions was evident following the 1979 Islamic Revolution. In this time, many educational and medical centres have been turned into prisons or bases for Islamic militia forces. The famous UNESCO building in the city of Dezful in the southwest of the country was changed to a horrific detention center, where thousands of mostly young political prisoners were executed in cold blood.

The constitution of the Islamic Republic of Iran ratified in October 1979 and amended in 1989 arose based on a series of fundamental religious criteria of Shiite Islam, which is in turn established on the traditional Twelver Ja'fari School, which cannot fully satisfy the needs and desires of a modern, democratic, and pluralistic society. Traces of traditional Shiite principles can also be easily found in the 1906 Iranian Constitutional Revolution's legislations. Under these legislative regulations, members of other religious and ethnic communities were not only eliminated from political power but also deprived of their fundamental rights. Although the constitution had tried to limit the vast power of the Shah while expanding the newly established national assembly (Majlis), many of its main articles were intensely coupled with the Shiite clergy's principles. It urged the Assembly to control all its legislations to comply with Sharia law, and the judicial system thus fell under control of the Shiite clergy. A lack of provisions that would grant citizens' rights and gender equality, support freedom of speech, assembly, or religion, or protect ethnic and religious minority rights further led to the institutionalization of discriminative policies. Ethnic and religious minorities as well as women were eliminated from the constitutional rights and legal preservations.

During the Constitutional Revolution in 1906, the British Embassy in Tehran ironically became a haven for constitutionalists to exchange their political ideas and debate on the ways out of the despotic Qajar monarchy. Some even have called such gathering as "open-air school of political science" (Abrahamian, 1982). Preposterously, Britain ceased their supports toward the constitutionalists and backed up the Shah: a behaviour which later costed them the Iranians' trust.

Kurdish people and their local leaders were mostly suspicious toward national Iranian political parties, such as the Iranian communist party ("Party of the Masses of Iran" – Tudah Party of Iran), significantly influenced Iranian social, cultural and political life during the Shah's reign and a short period after the Iranian revolution of 1979. In a formal report regarding a visit to Iran and the Urmia region in 1942, the British Consul in Tabriz revealed that Kurds disliked the Tudeh party immensely and that the party was not allowed to open any local offices in Kurdish areas. A few decades later, this political group became a major force behind the 1979 Islamic Revolution and Ayatollah Khomeini's wish to establish a fundamental clerical Islamic republic. One reason behind such an odd alliance is the ideological attachment of the Tudah Party to the Soviet communist regime. Second, there was a degree of harmony between Islamist fundamentalists and major communist groups in viewing United States and major western countries as imperialist superpowers whose major goals were to subjugate the entire world, including all developing countries. It is believed that the increased politicization of the clerical establishment in Iran was also a related consequence of fundamentally secular discourses propagated by the Soviet Union and their primary conduit into Iran, the Tudah Party (Amanat, 2009).

    Many call the 1906 Iranian Constitutional Revolution an intellectual revolution, which had led to enlightenment within the country's socio-political structure. But the truth is that despite the possible transformations and slight political reforms this movement might have caused, the footprints of a traditional Islamic-Shiite culture were easily recognizable in all "modern" establishments and institutions. Even modern political parties of this era (the period of Constitutional Revolution) did not accept members from non-Muslim Iranian communities, and according Erwand Abrahamian (1982), non-Muslims were not welcomed as members of the secular socialist and nationalist party, the Iran Party. Even then, the situation within other political parties was more hostile. The radical "freedom" party spread hatred and disputes against religious minorities by publishing many articles and writings that demonized them. (Abrahamian, 1982).

    According to Erwan Abrahamian (1982), only one communist party was established in 1941 due to a sense of fear of the clergies, which at the time had made citizens feel uncomfortable to refer to themselves openly as communist or socialist. Therefore, the founders referred to themselves as the "Tudeh" party instead of the Communist party. Later on, some prominent leaders of the radical revolutionary Marxist organizations openly called themselves true Muslims with a Marxist ideology: clearly a contradictive, opportunistic eclecticism which led to horrible political confusion and inconsistency during and after the national uprisings leading up to the 1979 Iranian revolution. The Tudeh Party and the Fadaian Khalgh or "Aksariyat" (Organization of self-sacrificers of the people of Iran-Majority) as the two largest left-wing political parties in Tehran after the revolution furiously supported Ayatollah Khomeini's Islamic revolution just because of his anti-capitalist and anti-imperialist capacities. Noureddin Kianouri, the General Secretary of the Tudeh Party, openly defended the Imam's Line (*Khat-e Imam*) which promoted the fundamentalist Shiite thoughts of Ayatollah Khomeini.

Kianouri (1982) "believed [...] Imam Lines to be an anti-Imperialistic, anti-American movement, which guarantees masses' fundamental rights and freedom, initiator of essential economic changes, exterminator of dependent capitalism and grand-feudalism's plunder, and finally the savior and instigator of improvement in the Iranian toilers' and impoverished peoples' living conditions" (Author's translation from Persian of Kianouri, 1982, p. 258). In a gesture of extreme affection toward the Stalinist dictatorial regime, another leader and rhetorician of this political faction named Anwar Khamei (1983) wrote that "there isn't any real God than Stalin!", which ended up being an extremely humiliating proclamation. Entire members of the central committee of the time's Iranian Communist Party (Hezb-e Komonist-e Iran) under the leadership of Hamid Azariyoun went behind Ayatollah Khomeini's movement and voted for an Islamic Republic. In his 1974 military court trial, the Iranian Marxist revolutionary Khosro Golsorkhi announced that he had found social justice in the school of Islam and had then reached socialism. He also believed that Imam Hussein (the third Shiite Imam) was the great martyr of the people of the Middle East (Samakar, 2006).

With the greatest level of support coming from the Soviet regime in Moscow and its security agency (the KGB), the major Iranian leftist political parties paved the way for the Iranian Ayatollahs to establish the most horrific Shiite-Islamic fundamental system in Iran's history. The irony here is that for Marxism, religion was considered to be a false consciousness and a source of human servitude rather than human emancipation. Similar to some counterpart organizations in other Islamic countries around the world however, religion became a major source of liberation and independence for many Iranian Marxist organizations.

Iranians have experienced extremist-despotic Shiite regimes since 1501, when the militant Sufi leader Shah Ismail of Safavids declared twelve-Imam Shi'ism as the official state religion in Iran and used force to convert most Iranians to the Shia sect. Under Safavids, Iran became a theocracy that intertwined state and religion, and the Shah became called the *murshid-e kamil, or* the perfect guide and emanation of the Godhead. Under these theocratic regimes, Iranians went through extreme public disorder, turmoil, and series of national and international wars. Accompanied by millions of other Iranians, ethnic and religious minorities suffered from torture, extermination, genocide, forced displacements, and the worst forms of assimilation and culturicide.

One important reason for the Islamic traditional forces' breakthroughs in claiming power in countries like Iran and Iraq might be their cunning adaptation of "left" political philosophies or western ideological approaches into traditional Islamic thoughts and teachings. In pre-revolution years, the Iranian clergy member Ayatollah Morteza Motahari used Marxist philosophy and critical analysis in his writings. Similarly, Ayatollah Mahmoud Taleqani also wrote a book on "Islam and Property" (Islam va Malekiyat) where he supported Marxist theory of collective property rights. Ali Shariati was also an Islamic ideologist and intellectual deeply aware of Shia theology, but his thoughts were still immensely influenced by Marxism and Third World theories. Shariati was sold on Marxist ideology and believed in class struggle, workers' revolutions, and establishing a classless society, while at the same time he interpreted Shiism as a creed of revolution. Like his communist revolutionary counterparts, he did not hesitate to step further and called his model "red Shiism", which existed in contrast with the traditional, clerical Safavid Shiism, which he referred to as "Black Shiism" (Vali Nasr, 2007). Shariati was not the only one who labeled the Shiites as oppressed, deprived, and revolutionary masses. Indeed, many others like Louis Périllier (1985), Henry Corbin (1991), and Francois Thual (1995) have also assigned such revolutionary characteristic to Shiite masses.

Other clerical characters like Mohammad Baqir al-Sadr in Iraq also used western philosophical and political economic discourse and language to win over the attention of the younger generations for their future political endeavours. In sum, such devious amalgamations of modern thought with local traditional ideologies by many Islamic clergies has helped fundamental Islamic forces hold political power in many Middle Eastern countries.

The Middle Eastern nations' economic plans and recommended policies could also be seen as irritating elements which have initiated dual economies and not real development, as lamented by Joseph E. Stiglitz, the former senior vice president and chief economist of the World Bank (Stiglitz, 2003). The reality is that the rising tide in the Middle East rarely lifts all boats. The underlying characteristics of such unjust and uneven developments are nothing but persistent exploitation, poverty, inequality, ethno-racial injustice, and discrimination against the majority, while the ruling elites enjoy luxurious conditions and inclusiveness. The unstable oil regimes in the Middle East have focused on transforming their economies rather than the lives of their citizens. In contrast, Joseph Stiglitz believes that "development is about transforming the lives of people, not just transforming economies" (Stiglitz, 2003).

VI. Intellectuals' Antagonistic Stances on Modernity

Colonial forces have been continuously present across the Middle East for centuries, but it was neither the British nor the French agents who strived for modernization in these countries. Rather, it has been the local rulers and endemic intellectuals who took the lead to modernization. Amanullah Khan in Afghanistan, Reza Khan in Iran, Mustafa Kemal in Turkey, Gamal Abdel Nasser of Egypt, and many others were the driving forces behind the ideas and undertakings of modernization in these countries, though no such initiatives ended up being adopted smoothly, and confusion, contradiction, and animosity became entrenched *en route*. On the one hand, clashes and rival positioning has permeated between secular political forces and traditional clergies or religious layers of society. On the other hand, the opposing and conflictual stances of famed authors and intellectuals have played a tremendous role in moving the masses, forming the public opinion, and crafting the vox populi. Even then, Middle Eastern intellectuals and authors have had different stances toward modernity and tradition depending on their social class, family status, educational level and type, and ties to traditional or religious society. In some cases, the more populist ones try "to have it both ways"!

At the same time, while progressive scholars' major concerns lie in emancipatory social change (keeping in mind obvious social and political exigencies), Horkheimer (1937) and his associates (Herbert Marcuse and Theodor Adorno) at the Frankfurt School of Social Science emphasized helping oppressed peoples reach happiness by developing the critical consciousness necessary to gain correct knowledge. Horkheimer (1937) formulates a fundamental critique of bourgeois societies, which he identifies as a social formation torn apart by political and economic contradictions, ideological paradoxes, and social injustices. Departing from the classical academic social involvements such as that of Horkheimer and associates and moving into a newer era of scholar contribution, one can easily confront myriad number of works published to support deprived people and oppressed communities.[10]

Jalal Al-e Ahmad (1923-69) is an Iranian leftist intellectual unable to expound his ultimate position or his true "weltanschauung". In his iconic book namely "Westoxification" (*gharbzadehgi*), he sees Shiite-Islamic characteristics as predominant elements of the Iranian cultural identity and tries to distance himself from western cultural elements:

> [...] every schoolchild, in learning the "Imperial Anthem" as the national anthem, forgets the prayers. In setting foot in sixth grade, he departs the mosque. In going to the movies, he consigns religion to oblivion. Thus 90 percent of those of us with a secondary school education are irreligious, or rather, indifferent toward religion. They are suspended in a void. They have nothing to stand on, no certainty, and no faith. When they see that the state, for all its pomp and circumstance, its organization and budget, all the foreign aid, all the artillery and tanks, is incapable of solving a social problem such as the unemployment of graduates, and when they meanwhile see what a refuge an ancient religious faith is for the army of the poor and helpless, how they rejoice on 15 Sha'ban, they find themselves at a loss. The radio keeps murmuring spells in their ears; the cinema sets the worlds of our betters before their eyes. True, they are confronted with another reality, the reality of the content of religious faith. (Ahmad, 1983)

He refers to the Sassanid era's Zoroastrians who refused to join the Muslim conquerors and fled to India. He notes that they should have stayed and accepted to pay the *Jaiya* (a special tax imposed on non-Muslims) and not impose the pain of a trip on themselves. Al-e Ahmad died just ten years before Ayatollah Khomeini's ascension to power in 1979 and did not observe what a return to the Shiite fundamentalist identity meant; something which led the entire country into four decades of political, social and economic downturn and misery. Six years prior to his death however, he did witness Khomeini's fundamentalist rhetoric and extreme attitude on the state policies, which led to the June 1963 uprising in the holy city of Qom. However, this experience did not lead to any meaningful thoughts, revisions, or reconsiderations.

Numerous other authors and activists also preached and advocated for a return to Shiite-Iranian home culture and an avoidance of the western liberal way of life. Fred Halliday (1993) criticizes the fanaticism of calling a condition "gharbzadegi," and argues that if there is a condition such as "gharbzadegi," then there should be one also could be called "sharghzadgi" (Eastoxification). In his concluding statement, he notes: "I could sum this up by adapting a slogan: na gharbzadegi, na sharqzadegf, neither westoxification nor eastoxification. Let us therefore go beyond this unnecessarily polarized and in some ways methodologically impoverished debate and continue with the job of studying these societies" (Halliday, 1993, p.163).

Ale Ahmad's idea of "Westoxification" is just the other side of the coin in Edward Said's assertion about "orientalism" and the colonial domination of westerners and their scholars in downward-looking assessments of the Middle East (or perhaps more appropriately, Arab-Islamic countries). Said's theory of orientalism gives such exaggerative thoughts on how hegemonic the western intellectuals' and scholars' works or discourses could be toward the so called "primitive, irrational, violent, despotic, fanatic, and essentially inferior" oriental societies. He even accuses Marx of falling into Eurocentric orientalism and tags him as pro-colonial, while citing a passage from him in the 18th Brumaire of Louis Bonaparte: "Sie Können sich nicht vertreten, sie müssen vertreten warden," which means "if they cannot represent themselves, they must be represented" (Said, 2003). The same way, Said's and Ale Ahmad's fanatic texts are seen by many others as anti-western (Lewis, 1982). Sometimes it rather seems that Said has intentionally disregarded other non-western, especially Russian scholars in his denigrative writing. As Bernard Lewis has suitably noticed the Russians even in their most abusive and contemptuous statements about Islam have enjoyed a total exemption from Said's strictures. Here Russian academicians like *S. P.* Tolstov, who calls the prophet Muhammad a "shamanistic myth" or E. A. Belayev, who described the Qur'an as the ideological expression of slave-owning ruling class, remain unchallenged. Lewis (1982) roots such omissions in Edward Said's political devotions and points at Said's claim that South Yemen was "the only genuinely radical people's democracy in the Middle East".

Unfortunately, such double-standards and hypocrisy along with pessimistic, biased, and unidimensional assertions against western society and its scholars exculpates the people, culture, and ruling elites within the oriental societies from their historical responsibilities of agency, self-awareness, and social cohesion. Ale Ahmad's thoughts of "Westoxification" as well as Edward Said's "Orientalism" are rather seen as "a generalized swear-word" (Keddie, 2007) against anyone who might take a different position regarding the ethnic or religious disputes within Middle Eastern societies.

At the opposite end, there are many Iranian intellectuals who either vehemently wish for a separation from the "Shiite-Arabic" elements drained into the Iranian culture and psyche. Here, such separation can refer to backing Iranian cultural and social purification or distancing Iranian society from Arabic culture while not necessarily emulating western culture or ways of life. Sadegh Hedayat (1903-51) is a prominent romantic nationalist author who was distanced from Shiite Islamic elements, which he viewed as having highjacked the more favourable Persian culture and language for many centuries. In 1924, he published his first impressions in a book entitled "*Ensan va Heyvan*" ("Man and Animal"), which condemns the killing of animals for any purpose (Heyadat, 2013), which is completely contrary to fundamental rituals in the Islamic school of thought. Hedayat does not hide his hatred of Arab Muslims and abhors Islam in his writings. Instead, he venerates Old-Iranian, Zoroastrian and pre-Islamic eras as the Golden Age of Iran in which a true cultural identity (i.e. the Aryan civilization) was glorified; an era which according to Hedayat was destroyed by the Arab Muslim invaders, who replaced Iran's superior culture and civilization with an inferior culture and a ruthless religion of their own. Furthermore, he portrays today's Iranian Muslims as corrupt and hypocritical.

Similarly, Mohammad Ali Jamalzadeh (1892-1997), Sadegh Chubak (1916-1998), Mehdi Akhavan (1929-1990), Nader Naderpour (1929-2000), and many other Iranian authors, novelists and intellectuals openly show their aversion towards the Islamic-Shiite Arabic culture and praise the "pure" Persian language and culture. They accuse Islam and the Arab Muslims of being historical enemies of Iran and Iranians, and believe that the only way out of such "historical misery" and "regression" would be only a return to a pure Iranian culture and civilization.

Sayed Jamal Adin Asadabadi (1838-1897) was an Iranian Islamic ideologist and political activist whose ideology, beliefs, and intentions—like his adopted names as discrepant ethnic-national identities—were ambiguous (Kasravi, 1999). He advocated for the modernization of Islam while the same time furiously acted against European countries. While he was not interested in Islamic theology, he supported the unification of all Islamic schools of thought. His idealisms were a confusing patchwork of inconsistent ideas and beliefs, and he would intentionally adjust his viewpoints according to the situation. While he was against British dominion and wished the western inclined rulers could be overthrown, he was described absurdly as a liberal thinker. He could easily pair himself with traditional clergies against Britain and at the same time be close to reformist intellectuals of other Islamic countries and preach for furnishings with modern western technologies. He identified himself as Sunni Pashtun when he was in Afghanistan or India, as Shia Jafari in Iran, and as a reformist Sunni clergy member in Istanbul while hiding his attachment to Shia denomination. Depending on the situation, Asadabadi named himself Al Afghani, Al Istanbuli, Al Kabuli, Al Rumi, or Isfahani. It is known that at the beginning he belonged to the two Shiite religious movements of Sheykhism and Babism (Abrahamian, 1982). He was also not consolidated at all on his approach to dealing with Western powers. His vehement hostility against Britain was lacking towards Russians, something that many Iranians today still latch on to. Not only was he accused of being an agent to the Russians, but his faith toward Islam was also questioned. His controversial voyage to Russia in 1887 took two years in an era where both powers were immensely competing against one another (Keddie & Richard, 2006). Ahmad Kasravi (1999) states that "Seyyed Jamal despite wearing all clerical dress and his job as Shiite Preacher did not have really a strong faith in Islam or in its founder; and he had been telling this to many people secretly." He continues "… especially he counted as one of the founders of Constitutional Revolution and the truth is that his words in advancing the movement have been very effective." The problem with Asadabadi has been his altering characteristics, which made him both mysterious and suspicious. None of the historians or scholars of the Iranian Constitutional Revolution (Kasravi, Abrahamian, Keddie, Parizi, etc.) could give a reliable update on his last known position.

One of the leading characters in the 1905 Constitutional Revolution, which led to the establishment of the country's first parliament, was Mirza Malkom Khan. He was born in an Armenian family but converted to Islam and was educated in

Europe. He counted as an important 19th century pro-west modernist intellectual and advocated for a system of law and order for Iran. He was in favour of introducing modern concepts and ideas to the public by making them compatible with acceptable Islamic formats. He is known having been deceitful in his career, dubiously patriotic toward Iran, and had reportedly converted back and forth between different religions (Rain, 1974). He had even changed his citizenship due to his relationship with the Qajars, or Ottomans. Malkom Khan's involvement in establishing the Faramoshkhaneh (an Iranian version of Freemasonry) in 1858 has also been a significant source of contention. While some may still believe in "its lack of affiliation to any of the European obedience" (Algar, 2012), there is no doubt that Faramoshkhaneh has been preserving foreign interests in Iran.

Malkom Khan had announced his establishment having thirty thousand members, which indicates an immense foreign influence within the country, though this number may be exaggerated. A roster presented by Malkom Khan shows how most the Persian elites including Qajar family members and princes such as Soltan Oways Mirza Ehtesam-al-Dawla and Sayf-Allah Mirza were involved in the disputed arrangement. An important concern is how such critical writings of "Qanun" published by Malkom Khan in Europe could have regularly reached readers throughout Iran including Kermanshah[11] (a large Kurdish city in Western Iran about 600 kilometers distanced from Tehran) without direct involvement of a foreign country (Rain, 1974).

Apart from his political affiliations with foreign countries' interests and interventions, Molkom Khan had been actively publishing on modern politics and philosophy as well as on the rule of law, democracy, and freedom. He had written about the famous French philosopher and father of modern Sociology, August Conte, for the first time in Iran (Adamian, n.d.). While he was a key player in the Iranian intellectual movement of the 19th century, he could never be purged from business disputes such the Iranian Lottery concession corruption scandal or the freemasonry club's hidden agendas. According to Ismail Rain however, a main reason for the legionary's eventual defeat in Iran was the inextricable internal enmity between the political figures and the court. Although these people had been participating in British freemasonry associations and doing all duties dictated and assigned to them individually, they could never work together collectively (Rain, 1987).

VII. The Dilemma of Double Standards and Dualistic Journalism

Societies' intellectuals are allegedly believed to think ahead of their people and perceive everyone objectively and with equality and justice. However, there are numerous Iranian intellectuals and activists who divide citizens into categories and view each with antagonism instead of leading mainstream politics and public opinion through fair and just humanistic constructs. Here, a content analysis of the socio-political texts and writings published by major Iranian authors proves the existence of extreme bias and dualism toward socio-political events and occurrences.

Reza Fani Yazdi is an author who had been leading the communist party in the 1980s in the Iranian province of Khorasan and was captured by authorities of Islamic Republic. While he was originally sentenced to death, he was instead freed from prison and sent abroad for unknown reasons. Almost all his quasi-journalistic writings convey identical messages and assume the formal position of hardline members of the Iranian Islamic regime. In this, he calls Sunni–Arab countries "Mortaje" (reactionist) or Israelis, Americans, and other western countries "Vahshi" (Savage) and calls upon Palestinians to radicalize further against Israelis while Arafat was signing the peace pact with Israel 1991. Here, he criticizes "the Israeli's savage and barbaric invasion of Lebanon and their massacre" (Fani, 2012). In his article he praises the Islamic regime and believes that the country has been very successful in spreading its own type of Islam, while the Iranian Shiite leaders have become very popular figures in the Middle East:

> The Muslim Brotherhood model of Islamism, which had been leading in Egypt in the past, had almost lost its popularity in the Middle East. Large populations of Muslim and Arab peoples were now embracing Islamism in the manner of the Islamic Republic of Iran. Shiite figures like Hassan Nasrallah, Ruhollah Khomeini, Ali Khamenei, and even Iranian President Mahmoud Ahmadinejad have become popular regional figures among Sunni Muslims. (Fani, 2012)

There are myriad other personalities in the political sphere of Iran known as intellectuals, reformists, oppositional leaders, or journalists, who claim to be on the oppressed side rather being with the formal power. People like Shayegan, Ehsan Naraghi and Husein Nasr have written papers on the social or political stances of the Iranian society or even on the regional or international status quo, in which they claim to have presented fair and unbiased synopses of the 'true' story. While they try to prove themselves to have supported the troubled and marginalized masses, they have often ended up being discriminatory and unfair in their assertions. Additionally, they present themselves as worried about the world's oppressed while remaining completely silent toward their own countrymen. Such proud intellectual faces unfoundedly relate communist ideological aggression and violence against their citizens (e.g. the Cambodian genocide by Khmer Rouge, 1975-79) to the "western intruders", though none of them acknowledge the 1988 prisoners' mass-execution committed by the Iranian clerical regime. Similarly, the post-revolutionary authors and ideologues in addition to official authorities of the Islamic Republic labelled the regime's dissidents as agents of the west or Zionism, or hirelings of foreign countries.

Such populist and dualistic statements can also be uncovered within Ayatollah Khomeini's proclamations, in which he at once deceitfully covers his true identity and position, while also promoting a discriminatory attitude toward religious minorities such as Bahá'ís:

> In his fifteen years of exile, he carefully avoided making public pronouncements, especially written ones, on issues that would alienate segments of the opposition — issues such as land reform, clerical power, and sexual equality. Instead, he hammered the regime on topics that outraged all sectors of the opposition: the concessions granted to the West, the tacit alliance with Israel, the wasteful expenditures or arms, the rampant corruption in high places, the decay of agriculture, the rise in the cost of living, the housing shortage and the sprawling slums, the widening gap between the rich and the poor, the suppression of newspapers and political parties, the creation of a vast bureaucratic state, and the gross violations of the constitutional laws. In denouncing the regime, Khomeini promised to liberate the country from foreign domination; extend freedom to all political parties, even "atheistic" ones; guarantee the rights of all religious minorities,

except those of the "heretical" Bahá'ís; and bring social justice to all, particularly to the bazaaris, the intelligentsia (rushanfekran), the peasantry (dehqanan), and, most mentioned of all, the dispossessed masses (mostazafin). These promises, especially the populist and anti-imperialist themes, succeeded in winning over a wide range of political forces, from the followers of the late Ayatallah Kashani and remnants of the Feda'iyan-i Islam at one end of the spectrum, to the Liberation Movement and the National Front at the center, and to the Tudeh, Mujahedin, and the Marxist Feda'i at the other end of the spectrum". (Abrahamian, 1982)

Such bigoted rhetoric occurred in later years of the Iranian Islamic Revolution along with the instrumental use of people for its political purposes, such as suppressing any opposition and strengthening the foundation of power domestically, and the use of Shiite Afghan and Iraqi refugees to fight in Syria and against Iranian anti-regime protesters internationally.

There are many more journalists, activists or scholars in Iran and other Middle Eastern countries that have chosen to rather be bought off by the wealthy elite than destroyed by men of the sword. Millions of petrodollars have been spent to keep contemporary authors, activists, and intellectuals in line with the formal political affairs of any given state within the Middle East. Authors or activists who resist the formal procedures will pay a big price for their deviancy such as imprisonment, loss of licensing or professional activism, exile, torture, or death. As the Lebanese political scientist Fouad Ajami accurately indicates, "In the Arab world today, intellectuals are either beaten down by the stick or seduced by the carrot," (Miller, 1985). Political activists, intellectuals, academics, and journalists in countries like Syria, Egypt, Iran, Palestine, and Turkey are targeted daily by their governments, and in many cases, they have languished in prison for years. In the absence of free democratic institutions and a lack of free press and free speech these people are targeted for all kinds of torture, discrimination, and life imprisonment. In 2009, the courageous Iranian journalist and human and women's rights activist, Narges Mohammadi, was sentenced to 11 years in prison for "assembly and collusion against national security" after protesting the fraudulent election of Mahmoud Ahmadinejad. Similarly, the Kurdish politician and intellectual

Selahattin Demirtas has been in detention for his open criticism toward Erdogan's oppressive policies in Turkey and is unjustly facing 142 years in prison. Finally, the Saudi women's rights activist and social media figure, Loujain al-Hathloul, has been imprisoned since 2014 for opposing the Saudi male guardianship system and driving ban against women.

Located in Tehran, "Evin" is the name of what is perhaps one of the world's most brutal and notorious prisons. Because of its undue number of incarcerated intellectuals, political activists, scholars, and journalists, it is euphemistically referred to as "Evin University" by Iranians. After extensively documenting mass hangings at the Saydnaya detention center, Amnesty International in a 2017 report referred to the prison as "the human slaughterhouse".

Nevertheless, the conspiratorial application of politics and social affairs is not, of course, unique to Iran. Elsewhere in the Middle East, one can easily distinguish literature and oratories which were either rejected by the public or political system and were very much contradictory. Arab philosophers and intellectuals also sometimes used western philosophical theories, concepts, and values in an irrelevant and self-imaginary manner. The concepts of feminism, democracy, human rights, and existentialism have been incompletely borrowed or adopted from European intelligentsia. "A salient feature of the current literature on decolonization is that if it addresses intellectual exchange at all, it does so within the framework of an incomplete and unsatisfactory borrowing or adaptation of European ideas to Third World realities" (Di-Capua, 2012). For example "if evaluated against the original existentialism of Heidegger and Sartre, Arab existentialism might indeed be condemned as a "poor application" that was philosophically eclectic and politically incoherent" (Di-Capua, 2012).

In the 1950s, the Egyptian philosopher Abd al-Rahman Badawi declared his new Arab existentialistic-based (wujudiya) philosophy a "philosophy for our generation." Di-Capua (2012) indicates that Badawi processed "the ideas of Martin Heidegger and Jean-Paul Sartre into an entirely new intellectual tradition that was European in origin and Middle Eastern by design". He adds that "by the early 1960s, Arab culture was dominated by the language, assumptions, and politics of existentialism" (Di-Capua, 2012). A dilemma began when such use of European philosophy became entangled in anticolonial nationalism while also becoming fused with Islamic tradition. This extraordinary amalgamation of modernity and tradition caused tumultuous socio-political relations within the Arab nations in the coming decades. The catastrophic events following the Arab Spring at the dawn of the 21st century for example are just the latest in a chain of issues in Arab national intellectualism and politics.

Many rival Arab thinkers and authors associated the philosophy of existentialism in western societies with caricaturized scenarios where "people kissed one another in the streets" and moral laxity and sexual misconduct prevailed throughout the entire nation. They saw existentialism either as antithetical to the Middle Eastern way of life or as an idea that would bring nothing but social decay and egotistic indifference. In contrast, authors and activists such as Suhayl Idris endorsed a different model of political existentialism longing for freedom and democracy within Arab nations. Idris saw existentialism as an emancipatory socio-political doctrine that Arab nations urgently needed. He believed that the values of liberty and social responsibility must be made centrally important for ethical behaviour in the Arab world (Klemm, 2000). Any Arab nations' affinities toward western philosophers like Jean Paul Sartre have either been opportunistic or antagonistic in nature. When Sartre refused to accept the 1964 Nobel Prize in Literature because he believed that Americans were in control of the Prize, he became a significant symbol of freedom within the Arab nations, and it led him to be called the "greatest thinker of freedom in the twentieth century" (Klemm, 2000). In the Iraqi novel "Papa Sartre" (Badr, 2006), an "Iraqi Arab's Sartre" is dispatched to save the nation and turn Baghdad into another Paris. However, the reality of the day differed from the author's yearning and in addition to Iraq, other Arab nations including Egypt, Syria, Yemen, and Algeria turned to violent dictatorial regimes of repression and injustice. In an ideological amalgam of pan-Arabic nationalism and Marxist-Leninist concepts, Anouar Abdel-Malek (1962) referred to post-WWII Egyptian society as a "société militaire," where a new middle class viciously seized political power. Along with authoritarian and militaristic political systems, Baathist regimes claimed the reputations, freedom, and lives of many intellectuals, journalists, and university professors.

> Indeed, the repression and violence of the 1960s pushed Iraqi, as well as Egyptian, writers to question the fate of personal freedom. For writers such as Sarkun Bulus,

Yusuf al-Haydari, and Adil Kazim, to name only a few, it was a struggle over the fundamentals of human dignity". (Di-Capua, 2012)

During the 1967 Arab-Israeli War when Jean Paul Sartre signed a pro-Israeli manifesto criticizing Arab hostility and aggression towards Israelis, not only the politicians but also the Arab intellectuals accused Sartre of hypocrisy and logical inconsistency towards their griefs. Here also, Sartre's anti-colonialist ideology sharply contradicted his unconditional support toward the Israeli State, which Palestinians and Arab nationalists furiously detested. In strides toward reconciling Islamic and western traditions, the Egyptian intellectual Rifa'a al-Tahtawi exemplifies the Roman civilization as an example what could become of Islamic civilization. In addition, a western-educated Malaysian Islamic scholar by the name of Syed Muhammad Naquib al-Attas (1978) who published both Islamic theology and philosophy, preaches "de-westernization of knowledge" or "Islamization of knowledge" without properly identifying their connotations or providing examples of any real-world applications. When *al-Attas* and his Iranian counterpart Prof. Gholamabas Tawasoli, a liberal-Islamic sociologist, were invited our Faculty of Social Sciences at the University of Tehran in the 1980s, they were markedly enthusiastic about the recent Iranian revolution's outlook. Several years later when hundreds of thousands of Iranian dissidents, intellectuals, journalists, and liberal-Islamists were unjustly incarcerated, tortured, or executed, *al-Attas* and his comrades kept quiet and showed little concern. In the same year that saw the Ayatollah's regime execute over 20,000 political prisoners in a matter of weeks, the major concern of al-Attas and his Muslim intellectuals was to hold Palestinian leader Yasser Arafat out of peace with Israel.

The Islamic awakening in the Middle East demonstrates some critical inconsistencies and contradictions. Many intellectuals within this region reject or fail to acknowledge Greek, Zoroastrian, Hindu, and Jewish influences on Islamic Middle Eastern cultures and philosophy. In countless cases, contributions of non-Muslim Arabs as well as non-Arab Muslims around the Middle East are erroneously or intentionally overlooked, or the contributor's ethnic background is not acknowledged. In an article, Obiedat (2019) lists some paradoxes within the Arab Islamic awakening:

"First, it calls for the authentic return to Arab-Islamic heritage, while deeming as heretical several traditional doctrines; second, it strives for Arab unity without recognizing the needed concessions that should be given to unify non-Muslim Arabs; third, it is proud of the creativity of Islamic heritage in natural and philosophical fields while rejecting the indebtedness to Greek or Zoroastrian influences; fourth, it embraces the Abrahamic path in response to atheistic trends and calling for unity with Jewish and Christian monotheisms, without accepting the possibility of tracing the influence of these traditions on the Qur'an and without admitting the non-Abrahamic traditions such as Hinduism into the spiritual camp; and fifth, it admits the primacy of scientific knowledge, while disparaging its methodological presumptions seen in materialism. The articulation of critical views to resolve these contradictions in the Arab world present creative reformation attempts to harmonise intellectual spheres of identity". (Obiedat, 2019)

When the realization of political power is involved this paradoxical worldview risks becoming more fanatic and contributing to total elimination and destruction. In 2001 for instance, the Egyptian Ministry of Culture burned approximately 6,000 volumes of the 8th century classical Arabic poet, Abu Nuwas.

In a candid assessment of Arab media and journalism, the prominent Lebanese journalist and editor Jihad al-Khazen admits that he and his colleagues had extensively committed self-censorship in their writings and instead of covering news stories, they had covered up the stories. He explains how Arab authors had been denying the news and instead praising the ruler, and acknowledges how Arab editors consider the cost of their writings: "We can afford to be banned in Sudan, where the currency is almost worthless, but if we are banned in Saudi Arabia, we stand to lose tens of thousands of dollars in advertising revenue. Consequently, we are more careful with Saudi news; it is a matter of economics, even of survival" (Rubin, 2002).

A significant reason for the ease at which Islamic traditional forces claim power in Middle Eastern countries such as Iran and Iraq might be the adaptation of "left" political thoughts and teachings or western ideological approaches into their Islamic traditional philosophy. In pre-revolution years, the

Iranian clergy member Ayatollah Morteza Motahari hypocritically used Marxist philosophy and critical analysis in his writings. Ayatollah Mahmoud Taleqani also wrote a book on "Islam and Property" (Islam va Malekiyat) where he supported Marxist theories of collective property rights. The Islamic ideologist, Ali Shariati, was also deeply aware of Shia theology, but his thoughts were still heavily influenced by the Marxism and Third World theories. He was sold on Marxism and believed in class struggle, workers' revolution, and establishing a classless society, while the same time interpreted Shia as a creed of revolution. In Iraq, clerical characters like Mohammad Baqir al-Sadr mixed the western philosophical discourse and modern political economy into his Shiite traditional ideology to win the attention of younger generations for his future political aspirations. Such reluctant amalgamations of modern thought with local traditional ideologies by many Islamic clergies has helped many fundamental Islamic forces take control over the political power in many Middle Eastern countries.

In 1979, Iranians overthrew the more secular regime of Shah and replaced it with the most fundamental clerical political system of twentieth century, led by Ayatollah Khomeini, who took control with absolute power and enforced the most repressive ideological views seen yet. When Saddam's regime fell before US tanks in 2003, it was not the secular forces but rather most repressive Islamic brains such as Muqtada al-Sadr, Ali al-Sistani, Nouri al-Maliki, and the fundamental clerics of the Supreme Council for Islamic Revolution in Iraq (SCIRI) such as Mohammad Baqir al-Hakim who assumed power in the country. In Afghanistan, Pakistan, Algeria, and even more secular countries like Turkey and Lebanon, such fundamentalist takeovers are easily evident. The key question is now why, despite a history of modernization and the existence of civic organizations and secular forces, do only the major traditional, ideological, and repressive groups gain control over the socio-political destiny of their citizens? Many scholars blame the traditional ties between clergies (the Ulama) and their flock (the Umma) as the main cause of such adversity (e.g. see Nasr Vali, 2006). Even Edward Said's (1978) concept of orientalism did not do much to help the Arab nations' breakthrough with decades of national development and emancipation struggles. Said's theory appears instead to have received support from the rising fundamental Islamic ideologies in Iraq, Lebanon, Syria, Egypt, Turkey, and Iraq.

Endnotes

1. The film is directed by Parisa Bakhtavar and written by Asghar Farhadi in Tehran.
2. In my personal interviews with Iraqis living in Baghdad after Saddam's Fall in 2003 many people have revealed their hidden access to satellite dishes on their home rooftops.
3. Reza Khan was pursuing a fatwa to perform the discovery of the veil: http://www.iichs.ir/News
4. https://negaam.news
5. http://arabic.cctv.com/2016/05/31/VIDE7LuWobR63Wz6vMUzGtzU160531.shtml
6. Ayatollah Khomeini's famous outcry for clergies' absolute rule over the entire population.
7. Taken from the CIA report 1975: From the Rise to the Fall; translated by Islamic students.
8. Tarikh al-Rusul wa al-Muluk (History of the Prophets and Kings) Farsi text.
9. The United Kingdom and United States orchestrated a 1953 coup d'état of Iran; the 1967 devastating defeat of Arab nations by Israelis; 1989 Russians invasion of Afghanistan; George Bush's War on Terror and subsequent 2003 Iraq invasion, etc.
10. For example, see published works by Blalock (1967); Blauner (1969); Blumer (1958); Brown & Strega (2005); Moynihan et al. (1967); Nisan (2002); Pager & Shepherd (2008); Patterson (1998); Thompson (1992); van den Berghe (2001); and others.
11. Abolghasem Lahuti has been reading copies of Qanun journal (Laws journal) regularly sent to his father's home in Kermanshah.

References

Abdel-Malek, A. (1962). *Égypte, société militaire.* Éditions du Seuil.

Abrahamian, E. (1982). *Iran between two revolutions.* Princeton University Press.

Adamiat, F. (n.d). *Fekre Azadi.* Tehran: Taban Publications.

Ahmad, J.A.I. (1983). *Occidentosis: a plague from the west.* Contemporary Islamic Thought Persian Series, Mizan Press.

al-Attas, S.M.N. (1978). *Islam and Secularism.* Kuala Lumpur: Art Printing Works.

Algar, H. (2012). *Freemasonry in the Qajar period, by online Encyclopedia Iranica.* Retrieved from http://www.iranicaonline.org/articles/freemasonry-ii-in-the-qajar-period

Amanat, A. (2009). *Apocalyptic Islam and Iranian Shi'ism.* London: I. B. Tauris.

Anglim, S. et al. (2013). *Fighting techniques of the ancient world 3000 BCE-500 CE.* Amber Books.

Anvar, K. (1983). Memories, the great opportunity lost: a narrative of Tudeh Party's organization. Tehran: Hafteh Publications.

Arendt, H. (1970). On violence. Harcourt Publishing Company.

Badr, A. (2006).Beirut: Baba Sartre.

Bakier, A.H. (2006). Lessons from al-Qaeda's attack on the Khobar compound. *Terrorism Monitor, 4*(6). Retrieved from https://jamestown.org/program/lessons-from-al-qaedas-attack-on-the-khobar-compound/

Barraclough, S. (2001) Satellite television in Iran: Prohibition, imitation and reform. *Middle Eastern Studies, 37*(3), 25-48.

Bellin, E. (2004). The robustness of authoritarianism in the Middle East: Exceptionalism in comparative perspective. *Comparative Politics, 36*(2),139-157.

Bishop, I.L.B. (1891). *Journeys in Persia and Kurdistan.* UK, London.

Bosworth, C.E. (1999). *The History of al-Tabari, The Sasanids, the Byzantines, the Lakhmids, and Yemen, Volume V.* The State University of New York Press.

Colaguori, C. (2012). *Agon culture: Competition, conflict and the problem of domination.* de Sitter Publications.

Di-Capua, Y. (2012). Arab existentialism: An invisible chapter in the intellectual history of decolonization. *American His-*

torical Review, Oxford. Retrieved from http://blogs.law.columbia.edu/nietzsche1313/files/2016/06/DiCapua-Arab-existentialism.pdf

Esfandiari, G. (2018). *Nothing comes between Iranians and their satellite dishes — not even the police.* Radio liberty. Retrieved from https://www.rferl.org/a/persian_letters_satellite_dishes_iran_police/24514665.html

Fani, R. (2012). Observation of the region's upheavals after Islamic Revolution: new waves of Islamism in the region. Retrieved from http://www.iichs.ir/Upload/Image/139410/Orginal/6bd50744_3371_4635_8c89_62d6c573d260.pdf

Fard, H.K. (n.d.). Scandal in Switzerland: Imperial court documents on drug trafficking of Amir Hooshang Dolu Ghajar. Retrieved from http://www.rezafani.com/index.php?/site/comments/regionalchangesafterrevolution/

Georgy, M. (2019). *Exclusive: Iran-backed militias deployed snipers in Iraq protests.* Retrieved from https://ca.reuters.com/article/topNews/idCAKBN1WW0B1-OCATP

Golkar, S. (2015). *Captive society: The Basij militia and social control in Iran.* Washington, D.C., Woodrow Wilson Center Press.

Grabar, O., Said, E.W., & Lewis, B. (1982). Orientalism: an exchange. *New York Review of Books, 29*(13).

Halliday, F. (1993). Orientalism and its critics. *British Journal of Middle Eastern Studies, 20*(2) 145-163.

Hedayat, S. (2013). *The Blind Owl.* Hedayat Foundation.

Henderson, B. (2011). *Yemeni rooftop snipers fire at random at anti-regime protesters.* The Telegraph. Retrieved from https://www.telegraph.co.uk/news/worldnews/middleeast/yemen/8774911/Yemeni-rooftop-snipers-fire-at-random-at-anti-regime-protesters.html

Horkheimer, M. (1992). *Traditionelle und kritische theorie: fünf aufsätze fischer-taschenbuch-verlag.* Pennsylvania State University.

Hutchinson, (1961). *M. R. Pahlavi, mission for my country.*

Kamshad, H. (1966). *Modern Persian prose literature.* Cambridge: At the University Press.

Kasravi, A. (1999). History of the Iranian Constitutional Revolution. Amir Kabir Publications, Tehran.

Katouzian, H. (2003). *Iranian history and politics: the dialectic of state and society.* Routlege Cruzon, London.

Keddie, N. R. (2007). *Women in the Middle East.* Princeton University Press.
Keddie, N.R. & Richard, Y. (2006). *Modern Iran: roots and results of revolution.* New Haven & London: Yale University Press,
Kermani, N.A.I. (1982). *Tarikh-e Bidari-e iranian* [history of Iran's awakening]. Tehran, Agah Publications.
Kianouri, N. (1982). Tudeh Party of Iran and the issues of our revolutionary homeland. Publication of Tudeh Party.
Klemm, V. (2000). Different notions of commitment (iltizam) and committed literature (al-adabal-multazim) in the literary circles of the Mashriq. *Middle Eastern Literatures 3*(1), 51–62.
Lewis, B. (1982). *The question of orientalism.* New York review of books.
Lewis, B. (2002). *The assassins: A radical sect in Islam.* Oxford University Press.
Mark, J. J. (2009, September 02). *War in ancient times.* Ancient History Encyclopedia. Retrieved from https://www.ancient.eu/war/
Miklos, J.C. (1983). *The Iranian Revolution and modernization: Waystations to anarchy.* Washington, D.C. The National Defense University Press.
Miller, J. (1985). *The embattled Arab intellectual.* Retrieved from https://www.nytimes.com/1985/06/09/magazine/the-embattled-arab-intellectual.html
Mish, F. C. (1985). *Akkad.* Webster's Ninth New Collegiate Dictionary. Springfield, MA, Merriam-Webster.
Nasr, V. (2007). *The Shia Revival: How conflicts within Islam will shape the future.* W. W. Norton & Company.
Obiedat, A. Z. (2019). Identity contradictions in Islamic awakening: harmonising intellectual spheres of identity. *Asian Journal of Middle Eastern and Islamic Studies, (13)*3.
Orwell, G. (2013). *Nineteen Eighty-Four.* London: Arcturus Publishing Limited.
R. W. Ferrier (Ed., 1996). *A journey to Persia: Jean Chardin's portrait of a seventeenth-century empire.* I.B. Tauris.
Rain, I. (1974). *Mirza Molkom Khan, zendegi wa koshesh-haie siasi-ou* [Life and political struggles of Miraza Malkolm Khan]. Tehran: Safialishah Publications.
Rain, I. (1987). *Faramushkhanah va faramasuniri dar Iran.* Tehran: Amir Kabir Publications.

Rubin, B.M. (2002). *The tragedy of the Middle East.* New York: Cambridge university Press.
Said, E.W. (2003) *Orientalism.* Penguin Books.
Samakar, A. (2006). *Man yek shooreshi hastam* [I am a rebel]. Sherkat-e Ketab-e Los Angeles.
Saman, S. (2019). Stalemate in Victory Bridge. Retrieved from https://saeedsaman.word press.com
Saravi, M., & Taghi, F.B.M. (1992). *Tarikh-e Mohamadi (Ahsan Altawarikh).* Amirkabir Publications.
Schmidinger, T. (n.d). *Der Mazdakismus im Iran.* Widerstand gegen eine Theokratie.
Shafizadeh, J. (2000). *Poshte-h pardehaye enghlab* [behind the curtains of the revolution]. Nima Verlag, Germany.
Stiglitz, J.E. (2003). *Globalization and its discontents.* New York: W. W. Norton.
Tabrizi, T., & Rahim, A. (1968). *Masālek ol-moḥsenīn* [The ways of the charitable]. Tehran: Sherkat-i Sahami.
Tétreault, M.A. (1983). *The organization of arab petroleum exporting countries: history, policies, and prospects.* Pennsylvania State University.
Thual, F., & Basser, K. (1997). *Francois Thual: Geopolitique du Chiisme.* France: Khavaran publishers.

Chapter 2

The Middle Eastern Militarism

I. The Middle East Perpetual Longing Towards Militarization

> *"Tame the savageness of man and make gentle the life of this world."*
> ~ Aeschylus

The role of the military and armed forces as well as the use of "hard power" among Middle Eastern countries and their ethnic groups has since long become a common part of life, and the region's history is full of vigorous antagonism and agony. Such a state of existence involving a seemingly endless array of threats and anxieties dominate not only the socio-cultural system but also the political institutions. A brief historical appraisal of the Middle East could lead to a perception that a perpetual and inextricable conflict exists, which brings to mind existing theories of natural or structural enmity within humankind. One might consider Thomas Hobbes' theory of civil violence for example, which states that human beings are naturally violent against toward other. One may rightfully criticize Hobbes however, and dispute his theory's adoptability to the Middle East's countries and communities. In reality, Hobbes's suggestion that the people should give their rights up to a sovereign entity serves to legitimize authoritarian powers and recommends that civilians obey their rulers unconditionally. Similarly, social Darwinism, as taken from Charles Darwin's 1870 evolutionist theory of natural selection and survival of the fittest, could also be brought up as a model to portray the situation in the Middle East today. Recorded histories of the region have demonstrated that those with more vigorous power and brutality happen to be those who had survived, while more passive and less coercive groups have tended to become oppressed.

The "Agon Culture" is also a concept which might explain the situations faced by many societies and ethno-cultural units which have experienced war and conflict. Contrary to the aforementioned theories such as social Darwinism, which views social conflicts and competitions as the result biological drives, Agon Culture sees social relations as based from cycles of domination and control. In support of this notion, Claudio Colaguori (2012) depicts the human condition in the form of a culture of domination and system of competition. In this approach, a culture of winners and losers or a culture of permanent conflict and competition governs social relationships and human capacity as a whole and Colaguori (2012) claims the world to have become an arena of perpetual competition and antagonism. Even though such a theory might appear dubious throughout much of the world, Colaguori's concept appears to hold true in the Middle East.

The Middle East of today has become an extreme picture of conflicting rivals and ruling tyrants without the slightest degree of tolerance or compromise toward "others". "Others" in this case refer to the easiest targets of violence, which are most often normal citizens, ethnic and religious minorities, members of diverse political, ideological or cultural institutions, or even members of labor unions, syndicates, and student groups. The ruthless warlords and tyrants of the Middle East and their continuing fight for power, control, domination, and supremacy have been a major source of instability, violence, and human rights abuse. Force and violence are and mostly have been pervasive in the Middle East to the extent that few parts of the rest of the modern world are familiar with violence to this extent. In his book, The Egyptian-Coptic and Marxist scholar Anouar Abdel-Malek calls Egyptian society rather militaristic, especially after 1952. One major reason for such militarism is the existence of countless disputes and unsettled domestic issues, which local rulers and international players did not feel the need to address.

Land disputes are made worse with the arbitrariness of nation-states' artificial boundaries, which on one hand contain within them divided social, ethnic, and sectarian communities, and on the other hand, possess unique geopolitical locations along with an excessive amount of valuable natural resources. The lines drawn to delineate the respective spheres of influence between the European colonial forces secretly arranged through the 1916 Sykes-Picot Agreement became the official borders of the newly established arbitrary countries, which since then have contributed to ethnic and religious conflict. Protecting such borders has been an extraordinary task and national security concern across the Middle East; a task seen by controlling powers to be much more vital than protecting the countries' inhabitants themselves.

A country's military expenditure and the percentage of the GDP spent for armed forces and related activities could plausibly indicate that country's level of tolerance and the desire to seek hegemony over others, including its own people. Importantly, most countries in the Middle East show a high volume of military spending. The aspiration for military expansion coupled with the desire for hegemony, are characteristics of most rulers and political leaders in the Middle East. A history of continuous rivalry and invasion along with tribal hit-and-runs has erected a horrible state of cynicism, socio-cultural segregation, and hatred and hostility. Along with regional and global intrusions in the internal affairs of ethnic groups in the Middle East, these factors have driven most of these countries to engage in a permanent arms race.

Contrary to many writings which try to prove positive relationships between military expenditures and economic growth or the degree of a country or region's development, extreme rearmament and fervent militaristic expenditures have always been a major factor depriving people from accessing their necessities. Some conservative commentators or extreme theorists might claim that defense expenditures—especially regarding the development of indigenous defense industries—stimulate economic growth or buy stability, which in turn improves the investment climate. However, countries in the Middle East have experienced the contrary: over the course of half a century, the trillions of petrodollars spent by Middle Eastern countries have proven akin to pouring gasoline on the fire, instead of leading to any political or economic stability. The amount and degree of wars, genocides, ethnic cleansing, constant military coups, ethnic uprisings, revolutions, and terrorist incidents are diverse forms of violence which the extraordinary military expenditures and rearmaments could not prevent from happening.

According to the Stockholm International Peace Research Institute (SIPRI), of the 10 countries with the highest military expenditures in the world in 2017, seven are in the Middle East: Oman (12 percent of the GDP), Saudi Arabia (10%), Kuwait

(5.8%), Jordan (4.8%), Israel (4.7%), Lebanon (4.5%), and Bahrain (4.1%), (Tian, Fleurant, Kuimova, Wezeman, & Wezeman, 2018). Saudi Arabia, Turkey, Iran, and Iraq have the region's highest shares of military expenditure and indicate a permanent increase in their annual purchasing. Saudi Arabia is by far the largest military spender in the Middle East and was the third largest spender in the world in 2017. Its military spending shows an increase of 74 per cent just between 2008 and 2015 to a peak of $90.3 billion (Gaub, 2014). Turkey's military expenditure also shows an increase of 46 percent between 2008 and 2017 reaching $18.2 billion dollars, which makes the country the 15th largest spender globally. The situation for the Iranian clerical system is not any better. While Iran does not share its exact military expenses and many of its international military allocations and costs of interferences are not formally publicized, an immense increase of 37% in its military expenditures between 2014 and 2017 can be found simply by focusing on existing data. It is not a coincidence that such increases happened at the same time that the Syrian civil war reached its peak. Since 2014, the Iranian economy has benefited from Obama's political compromises and the gradual lifting of European Union and United Nations sanctions, which facilitated enough of an increase in military spending to bring their 2017 expenditures to a $14.5 billion level.

The pervasive insecurity of Middle Eastern countries has bred high levels of spending on military and security arrangements. As Florence Gaub (2014) claims, the Arab nations continue to stay prone to conflict due to increased military spending. In her opinion, a higher spending in the military means a higher probability of armed conflict. The above data on military spending does not prove anything more than the likelihood of a conflict break out, and a war occurring. As Gaub (2014) also explains, modern European military expenditures are mainly a budgetary affair, while increased spending in the Arab world is an important factor in assessing if and where wars may occur.[1]

The Middle East's fragile security and pervading instability is evidenced by the extraordinary dimensions of the state's control over most aspects of people's public or even private affairs, and the autocratic regimes' distrust towards its citizens and their inevitable fear for survival. Military procurement mostly goes hand in hand with civil war, economic deterioration, underdevelopment, and even corruption and nepotism. It is estimated that up to 15 percent of the defense budget transactions account for corruption; a factor of further discrimination and economic deterioration. The regions' resources are sucked out of the civilian economy into the military, where they are then mostly subject to massive corruption.

The Middle East and North African (MENA) region is today the most militarized region in the world, not only due to a rapid increase in logistics and defense spending but also because of the demographic proportion and its share from the GDP. While EU countries spend on average 1 percent of their GDP on the military, the Middle Eastern countries spend more than 5.1 percent. Even the non-state-militarized actors are also more prevalent—and destructive—in MENA than in any other region in the world. Nine of the top twenty countries in the Global Terrorism Index are found in the MENA region (Bashiriyeh, 2011). Steve Killelea, Founder of the Institute for Economics and Peace believes reducing conflict is essential for ensuring a continued worldwide economic recovery. Furthermore, a 10 percent decrease in global violence could add an additional US$1.4 trillion to the world economy. His 2015 Global Peace Index reveals an increasingly divided world in which peacefulness in Europe has reached a historic high while the Middle East is spiralling into deepening violence. Conversely, reports show that a country's democratization will positively impact the economic and GDP growth: "In the long run (about 30 years), GDP per capita will be about 20% higher in a nation with democracy than one without it. If, hypothetically, MENA nations had shifted to democracy in 2015, GDP per capita could have reached at 7.8% in five years, against 3.3% in its absence" (Palmer, 1941).

Apart from the fact that the high military expenditures for defense or civil conflicts burden the economy and impede growth, Middle Eastern leaders have shown very little interest and any possible strides have made trivial and insignificant impacts on human development. An important part of the problem is that international organizations, political entities, and human rights organizations too infrequently question the notion of selling armaments including sophisticated weaponry to the mostly dictatorial regimes in the Middle East, which typically rely on a single autocratic ruler.

Dealing with the daily socio-cultural, ethnic, or economic problems through the use of militaristic force is a typical approach for various rulers in the Middle East. The Iranian

Shah's official response for dealing with the extreme inflation rates of 1970s was to declare war on the profiteers, arrest and ban the country's industrial and commercial characters, and make many others afraid in the hopes of controlling the steeply rising market prices.[2]

Wherever Middle Eastern countries faced a budget shortfall of some kind, the military's door was the last to be knocked on, supposing the issue could be brought up to the authoritative rulers in the first place. While the Iranian Premiers have been unable to persuade the Shah to reduce the military budget, drastic cutting of the civilian and development expenditures has not been a big question. In 1977, the Premier Amouzegar was unable to convince the Shah to touch the military expenses, but still easily eliminated $3.5 billion from the country's Five-Year Economic Plan and postponed many developmental and social programs in the country.[3]

Following the 1953 American-British orchestrated coup d'état to overthrow the democratically elected Prime Minister Mohammad Mosaddegh and re-establish Mohammad Reza Pahlavi's autocratic rule, military reform under American supervision began. When commenting on the Shah, Stephen McGlinchey notes in his graduation thesis (2012):

> His desire for military supremacy over his neighbors, and his distrust of the Soviets led him to seek an arms relationship with the U.S. following the end of the Second World War. This relationship gradually deepened throughout his reign, eventually resulting in Iran wielding a military that was, on paper, within reach of becoming the world's fifth most advanced force in 1978.[4]

The Shah not only increased the number of his soldiers from 120 000 in 1941 to over 400 000 in 1977, but over 30 percent of the country's budgets went to military resources and weaponization. The Shah's desire that Iran become a regional military power further drained the country of its resources. Benefiting from the implementation of the Nixon Doctrine, which sought to lessen reliance on American forces by providing countries like Iran with advanced weaponry, and using his new-found oil-generated wealth, the Shah went on a military spending spree. Between 1972 and 1976, Iran purchased $10 billion in American arms.

The reports indicate that despite considerable skepticism toward the Shah regime, Americans were hoping Iran could be turned from a "liability" into an anti-Communist asset in Asia (World Bank, 2016). The emergence of the Bagdad pact in 1955, along with Iran's membership and central role, fortified the above assertion further which in turn led to further militarization of the country. Along with his aversion toward his own people and Moscow's Communist regime, the Shah's greed toward regional power did not recognize any limits. According to formal reports, he had an extraordinary desire for the further expansion of forces within the country:

> One month later, William M. Rountree, Assistant Secretary for Near Eastern, South Asian and African Affairs wrote to Dulles after the Shah had delivered a list of military requirements to the Pentagon, costed between $300 and $500 million. Rountree asserted that the Shah expects far more military aid from us than we can give him". (Zisser, n.d.)

It is slightly ironic that just two years prior to the Iranian Revolution, the Shah was vehemently pressuring the Carter administration to purchase freshly arrived AWACS (Airborne Warning and Control System) planes (Bligh, n.d.). Simultaneously erroneous CIA reports and briefings to President Carter that year had helped the Shah fall further into his own arrogance. A 1977 CIA study noted that "[t]he Shah seems to have no health or political problems at present that will prevent him from being the dominant figure in Iran into and possibly throughout the 1980s" (Gates, Hegre, Nyg, & Strand, 2010). This report gave President Carter the confidence to call Iran in 1977 "an island of stability in one of the more troubled areas of the world" just months before Ayatollah Khomeini's ascension to power.

Militarism in the Middle East has not only slowed economic growth which in turn has contributed to underdevelopment, but also has put some of these countries on the verge of civil strife or outright international war. Since the Akkadian ruler Sargon the Great invaded the Sumerian civilization in Mesopotamia (today Iraq) and erected the Akkadian empire in about 2430 B.C.E, possibly the first empire in the human history has become the epicenter for countless wars and ethnic conflicts. Although the Middle East is known as "the cradle of civilization," one might have forgotten that this region has unremittingly been home to dozens of diverse civilizations which have mostly become consciously or unconsciously trapped into awful conflicts. The ubiquity of militaristic and despotic rule in the region has operated as a mechanism for the creation of violence and war between major inhabitants and civilizations. Diffusion of such a culture of wreaking enormous havoc on the Middle Eastern countries along with the unique mosaic of socio-cultural, religious, and ethnic divergence facilitated the continuation of violence, enslavement, revolts, mass killing, genocide, deportations, and forced migrations throughout both the modern and ancient histories of this region. The brutal events of past centuries notwithstanding, the Middle East from the dawn of the twentieth century to today have been relentlessly witnessing all forms of wars, violence, coups, and humiliation within and between ethnic and religious groups. Areas which might be less affected by war currently still face considerable risk of conflict.

In May 1977, fifty-three lawyers sent an open letter to the Shah accusing the regime of interfering in court proceedings and announced the formation of a special commission to safeguard the judiciary's sovereignty and independence and protect it from the legislative branch's intrusion. In June of the same year, some of the Iranian National Front leaders (Sanjabi, Foruhar, and Bakhtiyar) sent a more daring letter to the Shah which warned him in vain to avoid tending toward despotism, advised him to observe the Universal Declaration of Human Rights, and requested that he abolish the one-party system in the country.

Institutionalization of the military and coercive apparatus in the Middle East is essentially curbed or not really in full swing. Staffing policies, military ranking, and positioning of appointments are rather an issue of personal taste. In much of the Middle East, the country's supreme ruler appoints his most trusted male relatives to key military and intelligence positions to guarantee against any possible coup or rebellion. In Arab nations such as Saudi Arabia, Syria, Yemen, Bahrain, the United Arab Emirates, and Qatar, the military and intelligence have become a family or tribal affair rather than a professional or organizational body. The military—like many other institutions in post-revolutionary Iran—has assumed a parallel format is based on a history of full submission to the system and total obedience towards the supreme leader, who has the entire military apparatus under his personal control. Like many other institutions in the Islamic republic of Iran, religious and political reliability toward the system supersedes merit and competence. The Syrian president

Hafiz al-Assad appointed a trusted man of his tribe as commander of the Air Force without ever having trained as a pilot (Kaplan, 1994). The high ranking military and intelligence officers and elite authorities in Iraq during Saddam Hussein's rule were Sunnis, in Syria they are Alawi, in Iran they are Shiite Isna Ashari and believers in the Velayat-e Faghih, while in Saudi Arabia they are members of the Al Saud family. Finally, "In Jordan Palestinians cannot rise above the rank of major or lieutenant colonel in combat units" (Kaplan, 1996).

II. Militarism and Regimes' Legitimacy and Democratization Process

Countries with a higher average educational attainment in the past are more likely to have democratic political regimes today. Additionally, historical records indicate that democratic governments are much less likely to engage in wars with each other. The most immediate political consequence of armed conflict is that large parts of society become securitized. Policies usually deemed unacceptable by the public can be implemented with reference to the security of the state. Freedom of speech can be limited effectively through associating certain political stances with terrorism. Securitization can lead to political and social exclusion, which in turn is highly destabilizing. Several regimes in the MENA regions have attempted to combine authoritarian rule with an open and inclusive political strategy. When this inclusive strategy fails, the only way to voice opposition is through riots and violence. Suppressing popular revolts is very costly, and leads to further securitization of the political climate. In the end, these half-successful attempts at opening up have often led to further suppression or a return to armed conflict (Transparency International, 2018).

The growth of Islamist movements and the possible rise of new Islamic regimes will have potentially important implications for conflict within and among Middle Eastern societies, as well as between the Muslim world and the west. Such situations have caused deterioration in the existing meagre civil societies' endeavours towards introducing more inclusive, just, and democratic societies. Furthermore, moderate movements in power may establish an acceptable modus vivendi with the west. As mentioned by the American historian Robert Russwell Palmer (1989) regarding the French Revolution, the wars of kings were replaced by the wars of people (Transparency International, 2018). In a similar statement, Samuel Huntington (1993) also believes that the conflict of nations following the Russian Revolution yielded to a conflict of ideologies. Furthermore, he claims that categorizing the world's countries on the basis of their political or economic system or their level of development is no longer relevant, and a more appropriate approach would be to focus on them in terms of their culture and civilization.

The growing economic disparity between "haves" and "have-nots," political chaos, fundamentalism, rampant urban violence, large-scale ethnic conflict, environmental degradation and epidemics, and new risks to stability[5] might seem Malthusian at first blush, but in reality they are undeniable sources of conflict in the Middle East and elsewhere. These are also used by coercive rulers of the Middle East and elsewhere as reasons behind their militaristic philosophies of slaughter and massacre.

One major cause of the long-lasting military supremacy over Egyptian people for over half a century lies in the extraordinary large share and involvement of the country's military in the national economy. According to estimates, Egyptian armed forces controls over 40 percent of the entire national economy and enjoy:

> uncontested and broad regulatory control over planning, allocation, and management. Under a 1981 law, the Minister of Defence has wide-ranging powers over desert land, which constitutes about 94 per cent of Egypt: including to determine whether plots can be allocated to the private sector, and to allocate land specifically for military or strategic use. (Transparency International, 2018)

Some analysts argue that the tension between Muhamed Morsi—who represents the Muslim Brotherhood—and the Egyptian armed forces over the Suez development project was the major factor in his toppling by the military. Extreme levels of corruption and bribes also happened to be a major reason for Hosni Mubarak's overthrowing. The reports show that Mubarak and his family had garnered up to 70 billion US dollars from corruption (Inman, 2011).

Sometimes in an ethnic or national as well as partisan dispute, the entire society or members of a political party or ideology are pushed into conflict. In ethnic and national conflicts where citizens feel politically and/or economically oppressed by elites who are mostly from a different nation, the entire society gets involved in the process of the conflict. It is also sometimes difficult to distinguish between innocent civilians and dangerous combatants. In some cases, many members of a society become involved by providing moral support and provisions of food, shelter, or funds, while others take up arms and become involved in the military effort.

During the Syrian civil war, the entire population including Kurdish and Sunni Arabs in diverse political factions took up arms against ruling dictator Bashar Al Assad who at best represented only the minority Alawite-Shiite community supported by Russians and Iranians. The Assad family seized political power and took control over the entire country through a coup d'état in 1970 and stripped the Kurdish population in northern part of the country of their citizenship rights. Furthermore, all other ethnic groups including Sunni Arabs, the Druze, and Ismailis were removed from the party leadership and from sensitive political and military positions. Similarly, the Iranian Kurdish society faced Ayatollah Khomeini's Fatwa of Jihad after the Islamic Revolution, when they had requested that the newly established Islamic authorities ensure and respect their fundamental ethno-cultural rights. Just several months after taking control, Khomeini declared Jihad (the holy war) against millions of innocent Kurdish citizens in Iran, and effectively turned all four Kurdish populated provinces in the western part of the country into a battlefield. The Kurds today call such an order by the founder of the Islamic Republic a cataclysmic round of state terrorism against themselves which after four decades still haunts Kurdish society. Following Khomeini's declaration, Kurdish youths took up arms and began fighting the Iranian Revolution Guards Corps (IRGC) and other militia groups in the region, while many others who could not or did not want to participate in such political resistance either provided financial and logistic provisions or ensured moral support toward their Kurdish resistance forces.

Trends towards involvement of the entire community in war against a national enemy are also apparent in Turkey, similar to Iran under Ayatollah's regime. Since the establishment of an ultra-nationalist and militaristic political system of total subjugation and oppression in 1924, the Kurdish population in Turkey has found the need to resist, and finally in the 1980s, a new generation of stubborn Kurdish Marxist students came to political life as to resist the most brutal forms of oppression and coercion and reinstate their fundamental rights as indigenous people. Since then, the entire country has turned into an immense battle ground between militaristic regimes and Kurdish guerilla fighters which has cost hundreds of thousands lives and billions of dollars' damage to the entire region's economy.

Some scholars trust that the Middle East's militarization and extensive events of violence are just by-products of western countries' intervention in the Middle Eastern nations' internal affairs, or see the introduction of western countries' ideas as taking their toll on the Middle East. Many others blame the Cold War as key factor in the extreme hostility of more local regimes. However, it might be more realistic if one looks to the reasons for why such coercive and oppressive regimes exist in the first place, rather than just at these countries' current circumstances. The millennia of segregation between the state or God-appointed rulers and their subjects on the one hand point to the Middle East's inextricable linkage to the political legacy of Islam, while on the other hand the millenarian imperialistic tradition of the region's rulers are also to be blamed for the long history of incessant hostility. Fred Halliday is of the view that "the Cold War ... had a limited impact on the Middle East," (Halliday, 1997).

In contrast however, Gerges (1997) argues that the Cold War and west-east polarization was a major element in the militaristic antagonism of the Middle Eastern nations. He believes "the intrusion of the Cold War into regional politics exacerbated regional conflicts and made their resolution more difficult" (Gerges, 1997). No matter where we stand, the militarization of the Middle East originates from miscellaneous factors, which, despite a long history of foreign intervention, differ from state to state. However, one should not forget that the ultimate architect of the brutal Middle Eastern culture of abuse, oppression, and butchery is found in the historical and socio-cultural constructs of the region itself as well as in its continuing renewal of the corrupt elite and political leadership.

Endnotes

1. Global Terrorism Index is an annual report published by an international Think Tank in Australia called "Institute for Economic and Peace".
2. Memorandum from the JCS to Wilson, Washington, 7 January 1955. FRUS 1955-57, Vol. XII: 287.
3. Memorandum from Rountree to Dulles, Washington, 12 October 1957. FRUS 1955-57, Vol. XII: 409.
4. Memorandum from the JCS to Wilson, Washington, 7 January 1955. FRUS 1955-57, Vol. XII: 287.
5. These issues and disparities are discussed in Robert D. Kaplan's works, such as "the coming anarchy," and "the ends of the earth".

References

Abrahamian, E. (1982). *Iran between two revolutions*. Princeton University Press.

Anouar Abdel-Malek, (1962). *Égypte, société militaire*. Éditions du Seuil.

Bashiriyeh, H. (2011). *The state and revolution in Iran: 1962-1982*. New York: Routledge Library Editions.

Bligh, A. The Jordanian army: between domestic and external challenges. In Rubin & Keaney (Eds.), *Armed Forces in the Middle East* (p.150). London: Frank Cass.

Colaguori, C. (2012). *Agon culture: Competition, conflict and the problem of domination*. de Sitter Publications.

Field, M. (1977). *Middle East Annual Report*. London.

Gates, S., Hegre, H., Nyg, M., & Strand, H. (2010). *Consequences of armed conflict in the Middle East and North Africa region*. University of Oslo: Norwegian University of Science & Technology.

Gaub, F. (2014). *Arab military spending: behind the figures*. European Union Institute for Security Studies.

Gerges, F. (1997). *The superpowers in the Middle East: Regional and international politics, 1955-67*. Boulder: Westview Press.

Halliday, F. (1997). The Middle East and the great powers. In Sayigh, Y., & Shlaim, A. (Eds.), *The Cold War in the Middle East*. Oxford: Clarendon Press.

Inman, P. (2011). *Mubarak family fortune could reach $70bn, says expert*. The Guardian. Retrieved from https://www.theguardian.com/world/2011/feb/04/hosni-mubarak-family-fortune

Kaplan, R.D. (1994). *The coming anarchy.* the Atlantic Monthly.
Kaplan, R.D. (1996). *The ends of the earth: a journey at the dawn of the 21st century.* New York: Random House.
McGlinchey, S. (2012). *Arming the Shah: U.S. arms policies towards Iran, 1950-1979.* [Dissertation]. Cardiff University Press.
Palmer, R. R. (1941). Twelve who ruled: the committee of public safety, during the terror. *The American Historical Review, 47*(3), 589–591.
Tian, N., Fleurant, A., Kuimova, A., Wezeman, P.D., & Wezeman, S.T. (2018) *Trends in world military expenditure.* Retrieved from https://www.sipri.org/sites/default/files/2018-05/sipri_fs_1805_milex_2017.pdf
Transparency International. (2018). *The officers' republic: the Egyptian military and the abuse of power.* UK.
World Bank, (2016). *The cost of war & peace in the Middle East.* Retrieved from http://www.worldbank.org/en/news/feature/2016/02/03/by-the-numbers-the-cost-of-war-and-peace-in-mena
Zisser, E. The Syrian army on the domestic and external fronts. In Rubin & Keaney (Eds.), *Armed Forces in the Middle East* (pp. 118-22). London: Frank Cass.

Chapter 3

The Middle Eastern Genocide

I. Genocide: A Multilayer Concept

The term "Genocide" is a combination of the Greek term "genos" (tribe, race or people) and the Latin word "caedo" (killing), which was first coined time 1944 by the Polish-Jewish lawyer Raphael Lemkin. In chapter IX of his famous book "Axis Rule in Occupied Europe: Laws of occupation, Analysis of Government, Proposals for Redress," he defines the act of genocide as a synchronized attack on diverse aspects of the captive people's lives. This can range from political aspects (destroying self-government and imposing other models of administration), to their social lives (destroying social cohesion), culture (destroying cultural activities and institutions), economic lives (marginalization, shifting wealth, and exclusion), reproductively (depopulation and procreation policies), and other aspects including religion, morality, and physical existence (Lemkin, 2005). For Lemkin (2005), genocide encompasses the destruction of a nation or an ethnic group; His tireless campaign for recognizing the Jewish extermination by the Nazi regime as an act of genocide lead to initiation of the United Nation's Convention on the Prevention and Punishment of the Crime of Genocide on December 9, 1948. According to Article II of the Convention, genocide is defined as any of the following acts committed with intent to destroy, in whole or in part, a national, ethnical, racial, or religious group:

(a) Killing members of the group;
(b) Causing serious bodily or mental harm to members of the group;
(c) Deliberately inflicting on the group conditions of life calculated to bring about its physical destruction in whole or in part;

(d) Imposing measures intended to prevent births within the group; and/or
(e) Forcibly transferring children of the group to another group. (United Nations, n.d.)

Indeed, genocide has become a multilayer issue which requires the involvement of socio-political, cultural, medical, psychological, juridical, and diplomatic reasoning. Furthermore, for many, especially for statesmen and politicians at an international level, it is an intricate subject to contend with. Even for many scholars of social sciences and humanities, determining what historical events constitute a genocide or crime against humanity is not a straightforward task. At the beginning of the 20th century for example, one and half million Armenians were murdered by Turkish Ottomans, which has only been recognized by 32 countries around the globe. A major reason for such a low level of recognition toward these atrocities is nothing but reprehensible diplomatic considerations. There is no doubt that with the erection and expansion of the first global-magnitude human empires in written history came extraordinary destructions incurred to others and their civilizations.

As a solution to maintain their pervasive grip on power, the tyrant regimes and their regional rulers have orchestrated ethnic or religious massacres against local minorities time and time again. Throughout the diverse history of the Middle East, communities and minorities have been forced by their ruling tyrants (Sultan, Shah, and Sheik) or religious institutions into exodus, assimilation, and/or conversion, or have faced massacres. In the name of God, religion, national security, territorial integrity, or ethnic purification, masses of people have easily been mobilized to participate in state-sanctioned murders throughout the country. Quite often, western democratic countries as well as the international organizations have turned their backs to the brutal acts of genocide, mass deportation, and displacement across the Middle East.

Only in the last century have millions of innocent people in the Middle East been massacred and millions more forced to leave their hometowns. However, their misery is still not considered an act of genocide since the instigators' goals were not aimed to exterminate the entire population, but rather instigate displacement and political control. From this, it appears that the international community is less sensitive to recognizing the vicious genocidal acts of sovereign countries, and instead views them as crimes against humanity.

The term "crime against humanity" was used for the first time by the African-American civil war veteran and historian George Washington Williams in a report to the Belgian King Leopold II about his local administrators' and agents' atrocities against native Africans in the Congo Free State (today's Democratic Republic of the Congo). The term had also been used by European countries in 1915 to condemn the Ottomans' atrocities against their non-Turkish subjects, and prior to the Nuremberg trials against Nazi regime leaders in 1948, the United Nations had formally used the term in a report concerning Armenian genocide. Since then, the term has been used frequently by several states and international institutions to describe diverse war crimes and atrocities in Japan, Bosnia and Herzegovina, Iraq, Rwanda, Turkey, and Syria. There are many other recorded crimes which have not found appropriate international recognition, have simply been viewed as war crimes, or as quoted in a report by Guy Horton (2005) are "grave infringements of human rights".

Importantly, ethnicity is viewed as a central element in genocide, war crimes, crimes against humanity, and in mass deportations. The targeted destruction or killing of ethnic civilians counts as a fundamental motive underlying genocide and is considered both extrajudicial and arbitrary. However, history has demonstrated that instead of genocides occurring on an arbitrary basis, they are the result of a series of formal policies. For many despotic-militaristic regimes around the globe—and especially in the Middle East—the state policy is regrettably based on a genocidal mindset in which the very existence and identity of another group is viewed as a threat. In addition to ethnicity and language identity, the parameters of religion and political ideology in the Middle East play a crucial role in human rights violations, widespread physical elimination or mental harm, and obliteration.

Political despotism, tribal patriarchy, and military conquests have facilitated genocide, massacre, and exoduses by promoting an enduring sense of indifference within particular regional groups. There are myriad historical examples where ethno-religious groups have acted as accomplices or collaborators in state sponsored acts of genocide and displacement. Instead of referring to the Rwandan genocide as an urban-rural antagonism, some scholars see the atrocities as being brought about by inter-peasant conflict about access to land. Following this logic, some scholars additional view ideological conflicts as being responsible for the Khmer genocide. As Neil Davidson notes:

> The genocide in Rwanda took the form of an inter-peasant conflict about access to land and was neither a rural revolt against the towns nor a national struggle in any recognizable sense. Cambodian Stalinism certainly embodied a ferocious anti-urban bias, but the victims of Khmer nationalism were not, in the main, killed because of their ethnicity, but because of their supposed opposition to the New Order: most of the bones now preserved in Tual Sleng extermination center are of 'ethnic' Khmers. Indeed, the second greatest example of systematic internal violence in the 20th century (after Nazi Germany), Stalinist Russia between 1929 and 1956, can scarcely be said to have rested on peasant support, since at one level the industrialization of the Soviet Union can be seen as a civil war waged by the bureaucracy against the peasantry. (Davidson, n.d.)

The history of Middle Eastern ethno-religious minorities is full of genocidal atrocities, from ethno-cultural massacres, mass displacements, forced conversions, assimilation/culturicide, to the complete destruction of minority settlements. The stories of such tragic incidents continue to exist in the memories of millions of people, and such narratives are spreading across the generations, often being recorded in astounding detail. While historical mass killings and displacements led by Persians, Arabs, Turks, or Mongolians would barely meet modern genocidal criteria, more obvious cases of genocide, ethnic cleansing, and displacement had begun to materialize at the beginning of colonization in the 19th century. The following events in the Middle East are just a handful of internationally recognized acts of genocide or crimes against humanity and violations of human rights:

- **French military operation against Algerian people and tribal rebellions.** Known as the Pacification of Algeria, this operation cost more than one million lives, which many scholars this consider an act of genocide (Kiernan, 2007).

- **Armenian genocide** instigated during and after the First World War by the Ottoman Empire, which cost the lives of up to 1.8 million people (or 50 percent of the Ottoman Empire's Armenian population) (Ginsborg, 2014).
- **Greek and Pontic genocide** by Turkish Ottomans in 1914-22, which created more than one million casualties.
- **Assyrian genocide** and mass slaughter by the Turkish Ottomans in 1915-1922 with close to half a million casualties,
- **Libyan genocide** by Italian colonial forces between 1923 and 1931, massacring over hundred thousand indigenous Libyans (Duggan, 2007), such as the Senussi. About 25 percent of the Cyrenaican population was also killed in these conflicts (Duggan, 2007).
- **Dersim genocide** in Turkey initiated by the Young Turks in 1937-38. The Kurdish Alevis in the Dersim region of Turkish Kurdistan revolted against brutality Ataturk's regime, but their rebellion was brutally extinguished. Tens of thousands were massacred and displaced.
- **Al-Anfal campaign** or Iraqi genocide against Kurdish civilians in 1980s by Saddam's regime, which led to the extermination of about 380,000 people, destroying 3800 villages or towns, and displacing over two million. During this period chemical weapons were used against civilians by the Iraqi army.
- **Kurdish Izadi genocide** led by ISIS in 2014, which led to the massacre of up to 10,000 civilians and the expulsion of hundreds of thousands from their ancestral lands in the Shangal region. Abduction of Izadi women, sexual slavery, and forced conversions were unfortunately characteristic of this brutal campaign.

After Hitler's Germany, the Ottomans lead as the global top genocidal regime and are responsible for potentially the most genocides within the Middle East to date. The modern Turkish state came to exist on the basis of such an appalling legacy and has continued the same policy of extermination and apartheid into the 21st century. In a recent interview on Turkish national television,[1] President Recep Tayyip Erdogan made clear his ambitions for a military offensive against Kurds in northern Syria, and openly discussed his plan for demographic change and ethnic cleansing in the Kurdish region. The plan to build an "Arab belt" between Turkey and Syria (referred to euphemistically as a safe buffer zone) on Kurdish lands was originally a 1960s Syrian Baath regime project to separate Kurds from each other on both sides of the border and eliminate the possibility of a united territory. Today, Erdogan dreams of reviving the Ottoman Empire and presents himself as the present-day successor of the vicious Ottoman emperor Suleiman the Magnificent (1520-1566). However, he does not wish to accept that such aspirations at best only augment his public image in and around the capital city. Recent national and municipal elections reflected citizens' disapproval towards his political ambitions, indicating that he has lost ground in Istanbul and the eastern Kurdish regions.

Unlike many researchers who do not list Al Qaeda as a genocidal organization, Ben Kiernan (2007) argues convincingly in his historical analysis that Osama Bin-Laden's 1998 fatwa stating that it was the duty of Muslims to kill any Americans they encounter makes the organization genocidal in its aspirations. Such an argument can be expanded to other groups as well. When ISIS leader Albaghdadi, captured the Iraqi areas of al-Anbar, Nainawa, Mosul, and Shangal in 2014, he ordered massacre of non-Muslim citizens, including the Christians of Nainawa and Kurdish Yazidis of Shangal. Immediately after coming to power and establishing the Islamic republic, Ayatollah Khomeini ordered Jihad against the Kurdish nation and requested the country's militias "clean up the earth of corruption". Ayatollahs' campaign of slaughter and militarism has continued for over four decades, turning all four Kurdish provinces in the western part of the country into a security and intelligence fiasco. Similarly, according to Kiernan (2007), the Iraqi dictator Saddam Hussein wished to emulate Nebuchadnezzar, the Babylonian conqueror of Jerusalem, and Saladin (ironically a Kurd), who had defeated the Christian Crusaders. Saddam Hussein also committed one of the most brutal genocide campaigns in modern human history, which saw approximately two hundred thousand civilians slaughtered and millions of others forcibly displaced.

The revival of Islamic fundamentalist groups across the Middle East and North Africa in recent decades has not only escalated Shiite-Sunni hostilities but has also destabilized the region for millions of Christians, who have lived in the Middle East for centuries: "The rise of violent extremist ideologies in the Middle East, which follow an ultra-orthodox and skewed interpretation of Islam, has torn apart the already fragile social fabric of countries in the region and produced new threats against Christian communities" (Katulis, deLeon, & Craig, 2015). In Iraq, the capture of Mosul by ISIS in 2014 resulted in an estimated departure of 500,000 Christians, Yazidis, and other minorities in the first week alone (Nicolas, 2016; ACNUK, 2016; Katulis et al., 2015; Hanish, 2014). Christians were ultimately told to convert or be killed, triggering a mass exodus (ACNUK, 2016). The Arabic letter for "N", indicating 'Nazarene' (meaning 'Christians') was marked on all Christian homes (Haider, 2017), and became properties that were later considered *waqf*, or religious endowments of Muslim community (Hanish, 2014; Salameh, 2014). In March 2016, then U.S. Secretary of State, John Kerry, officially recognised that ISIS's atrocities against Christians and Yazidis counted as genocide and crimes against humanity. Thereafter, the UK Parliament similarly recognized these atrocities as genocide against Christians (Kraft & Manar, 2016).

In addition to regular citizens and regional minorities, the events immediately following the Islamic revolution in 1979 also targeted political prisoners. As the same time that Saddam's regime was committing genocide against opposing groups in Kurdistan and Shiite provinces in south, the Iranians, who had just lost a heavy war against Iraq, started a murderous campaign against their own children. "Those who said No" is a documentary produced by Nima Sarvestani dedicated to 20,000 Iranian political prisoners who refused to accept the Islamic regime and were sentenced to death in 1988 by the country's mysterious Death Commission. "Holy Crime" or Jenayat-e Moghadas is a documentary filmed during 90s by the Iranian director Reza Alamezadeh, which uncovers examples of the state-sponsored terrors committed by the supreme leader and authorities of Iran against the Kurdish opposition leaders in Europe.

For some scholars and historians, genocidal campaigns are products of the 20th century's modern nation-state building approaches; the complete breakdown of traditional multinational empires in the Middle East and Europe is perceived as a root cause for widespread genocides. Mark Leven in his varied contributions declares genocide to be a product of modernity and nation-state aspirations, which had first started in the west and spread into the Middle East and Eastern Anatolia on the ruins of the Ottoman Empire in the early 20th century. He believes "genocide is not an aberrant phenomenon in modern history but 'integral to a "mainstream" historical trajectory of development towards a single, global, political economy composed of nation states" (Levene, 2014).

In his work "Creating a Modern zone of genocide", Levene (1998) aptly refers to Eastern Anatolia as a "zone of genocide" (Levene, 2005), where Ottoman rulers in 1890 and later the Young Turks in 1920 committed unconscionable acts of genocide against ethno-religious minorities in the region which Kurds and Christians now call home. While there is no doubt that ruling ethnicities were involved in the genocidal campaigns and forced displacement of local minorities, linking genocide to modernization and 20th century nation-state aspirations seems overly reductionist. To only attribute political systems' genocidal acts to modernism risks neglecting a more intricate history of extermination within empires. Millennia-old tribal invasions[2] and conquests of rival empires cannot (and ought not) be accounted for as simple power transfers, and the human cost in such political transformations should not be overlooked. The Tartars, Mongolians, and Turkic and Arab nomadic tribes have historically tended to be the groups that massacred other ethno-religious minorities like Yazidis, Armenians, Assyrians, Chaldeans, Kurds, Zoroastrians, Palestinians, and Jews.

The rapid growth of genocide studies in recent years has further diversified the field and has opened new windows for the analysis of structural genocide, genocidal terrorism, and cultural genocide or "culturicide". Structural genocide is a socio-political strategy and application of demographic engineering arranged by modern states, which has become an open agenda. Structural genocide can take different forms, from planned starvation, disease, or socio-economic and political exclusion, to forced migration and displacement. Genocide Watch in United States views genocide as a process which develops in eight separate stages that are predictable but not inexorable (Stanton, 2012). The process starts with Classification, by which people are assigned to "us and them" roles. In the second stage, Symbolization, people are given names or symbols like "Gypsies" or "Jews." In the third stage, one group denies the humanity of the other and views the out-group as animals or parasites. In the fourth stage, or Organization, the state and related institutions, media, mobs, or terrorist organizations start institutionalizing the genocidal campaigns. Sometimes states use militias as to more easily divert responsibility. The post-revolutionary Iranian regime has extensively used this approach to carry out their terror and genocidal campaigns throughout the entire region. Turkey, Saudi Arabia, Syria, ISIL, and many other countries have each used foreign elements and militias in their genocides, war crimes, acts of terror, or instigations of mass exoduses. Iranian clergies have been known to hire Shiite militias from neighboring countries to fight in their proxy wars from Muscat to Rabat. Polarization is the fifth stage in the process of genocide whereby the state or/and extremist groups divide and polarize people and spread hatred toward the out-group. Typically, the state backs either openly or covertly oppressive elements, and helps them seize outgroups' assets while arresting and killing them. When the in-group starts to register members of the "out-groups" or prepare death lists, the Preparation stage becomes relevant. Almost all dictatorial regimes have been involved creating lists of members of the opposition or minority groups who do not fall in line with formal state politics. The most recent mass killing campaigns against political opponents in the last few decades are verified by the Islamic Republic of Iran. The regime is known to have sent terror squads not only to prisoners' cells or ethno-religious minority settlements, but also neighboring and European countries to slaughter their political dissidents. The worst and perhaps most tragic stage is called Extermination, where outgroup members fall victim to programs of systematic killing and massacres. In state-sponsored massacres, military and governmental agents work either openly or covertly with militia groups to perform mass killings. Such actions have been known to lead to revenge killings or bilateral genocides, as observed with Burundi and Rwanda. The final stage is called Denial, whereby the perpetrators of genocide attempt to cover up any evidence or intimidate the eyewitnesses, local reporters, and media. In this stage the culprits deny the genocide and their responsibility while blaming the victims for their actions.

From 10 countries identified by Genocide Watch in 2012 to be at the Extermination or Massacre stage, 3 countries (Syria, Afghanistan and Pakistan) belong to the greater Middle East, while out 12 countries at the Preparation stage, the 2 countries of Libya and Yemen are Middle Eastern. Seven other Middle Eastern countries of Iran, Iraq, Bahrain, Egypt, Algeria, Israel/Palestine, and Lebanon are categorized at the Polarization stage (Stanton, 2012).

The report unfortunately does not pay attention to the long-lasting genocidal policies of many other Middle Eastern countries such as Turkey and Saudi Arabia, where millions of ethno-religious minorities have been subjected to all forms of brutality and oppression. Typically, minorities' identities in these countries are either disregarded or annihilated. These quasi-genocidal policies along with the heavily militarized policies against minorities and political opponents need to be evaluated further, especially given the region.

The states' often sophisticated coercive apparatuses along with a continuing desire to use violence to deal with people's demands have created a permanent threat of extermination, displacement, and forced migration in these developing nations. While coercive systems of oppression and violence have been applied generously to repress native masses and subdue the grassroots community members, they have rarely been employed in the last century against Imperialist and colonialist forces in the Middle East. The several decades of political rivalry and enmity between states such as Iran, Turkey, Saudi Arabia, Iraq, Syria, Yemen, Israel, and Lebanon have only been transformed into regional wars in two cases: the first one was between Israel and surrounding Arab countries, while the second was between Iran and Iraq. Billions of dollars in annual military expenditure along with the high cost of enhancing the coercive apparatus in these countries have encouraged the ruling powers to further repress their own populations.

The absence of a real democracy and a lack of an effective and grassroots civil society along with an immense thirst for further militarization and securitization has emboldened Middle Eastern political regimes to strengthen their hold on power and view their entire realms as private possessions. In such circumstances, the state assumes full control over entire political powers and media, while leaving people with no choice but to take their grievances and discontent with them on to the streets. In a country where the parliament, courts, government, and media fail to fulfill citizens' needs and demands, streets and public spaces quickly become the only channel of protest and resistance; public spaces which are entirely under control of the tyrant regimes of oppression and violence.

II. Devastating Centuries of Ethno-Religious Massacre and Genocide

Farman is a Kurdish-Iranian term referring to a country's highest authoritarian decree, which must be obeyed by everyone. The term is used by Kurds (and especially Yazidis) to express the long history of genocide, massacre, and exodus against their people. The Yazidis believe that their community has gone through 72 cases of Farman or genocide campaigns, mostly at the hands of the Ottomans and Arab-Islamic Caliphate, and most recently in 2014 by the Islamic State of Iraq and Syria. In the 1640s, the ruthless Ottoman commander Firari Mustafa Pasha attacked the Kurdish Yazidis of Mount Sinjar with an army of 40,000 (Celebi, 1991) and within only seven hours, 3060 Yazidis were slain. The day following the battle, the Ottoman army raided and set fire to 300 Yazidi villages and massacred around 2000 women and children who had taken refuge in some caves around Sinjar with grenades and cannons (Çelebi, 1991).

The disastrous events of mass deportations, social displacements, and massacres against the Kurdish people, including the catastrophic gendercide against Barzani males and Saddam's infamous chemical attack in 1988 on Kurdish civilians, cost approximately 200 000 lives and destroyed 3800 villages, and created a need for new responsibilities and positions for Kurdish women. Since the majority of the male population in the 80s and 90s either joined the oppositional Peshmerga forces or fell victim to mass executions, imprisonments, or displacement and exile, the Kurdish women took over the harsh responsibilities of daily family life. Invasions by ruthless ISIS terrorists in regions of Iraq and Syria including Kobani, Efrin, Shingal, and Kirkuk between 2013 and 2017 shifted the responsibility of safety and security on to the newer generation of girls and women.

The Syrian poet Adonis once wrote, "God forgive the Kurds, who cannot keep the Qur'an memorized, when they reach at the Surah al-Anfal, then everyone dies." Adonis' poem refers to Saddam's brutal Anfal campaign, which claimed the lives of hundreds of thousands of victims. Starting in the early 1980s, the Iraqi regime under Saddam Hussein exacted a campaign of genocide against Kurdish population in the country' north, led by the infamous Ali Hassan al-Majid (Saddam Hussein's cousin), also known as "Chemical Ali". Anfal is the name of Qur'an capitol (Surah) which means "The Spoils of War" and describes the

Battle of Badr led by the Prophet Muhammad against his opponents in the Arabian Peninsula. Saddam used this title to justify his brutal campaigns as a holy war against Kafirs (infidels). Iraq's invasion and Saddam's fall in 2003 uncovered numerous mass graves in country's southern deserts, where tens of thousands Kurdish and Shiite populations were buried alive.

The most recent mass graves were discovered in July 2019 in the Samawa desert in the south, and contained about 2000 people, mostly women and children from Garmiyan area of the Kurdish Sulaymaniyah province (Shilani, 2019). Brutal attacks by ISIS against Iraqi and Syrian ethno-religious minority groups have been fuelled through concealed support from autocratic rulers in Turkey, Saudi Arabia, Iran, and Syria's Bashar Assad regime. Approximately 37% of ISIS detainees were registered in the official restrictions of the Turkish courts, while the others were involved in the Turkish attack on Afrin; fighting in place of Turkish soldiers. "On October 27, 2019, Abu Bakr al-Baghdadi was killed in a joint operation between the US military and the Syrian Democratic Forces (SDF) in Barisha village, near a Turkish checkpoint, about only five kilometres from the Turkish-controlled Hatay region."[3] The killing of al-Baghdadi in an area controlled by the Turkish occupation in the northern Syrian Kurdish region reveals Turkey's connection with this terrorist organization. Additionally, the Iranian Revolutionary Guards (IRGC) and their Quds Force—an extra-territorial branch responsible for supporting proxies in the region—continue to engage in interventions across the Middle East and large-scale illicit financing schemes to fund malign activities, which have further contributed to mass killings, displacements, and acts of genocide. The organization in Iraq:

> [directly] supports hardline elements associated with Iraqi Popular Mobilization Forces (PMF), including the designated foreign terrorist organization Kata'ib Hizballah. PMF units officially report to the Iraqi National Security Advisor, but several undisciplined units in practice are also responsive to the IRGC. There are numerous reports of intimidation, arbitrary detentions, and disappearances of Sunni persons by Iran-backed Shia militias. For example, Kata'ib Hizballah is reported to have kidnapped and intimidated local Arab Sunni residents in Diyala and Babil Governorates and prevented Arab Sunni internally displaced persons from returning to their homes.[4]

During the decade following the Islamic revolution in Iran, Shiite politics among neighbours like Lebanon, Iraq, Bahrain, Afghanistan, Pakistan, Saudi Arabia, Kuwait, and Syria began to stir. Shiite groups started to openly join the Shiite political movements and abandoned all forms of nationalism or leftist ideologies. These newly established organizations received all kinds of financial and political support from the Iranian regime pushing for Shiite political agendas originally introduced within Ayatollah Khomeini's export of the Islamic Revolution.

> It is not possible to tell how the sectarian struggle in Iraq will turn out, or when and where the next battle between Shias and Sunnis will be joined, or how many sectarian battles the Middle East must endure and for how long. What is clear is that the future for the Middle East will not be brighter than the past so long as the shadow of sectarian conflict hangs over it. This is the conflict that will shape the future. (Nasr, 2006).

The problem with most fundamentalist organizations is that instead of looking for political shares, they would rather eliminate entire "others" who do not align with their brutal ideologies. Benjamin and Simon explained in an New York Times editorial in the early 2000s:

> The terrorists allied with Mr. Bin Laden do not want a place at the table: they want to shatter the table. They are not constrained by secular political concerns. Their objective is not to influence, but to kill, and in large numbers—hence their declared interest in acquiring chemical and even nuclear weapons. It is just this combination—religious motivation and a desire to inflict catastrophic damage—that is new to terrorism. (Benjamin & Simons, 2000)

A different analysis led by Peter Bergen and Swati Pandey (2006, p.122) categorizes terrorism as a bourgeois endeavour and not a poor person's undertaking:

> History has taught that terrorism has been a largely bourgeois endeavour, from the Russian anarchists of the late nineteenth century to the German Marxists of the Bader-Meinhof gang of the 1970s to the apocalyptic Japanese terror cult Aum Shinrikyo of the 1990s. Islamist terrorists turn out to be no different. (Bergen & Pandey, 2006)

The bitter reality in the Middle East is that regional rivalries, interventionist policies, and proxy wars have all operated as major instigators of terrorism and violence within the most recent decades. Countries such as Turkey, Syria, Iran, Saudi Arabia, and Iraq have been equally responsible for the recent incidents of massacre, terrorism and forced displacements. Reports show that political players from farther away have also not hesitated to intervene or instigate devastating violent events. The Pakistani Prime Minister, Imran Khan, in his July 2019 visit to the White House revealed for the first time that his government had been assisting the Taliban in disrupting political developments in Afghanistan just to prevent an increased diplomatic proximity to India.

Some researchers and political activists would rather blame historical ethno-religious divides for the horrific cycle of killing and displacement in the Middle East and entire world than denounce western countries and American foreign policy. Stephen Kinzer (2003) cites the American interventionist policy as the main source of terrorism and calls the 1953 military coup in Iran a "haunting and terrible legacy" (Kinzer, 2003). He believes that the American military operation in Iran not only allowed a tyrant to restore absolute power, but ultimately contributed to the Islamic Revolution which resulted in more terrible changes towards fundamentalism. The revolution in turn spread terrorism and fundamentalism elsewhere in Middle East and to the whole world. While the irrefutability of such statements is essential, it is important that local or regional roots of war, violence, and displacements are not neglected or concealed.

We might encounter versions of genocide-like campaigns or exclusionist policies that are lesser penetrating in Iran than elsewhere in the Middle East. Iran has always been a multi-ethnic country with a higher diversity than any other country in the region. The Kurds and Persians are the oldest inhabitants of the Iranian plateau and many historians and ethnographers consider the Kurds—who have lived in the region for over four thousand years—to be indigenous. Regardless of these claims' validity, Kurds and other ethnic minorities within the Iranian plateau have always been major targets of historical abuse and oppression, culturally, politically, and economically. Importantly, Kurdistan and Baluchistan are the most underdeveloped and economically desperate regions in the country. Even the official data and field analyses easily indicate how the major ethnic minority areas of Iran are systemically neglected.

Ethno-Cultural Repression

The ferocious rise of Reza Pahlavi in Iran and Mostafa Kemal Ataturk in Turkey immediately following the First World War was accompanied by ethnic cleansing, assimilation, and forced migrations. In parallel with the rise of the atrocious European nationalism movements, many despotic Middle Eastern nations instigated a tremendous push for modern nation building on the false claims of "one nation, one language". Reza Shah in Iran and Ataturk in Turkey forcibly set a path toward a unified modern nation where everyone spoke the official language. Any ethnic or national claims other than the formal definitions dictated by the central authorities were seen as aberrant separatist deviations subject to immediate obliteration. Accordingly, a series of diverse socio-cultural assimilative and ethnic amalgamative approaches in forms of Turkification, Persification, and Arabization were presumed in many Middle Eastern countries. In many cases, harsh ethno-cultural annihilation known as culturicide transformed into real physical annihilation. A ruthless military that conducted genocide after genocide and took control over territory after territory in the name of the mother nation was used in the hopes of satisfying the dictatorial regimes' endless hegemonic desires. Without hesitation, one could simply claim that the ethnic minorities in Turkey, Iraq, Syria, and Iran had suffered a similar fate to the Jews in Nazi Germany or the Indigenous peoples of Australia, Canada, and the United States. Grigoris Balakian, one of the leaders of the Constantinople's Armenian community, who was arrested along with some 250 other people in April 1915, gave a tremendous and devastating eyewitness report of Turkish authorities' atrocities against the Armenians, which has been translated in English in 2010 (Balakian, 2010)

The situation is not much better in Syria than it is in Iraq or Turkey. In an interview with Yahoo News in Damascus, the educated and moderate Bashar Assad claimed that the allegations that over 1400 prisoners and protesters were massacred in a single prison were fake news. In early 2011, the Bashar Al-Assad regime deliberately released jihadists from prison to further radicalize the opposition and confirm the regime's claims that the entire rebellion was nothing more than a violent fundamental Islamist agitation. The leaders of two substantial Islamist militia groups, namely Hassan Aboud of Ahrar as-Sham and Zahran Alloush of Jaysh al-Islam, were both in Assad's prisons until mid-

2011, when they were intentionally set free by the regime. Importantly too, many future ISIS and Jubhat al-Nusra fighters were their cellmates.

The regime had prioritized the fight against moderate opponents while leaving jihadist groups and embryonic ISIS members unharmed. On many occasions, the Assad regime intentionally targeted non-violent or less violent opponents to ensure the rebellion turned violent. His regime's merciless barrel bombing of civilian population centers was just another example of massacre and brutality. His aggressions against the entire population supported by the Iranian clergies and the new Tsarist Putin of Russia turned the country into a bloodbath. It cost the Syrian people hundreds of thousands lives and created millions of refugees. The Syrian Observatory for Human Rights (SOHR), a monitoring group based in the UK, estimates the death toll since the start of the war to be as high as 511,000 as of March 2018 (Human Rights Watch, 2019). According to the United Nations High Commissioner for Refugees (UNHCR), the relentless fighting internally displaced 6.6 million refugees and scattered 5.6 million more around the globe (Human Rights Watch, 2019). The same report shows that the Syrian-Russian military alliance employed internationally banned cluster munitions and chemical weapons in re-taking areas from oppositional groups. Between July 2017 and June 2018 alone, troops were confirmed to have performed 36 cluster munitions attacks, with perhaps two dozen more unconfirmed cases. Ghouta and Daraa have been the major targets in these campaigns.

III. Political Discrimination and Violence Suppression

Political exclusion and socio-economic marginalization normally go hand in hand with one another, and suppressed minorities are usually deprived of fair access to existing services and national resources. In almost all despotic regimes, citizens deal with discrimination, double standards, and unjust or prejudiced treatment. Tyrant regimes have always targeted religious and ethno-linguistic minorities to prove and enforce their domination and apply their hegemonic superiority. As religion and language are important elements of people's identities, they have always been targets of ruling and political powers. Eliminating or excluding people from sharing political power on basis of their religious, ethnic, or linguistic roots is downright mundane compared to targeting people for genocide, mass killing and forced migration.

Scholars have approached the diverse elements of ethnic identity and its interactions with political power and violence differently. For some researchers (e.g. Huntington, 1997; Fox, 1998), religion is a salient aspect of ethnic identity that is can be likely to lead to further discrimination, oppression, and even sometimes conflict. Other scholars strongly believe that linguistic differences count as major causes of discrimination and ethnic conflict. Kürşad (2011, p.4) notes that "discrimination based on language tends to have a more direct impact on the individual's life".

The language policies adopted by many Middle Eastern states have been a major source of discrimination and linguistic assimilation, which have in turn escalated into ethnic conflicts and national disputes. States have frequently given direct or indirect advantages to the ruling ethnic language(s) while either restricting minority language education or banning the languages altogether. In a country where a dominant majority benefits from its language being pushed into minority communities as the only permitted national language, minorities' oppressed political and cultural rights are just one part of the story. Psychologically too, minorities with a weaker command of the official language risk having less access to education and national services, making them second class citizens. In such situations, the prestige differences between minority languages and the official language of the given country can lead to further discrimination. In dictatorial regimes with state-sponsored nationalism, ethnic minorities usually give up their mother tongue or at best only use it in the home. Parents in minority communities will often communicate with their own children in the official language rather than their own community language to avoid prosecution, as felt by the Kurdish citizens of Turkey up until the 90s. Additionally, many of these parents have felt the need to speak to their children in the official language as to provide them with more favourable educational and employment opportunities.

Due to minorities' political exclusion and marginalization, they are expected to desire political change and prodemocracy forces. Gurr (1993) notes that minorities who experience marginalization are expected to be prodemocracy because they expect to have a greater voice and protection in a more democratic system. (Gurr, 1993). Belge and Karakoç (2015) argue that some of the Middle Eastern regimes might include non-Muslim minorities in their ruling coalition but still they are often hesitant to include linguistic minorities. For example, the Berbers in Morocco and Kurds in Turkey were not considered to be possible partners in their countries' national political systems while Christian Copts in Egypt or in Jordan fared better.

In wars fought along lines of race, language, religion and ethnicity, people become targeted on the basis of such characteristics and inevitably undergo social disintegration, disorientation, and later on repression and violence. While neighbours become killers and rapists, members of mixed families tear each other apart; what had not previously been a meaningful factor like dialect, surname, or outfits, suddenly becomes a major source of hatred and exclusion. During and following the Islamic revolution in 1979 when Ayatollah Khomeini issued his Jihad decree against the Kurdish population, thousands of Kurdish civilians faced manifold forms of discrimination, exclusion, harassment, and violence in ways which had until then been rare in modern Iranian society. While Omar Koshan, the Eid-Al nationwide ceremonial burning of the second caliph of the Rashidun Caliphate is still practiced in some remote religious Iranian and Iraqi Shiite towns and districts, it has effectively been replaced by state-sponsored systems of discrimination and exclusion in others. Occasionally in mixed cultural gatherings for example, stories of ethno-cultural or religious differences become the material for bitter jokes against others and expatriates, and travel easily across generations to become an unobtrusive part of the dominating culture.

Land grab and land claims in the Middle East are other significant elements in the widespread violence and conflict which frequently transforms into mass displacements, massacres, or ethno-cultural cleansing. Like in many other parts in the world, complex disputes regarding historical land ownership exist in almost every corner in the Middle East. Disagreements on which ethnic or religious group have greater historical claims to a piece of land, region, or even an entire country reached their peak in the 20th century and have continued into the new millennium. From the Uyghurs' claim of the Xinjiang province in China to Palestinian disputes regarding Jerusalem and Kurdish claims to the oil rich city of Kirkuk in Iraqi Kurdistan, all count as potential sources of future violence and turmoil. Uyghurs in Xinjiang believe their ancestors were indigenous to the area, while Chinese authorities consider present-day Xinjiang to have belonged to

China since around 200 BC, meaning that Uyghurs are currently classified as a national minority who have no special land rights under Chinese law.

In the 16th and 17th centuries the two external imperial forces of Britain and Tsarist Russia along with Turkish Ottoman, Iranian Safavid, and Arab Kalifat regional forces were competing over a region which is known today as the Middle East. After almost four centuries, newer incarnations of the same players continue to shape the destinies of the region's peoples. The Iranian Islamic republic represents a new Safavid political power; Erdogan takes the role of new Ottomans; Saudis the role of Calafat of Baghdad; Putin the 21st century's Tsar, and Trump the old British Empire. Two centuries of war and conflict between both Iranian and Russian empires cost not only hundreds of thousands of lives but also led to the loss of over 3 million square kilometers of Iranian territory, which is known today as Dagestan, found in eastern Georgia, the Republic of Azerbaijan, and northern Armenia. While this defeat has not been the only defeat experienced by Iranians, it has proven to be the most disgraceful and embarrassing downfall in Iranian history. On one hand, Iran lost enough territory to halve its original size, while on the other, Russian agents' and officers' continuing oppressive acts toward the defeated area's inhabitants has been contributed to additional misery. Countless acts of hostility and assaults on part of the Russian armed forces within the Iranian territory of the Caucasus inspired grave complaints and protests from the locals. In this, local clergies and tribal leaders sent their written requests for salvation not only to the royal family but also to the Shiite-Islamic leaders residing in the holy cities of Najaf and Karbala in today's Iraq (Tarikh-e Now, Abasmirza, 1888, p.24).

Endnotes

1. TRT World, Exclusive: Turkish President Erdogan on developments in northern Syria (https://www.youtube.com/watch?v=O4hK-KqNRkA).
2. Sargon's conquest of Sumer, Ramses II's fight against Hittites, Hammurabi's war against Aššur, Medes' war against Urartu, Persians against the Medes and Assyrians, Alexander's conquest of Medes and Persia, Persia's wars with Byzantium, the Battle of Yarmuk between the Byzantines and the Muslim Rashidun Caliphate, the Arab invasion of Iran, and Mongolian conquests led by Genghis Khan throughout Eurasia are a handful of notable pre-modern war campaigns with genocidal characteristics.

3. Turkish state relations with the terrorist organization "Daesh".
4. https://www.state.gov/documents/organization/286410.pdf

References

Balakian, G. (2010). *Armenian Golgotha: a memoir of the Armenian genocide, 1915-1918.*

Belge, C. & Karakoç, E. (2015). Minorities in the Middle East: Ethnicity, religion, and support for authoritarianism. *Political Research Quarterly*, 1-13.

Benjamin, D. & Simon, S. (2000). The new face of terrorism. *The New York Times.*

Bergen, P. & Pandey, S. (2006). The Madrassa scapegoat. *The Washington Quarterly, 29*(2).

Çelebi, E. (1991). *The intimate life of an Ottoman statesman: Melek Ahmed Pasha (1588–1662).* SUNY Press, (pp. 169-171).

Davidson, N. (n.d.). In perspective: Tom Nairn. Retrieved from https://pureportal.strath.ac.uk/files-asset/4660428/In_perspective.pdf

Duggan, C. (2007). *The force of destiny: a history of Italy since 1796.* New York: Houghton Mifflin.

Fox, J. (1998). The effects of religion on domestic conflicts. *Terrorism and Political Violence, 10*(4), 43-63.

Ginsborg, P. (2014). *Family politics: domestic life, devastation and survival, 1900-1950.* Yale University Press.

Gurr, T. R. (1993). *Minorities at risk: A global view of ethnopolitical conflicts. Washington*, DC: United States Institute of Peace.

Haider, H. (2017). *The persecution of Christians in the Middle East.* University of Birmingham.

Horton, G. (2005). *Dying alive, a legal assessment of human rights violations in Burma.* Divine Master Print CO., LTD.

Human Right Watch. (2019). *Syria: Events of 2018.* Retrieved from https://www.hrw.org/world-report/2019/country-chapters/syria

Katulis, B., deLeon, R. & Craig, J. (2015). *The plight of Christians in the Middle East: supporting religious freedom, pluralism, and tolerance during a time of turmoil.* Washington, DC: Center for American Progress.

Kiernan, B. (2007). *Blood and soil: a world history of genocide and extermination from Sparta to Darfur.* New Haven: Yale University Press.

Kinzer, S. (2003). *All the Shah's men: An American coup and the roots of Middle East terror.* New Jersey: John Wiley and Sons.

Kürşad, T. (2011). Language and religion: Different salience for different aspects of identity. *International Journal of Business and Social Science, 2*(8).

Lemkin, R. (2005). *Axis rule in occupied Europe: laws of occupation, analysis of government, proposals for redress.* Washington: Carnegie Endowment for International Peace.

Levene, M. (1998). Creating a modern "zone of genocide": The impact of nation- and state-formation on Eastern Anatolia, 1878–1923. *Holocaust and Genocide Studies, 12*(3), 393-433.

Levene, M. (2005). *Genocide in the age of the nation state, volume. 2: The rise of the west and the coming of genocide.* London: I.B. Tauris and Co. Ltd.

Levene, M. (2014). *The crisis of genocide, volume 1: devastation. The European rimlands 1912-1938.* Oxford: Oxford University Press.

Nasr, V. (2006). *The Shia revival: How conflicts within Islam will shape the future.* New York: W. W. Norton & Company.

Shilani, H. (2019). *Mass grave in southern Iraq believed to contain remains of Kurdish Anfal victims.* Retrieved from https://www.kurdistan24.net/en/news/cfc66670-b1f2-4415-9c40-ccc296e5d519

Stanton, G.H. (2012). *Countries at risk report – 2012, the international alliance to end genocide.* Washington, D.C.: Genocide Watch.

UN. (n.d.). *Convention on the prevention and punishment of the crime of genocide.* Retrieved from https://www.ohchr.org/en/professionalinterest/pages/crimeofgenocide.aspx

Chapter 4

Sharia Law, Human Rights and Democracy

I. Sharia Law and Human Rights

"I have no hope of real change from this government unless they are forced. We face a catastrophe in this land and only the action of the international community by applying pressure can save us. Our children are dying. Our land is bleeding and burning and so I call the international community to apply punitive sanctions against this government to help us establish a new South Africa — non-racial, democratic, participatory and just. This is a non-violent strategy to help us do so. There is a great deal of goodwill still in our country between the races. Let us not be so wanton in destroying it. We can live together as one people, one family, black and white together." (Allen, 2006)
~ *Desmond Tutu, 1985*

While "Sharia" or Islamic traditional law has existed and been practiced since the early years of Islam in the seventh century, it was not until the expansion of the Muslim Empire and the 500-year absolute rule of the Abbasids dynasty (750-1258) that Sharia began to fully develop. The Turkish Ottomans and Iranian Safavids codified Sharia law differently, while many other sovereign countries thereafter interpreted a more tailor-made set of Islamic laws. While some Muslim countries today attempt to prevent or reconcile Sharia law in their political and judiciary systems with modern democratic values, many still vehemently use it to rule over hundreds of millions around the globe. Incorporating wide and diverse forms of the Islamic Sharia into national legislations, socio-political control systems, and codes of conduct has been interpreted as a major source of discrimination and injustice against both Muslims and non-Muslim minorities in almost all Middle Eastern countries. A tumultuous history exists within Sharia-dominated countries of veiled apartheid and state-sponsored violence against non-Islamic minorities, such as followers of the Bahai faith, Kurdish Yazadis, Yaresans, Zoroastrians, Jews, and diverse ancient Christian denominations.

These Islamic countries' domestic laws as well as the enigmatic Cairo Declaration on Human Rights in Islam (CDHRI) never considered the members of these faiths to be normal citizens or equal human beings. According the CDHRI, Muslim citizens of Islamic countries are called *Ummah,* and deserve special respect and attention in the eyes of the political powers, while non-Muslims are excluded. The *Ummat al-Islam* (or Islamic community), a supra-national community of Islamic people, views Muslims beyond its own national political borders as deserving of legislative or legal support, while its own non-Muslim citizens, who for millennia have lived within the same geographical and political spheres, are excluded. This provides a clear instance of discrimination and legal apartheid against often significant proportions of the national population.

Under Sharia law, non-Muslim subjects (*dhimmi*) permanently residing in Muslim lands were historically required to pay *Kharaj* (a land tax levied by Muslim rulers on their non-Muslim subjects) and *Jizya* (a per capita yearly taxation levied in the form of financial charges on non-Muslim subjects). Specifically involving Iran, discriminatory elements of the country's legal framework have continuously impacted the daily lives of religious minorities. For example, article 881 of the Civil Code bars non-Muslims from inheriting property from Muslims. In addition, if a non-Muslim leaves a Muslim heir, that Muslim heir is entitled to the entire inheritance, including the shares of non-Muslim heirs, regardless of these individuals' relationship with the deceased (United Nations, 2009).

In most Middle Eastern countries, only a few universal faiths (Christianity, Judaism, and in Iran, Zoroastrianism) are considered official within national legislations and laws, while immense discrimination exists toward smaller or regional religions. In many cases, even limited legislative supports toward such minorities are restricted to Islamic law and regulations, as demonstrated in the following analyses:

> The Constitution of the Islamic Republic of Iran, promulgated in 1979 (amended in 1989), establishes the

Twelver Ja'fari School of Shi'a Islam as the official State religion. According to article 13, Christians, Jews and Zoroastrians are the only recognized religious minorities. These religious groups are free to perform their religious ceremonies 'within the limits of the law'. Article 23 forbids the investigation of individuals' beliefs and states that 'none may be molested or taken to task simply for holding a certain belief', although as evident in articles 4, 10, 14, 20, 24, 26, 27 and 28 of the Constitution, a number of rights granted under the Constitution remain highly restrictive and qualified by the "compliance with Islam" criteria. (United Nations, 2009)

Similarly,

[...] a non-Muslim man regardless of his marital status is considered to have committed adultery when he has sexual intercourse with a Muslim woman and is subject to the death penalty (art. 224 (c) of the Islamic Penal Code). A Muslim man, on the other hand, must be married for the death penalty to be applied, and the state of being married is subject to broad exemptions, thereby providing exceptions to the enforcement of the death penalty (arts. 225–227). The punishment for adultery for a Muslim man with a Muslim woman is 100 lashes (art. 225). If a Muslim man commits adultery with a non-Muslim woman, the Penal Code does not specify any penalty. In response, the Government noted that, according to Islam, sexual relations between a man and a woman are permissible only through the contract of marriage." (United Nations, 2009)

Due to the *gozinesh* (Selection Law) process, which involves investigations conducted by the Supreme Selection Council and the Ministry of Intelligence, non-recognized religious minorities in Iran face serious hurdles in obtaining university degrees or gainful public sector employment. The acceptability of an applicant's beliefs, political affiliations, and repentance of any former political opinions and affiliations are going to be measured according the *gozinesh* process based on the Religious and Ethical Standards of 1995. A comprehensive description of such invasive measures is as follows:

These requirements are intended to ensure that applicants adhere to and have knowledge of Islam, follow the theory of Velayat-e-faqih (rule of an Islamic jurist under Shi'ite Islam) and are loyal to the Islamic Republic of Iran. Minorities unable or unwilling to accept the requirements are excluded from any possibility of employment in the public sector. Private employers have also reportedly followed the guidelines of the *gozinesh* requirements, thereby discriminating against potential non-Muslim employees. The gozinesh requirements are a violation of the International Covenant on Civil and Political Rights, the International Convention of the Elimination of All Forms of Racial Discrimination and the International Covenant on Economic, Social and Cultural Rights, as well as a violation of article 23 of the Constitution, which prohibits "investigation into one's ideas" and subjecting that person to aggression or questioning "for merely holding an opinion". "'gozinesh' criterion … may limit employment opportunities and political participation for, inter alios, persons of Arab, Azeri, Balochi, Jewish, Armenian and Kurdish communities." (United Nations, 2009)

Such examples of exclusion and discrimination do not stop at the non-Muslim members of the *Ummah*, as Muslim minorities, who do not follow the same Islamic branch formally sponsored by the state, are also at risk. The systematic abuse and discrimination against Islamic minorities, Sunni or Shiite, by different countries' Islamic authorities are deeply institutionalized and such discriminatory practices are molded into their national laws, rules, and regulations. In Iran, Iraq, Syria, and Saudi Arabia, Islamic minorities suffer from state-sponsored codes of conduct dictated by the ruling Islamic school. Over the course of four decades of Islamic Shiite rule, the Iranian regime has refused to integrate its Sunni population into the political system by depriving them of any political or administrative positions. The Iranian Shiite clerical regime has never allowed its Sunni population of over three million in Tehran to open a Mosque or a religious or cultural center. Even Khalid Mashal, the fundamentalist Sunni leader of the Palestinian Islamic Organization Hamas whose party has immensely benefited from Iranian financial and logistical support, needed to use the Pakistani Embassy for his

Friday prayers during his official visit to Tehran. As Faramarzi (2018) points out, "[t]he flare up of tensions between regional rivals Saudi Arabia and Iran over Lebanon, Syria, Iraq, and Yemen would seem to encourage interest in the state of Iranian Sunnis, if only because the Saudis present themselves as defenders of the world's Sunnis, and Iran the self-appointed champion of the Shia cause." (Faranarzi, 2018).

Iran registers more than 80 offenses punishable by death, including adultery, homosexuality, drug possession, waging war against God, corruption on Earth, blasphemy, and insulting of the Prophet Muhammad. Sharia law recognizes the hierarchy of the patriarchal society whereby the man is the head of the household and in his absence, the eldest son, the husband's brother or father, or any other male relative takes control of the family, while the wife remains disadvantaged and valued at best as half of her male counterpart.

With respect to the rules and regulations related to *Diya* (blood money), inheritance, and witness testimony, Sharia law views women as lesser than men. Almost three centuries after Rousseau's doubts regarding women's rationality and critical thinking abilities, Ayatollah Khomeini repeats the same antifeminist notions by citing the Qur'an and the prophet's traditions to assert that women require guidance from their men (usually the father or husband). His major oppositional stance against the Shah's reign was focused on the newly imposed women's voting rights. In an Instagram sermon for hundreds of women in Iran, a key Iranian Shiite cleric named Ayatollah Sadiq Hussaini Shirazi mentions that

> Allah had created three types of animals: One which are used for carrying people or staff such as horse or donkey; the second, which are used as source for food and meat consumption like sheep and cow, and the third are women for men's use. God has shaped women like human beings, so that men won't get frightened!

In living memory across the Middle East, groups exist who are regularly ridiculed, ostracized, and persecuted, and have been for centuries. Ayatollah Khomeini's stances on women's political participation and their right to work outside the home, and his vehement hatred against Bahais, Jews, and others were not concealed at all. His numerous invitations to majority religious and community leaders to take part in a broader fundamental movement against the Iranian regime in 1960s also indicated his fanatic ideas and an immense thirst for political power. Discriminatory attitudes against religious and cultural minorities, such as viewing Jews, Sunnis, Zoroastrians, and Baha'is as impure or unclean (*najis*) people who should be avoided by Shiite citizens, is something that has continued into current times. Such unjust, biased, and discriminatory statements and subsequent actions can be linked to the Ayatollah's interpretation of a verse in Quran, which states *Inama al-Moshrekoun Najis*[1] (the polytheists are nothing but impure). There is no doubt that such discriminatory forms of ostracization, especially toward vulnerable groups and minorities in despotic cultures, has continued into the modern era.

The concept of najis can be extended to other minorities within the Middle East, where it has been used to justify countless human rights violations. Muslim Arabs have been known to refer to the Iranians as *Mawali*, or freed slaves, while Islamic texts, and especially the Qur'an, state conversely that Muslim believers are brothers. However, the issue perhaps more precisely involved Arab supremacy over the *Ajam*, a pejorative term denoting non-Arab nations, which was also used to refer to Iranians. The Middle East today is full of violations of rights included in the Universal Declaration of Human Rights (UDHR), in which people are disadvantaged, discriminated against, or deprived of their rights because of religious, ethnic, or political affiliations, or even fashion sense or use of cultural symbols. Although such concepts and negative attitudes may not always be present in the actual laws to such a great extent, they are often enforced by ordinary people and encouraged by the clergies and formal authorities. For centuries, the targeting of minorities such as Kurdish Yazidis in Iraq, Berbers in Algeria, or the Bahais and Kurdish Yaresanis in Iran, has become an integral part of the agenda and concerns of international human rights organizations around the globe.

Based on the pure monotheistic faith with which Islam is built, all humankind is called to worship only the Islamic God, namely Allah, and nothing else. The real foundations of people's dignity, freedom, and integrity are built on such monotheistic beliefs, while any other beliefs are seen as *shirk* (polytheist) and in enmity with God. Although the Qur'an classifies Jews and Christians as "People of the Book" (Ahl al-Kitāb), it also labels them as polytheists—Jews for adhering to concepts of divine national selection, and Christians for their doctrines of the Trinity and Incarnation (Quran 2:94–95; 5:18; 62:6; 98).[2]

In August 1990, foreign ministers of the member states of the Organization for Islamic Cooperation (OIC) came together to ratify a framework for an Islamic human rights project which led to acceptance of a special format of Human rights called the Cairo Declaration on Human Rights in Islam (CDHRI). In reality, the conference was simply a response to the 1948 United Nations' Universal Declaration of Human Rights (UDHR). The ratified document essentially was supposed to provide OIC members with clear guidelines regarding how to deal with member states' disputes and ongoing human rights violations. While it protected Islamic authorities from being criticized for their countries' human rights violations, the CDHRI caused additional disputes and confusion, and did not help citizens of the Middle East or elsewhere in the world. This declaration does not clarify which Islamic laws ought to foundational for legal judgement and interpretation. According to the Declaration, followers of other religions are free to exercise their faith and perform their religious rites within the limits of the provisions of the states' laws, typically means Sharia law. In many cases, the Muslim countries' constitutions contain paucity clauses, which require that no law can be contrary to the tenets of Islam. As a result, the authorities and courts quite often have the power to invoke arbitrary conditions on religious minorities. Afghan Sikhs, Iranian Baha'is, Zoroastrians, and Yaresanis, Kurdish Yazidis of Iraq, and Christian-Assyrians in Baghdad are some minority religions of the Middle East who suffer from such legal deficiencies and discrepancies.

Importantly, there are huge discrepancies and heterogeneity within the major Islamic schools of thoughts (*Madhabs*), which are based on dissimilar religious jurisprudence (*fiqh*). Similarly, there are colossal differences between the liberal Sunni *Hanafi* (the school of law) and the absolutist Saudi *Wahhabi* religious laws, or Twelver *Jaffari* Shia and other schools of Islamic jurisprudence. Three major sources of Sharia legal reasoning after the Qur'an and Sunna (prophetic traditions) are Qiyas (deductive analogies), Ra'y (opinions), and Ijma (binding consensus), which have together caused tremendous confusion and differences of opinion within the Muslim community. There is no common understanding between Islamic clergies and authorities, even at the highest eminence on the use of Qiyas or Ra'y as a legal doctrine. While many theologians, such as those who founded the Hanafi school of Sunni jurisprudence (most widely practiced law school in the Sunni tradition) accepted its legitimacy, Ahmad Ibn Hanbal, founder of the Hanbali school of Sunni jurisprudence, as well as the prominent Islamic Scholar Muhammad al-Bukhari, rejected such methods as foundation for Sharia law along with many other scholars and clergies.

Even within the same school of jurisprudence there are sometimes considerable legal differences of opinion on the socio-economic and political matters of the Muslim community. An offense or action could be interpreted leniently by one Islamic jurist and strictly by other. Box 4.1 on the following page demonstrates how different Middle Eastern countries' legal systems deal with Sharia-related jurisdictions. While the majority of modern Islamic jurists regard apostasy and blasphemy as a crime deserving the death penalty (Omar, 2009; Rashied, 2009), many moderate Muslims see the death penalty as a violation of universal human rights and individuals' freedom (Ibrahim, 2006). Some others might even view the death penalty as morally wrong (Elliot, 2006) and inconsistent with the Qur'anic injunctions (El Fadl, 2007).

While the Shia Jaffari and Sunni Wahhabi schools have zero tolerance for Infidels or apostates to Islam, the Hanafi Sunni Muslim do not want to see the state's interference in such incidents:

> Hanafi scholars refuse to control a human religious or spiritual destiny, and refuse to give that right to any human institution. Among the *Hudud* crimes, those crimes against God, blasphemy is not listed by the Hanafis. Hanafis concluded that blasphemy could not be punished by the state. The state should not be involved in deciding God-human relationships. Rather, the state should be concerned only with the violation of human rights within the jurisdiction of the human affairs and human relationships. (GlobalSecurity, n.d.)

Anti-blasphemy laws have become part of the legal systems of 32 majority Muslim countries in the Middle East and any sentences carry the death penalty. While the right to convert to another religion is enshrined in Article 18 of the United Nations

Declaration of Human Rights, many Muslim-majority countries such as Saudi Arabia, Iran, and Pakistan count any departures as a violation of Sharia law and therefore punishable by death. In 2018 in Iran alone, 253 people were executed for such reasons. According Amnesty International the law in these countries is used to pursue vendettas and justify vigilante violence against "non-believers". "On the basis of little or no evidence, the accused will struggle to establish their innocence while angry and violent mobs seek to intimidate the police, witnesses, prosecutors, lawyers and judges" (Reality Check, 2018).

Box 4.1: Blasphemy and Related Laws in the Middle East and North Africa

Algeria
Algerian law criminalizes any behavior, whether through writings, drawings, statements, or any other means, that insults the prophet of Islam or the other prophets, or ridicules any Islamic religious rites. The penalty for such behavior is between three and five years' imprisonment and/or a fine of between 50,000 and 100,000 Algerian dinars (about US$455 to $909). The law was applied in the recent case of Slimane Bouhafs. In August 2016, Bouhafs, an evangelical Christian, was sentenced to five years in prison and ordered to pay a fine of 100,000 dinars (about US$900) for insulting Islam and its prophet. In September 2016, after filing an appeal, Bouhafs had his five-year sentence reduced to three years and the fine was dropped.

Bahrain
Article 309 of the Bahrain Penal Code of 1976 penalizes individuals who insult any religious sect with a term of imprisonment not exceeding one year or a fine not exceeding one hundred Bahraini dinars (approximately US$265). Article 310 also punishes any person who prints or publishes a holy book for members of a recognized religion but deliberately alters the text in a

manner intended to change the meaning of the book or ridicule its teachings and principles. Likewise, it sanctions any person who publicly insults a symbol or a person that is glorified or considered sacred by members of a particular sect. Finally, it prohibits any person from imitating in public a religious ritual or ceremony with the intention of ridiculing it. In August 2012, a Bahraini court sentenced a man to two years in prison for making insulting comments about one of the wives of Mohammed.

Egypt
Article 98(f) of Egypt's Penal Code, as amended by Law 147/2006, states that "whoever makes use of religion in propagating, either by words, in writing, or by any other means, extreme ideas for the purpose of inciting strife, ridiculing or insulting a heavenly religion or a sect following it, or damaging national unity" is punishable with six months to five years of imprisonment and/or a fine of five hundred to one thousand Egyptian pounds (approximately US$25 to $50). In May 2015, an Egyptian court of first instance found television show host Islam El-Beheiry guilty of insulting the religion of Islam. The court sentenced him to five years of imprisonment. In December 2015, the Court of Appeal reduced the sentence to one year.

Gaza Strip
The law applicable in the Gaza Strip criminalizes as a misdemeanor the publishing of any print, writing, picture or effigy intending to insult the religious feelings or belief of others. Offenders are subject to one year of imprisonment. The utterance in public and in the hearing of another person of a word or sound with the same intention is subject to the same penalty.

Iran
Chapter two of book five of the Penal Code of Iran is on "insulting sacred religious values and criminal attempt on national authorities." It com-

prises three articles, two of which relate to the crime of blasphemy. Article 513 states, anyone who insults the sacred values of Islam or any of the Great Prophets or [twelve] Shi'ite Imams or the Holy Fatima, if considered as Saab ul-nabi [as having committed actions warranting the hadd punishment for insulting the Prophet], shall be executed; otherwise, they shall be sentenced to one to five years' imprisonment.

Article 514 states, "anyone who, by any means, insults Imam Khomeini, the founder of the Islamic Republic, and/or the Supreme Leader shall be sentenced to six months to two years' imprisonment." In addition, there is a crime of "swearing at the Prophet" (Sabb-e nabi) under article 262 of the Penal Code: "anyone who swears at or commits qazf against the Great Prophet [of Islam] . . . or any of the Great Prophets, shall be considered as Sāb ul-nabi [a person who swears at the Prophet], and shall be sentenced to the death penalty." A note on the article states that swearing at the [twelve] Shi'ite Imams or the Holy Fatima will be considered Sab-e nabi. However, under article 263, if the accused claims that the statements were made under coercion or by mistake, in a state of drunkenness, in anger or by a slip of the tongue, by failing to pay attention to the meaning of one's words, or in quoting someone else, then the accused will not be considered to be a person who swears at the Prophet. According to one nongovernmental organization, the government of Iran "jails and executes periodically dozens of individuals on charges of 'enmity against God' (moharebeh)." In the view of IHEU, while "this crime is framed as a religious offense, and may be used against atheists and other religious dissenters, it is most often used as a punishment for political acts that challenge the regime (on the basis that to oppose the theocratic regime is to oppose Allah)." Examples of recent cases of possible charges of or conviction for blasphemy are as follows:

Four (and possibly more) Zoroastrians were convicted in 2011, and were still in prison as of April 2016, on charges of blasphemy, among other charges.

Members of the Iranian metal band Confess, Nikan Siyanor Khosravi and Khosravi Arash Chemical Ilkhani, were reported in February 2016 as having been imprisoned after being arrested "for promoting music considered to be Satanic, writing anti-religious lyrics, and granting interviews to forbidden foreign radio stations," and subjected to sentences of six months to six years in prison, unless found guilty of blasphemy, for which they could face execution.

In September 2014, Iranian blogger Soheil Arabi "was found guilty of insulting the Prophet Muhammad on Facebook and sentenced to death," but the Iranian Supreme Court struck down the sentence in 2015 and returned the case to a lower court, "which removed the charge of 'insulting the Prophet' and sentenced him to seven and a half years in prison, two years of religious studies (to prove his repentance), and a two-year ban from traveling abroad.

The May 2014 sentencing of eight people (arrested in 2013) "to a combined 123 years in prison for various charges including insulting the country's supreme leader on Facebook," with individual prison sentences "ranging from seven to 20 years for charges of blasphemy . . . and insulting Iran's Supreme Leader Ayatollah Ali Khamenei."

Iraq

Article 372 of Iraq's Penal Code of 1969 provides that any individual who insults the creed of a religious sect or its practices, or publicly insults a symbol or person that is an object of sanctification, worship, or reverence for a religious sect, may be punished with a term of imprisonment not exceeding three years or a fine not exceeding 300 Iraqi dinars (about US$0.25).

Israel

The infliction of "injury to religious sentiments" constitutes a criminal offense in Israel and is punishable by one year of imprisonment. Indictments under this offense, however, are extremely rare. As discussed below, under limited circumstances the potential for harming religious feelings may also constitute a ground for prohibiting the screening of movies or the distribution of publications. Section 173 of the Penal Law 5737-1977 provides as follows:

Injury to Religious Sentiments

173. If a person does any of the following, then he is liable to one year imprisonment:

(1) He publishes a publication that is liable crudely to offend the religious faith or sentiment of others;

(2) He voices in a public place and in the hearing of another person any word or sound that is liable crudely to offend the religious faith or sentiment of others.

In a 1998 decision the Supreme Court rejected an appeal from a conviction of attempting to injure religious sentiments by trying to post flyers in Hebron, a city with a majority of Muslims that had experienced a high level of tension between Jews and Arabs in recent years. The flyers depicted a pig wearing an Arab head cover and labeled "Muhammad" stepping on an open book titled "Quran." The Court noted that, considering that freedom of speech constitutes a basic principle of a democratic state, indictments under section 173 of the Penal Law were rare. In the circumstances of the case, however, there was no need for expert opinions to prove that the flyers could cause injury to the feelings of Muslims in Hebron and crossed the line of what was permitted as free speech.

Two leading decisions explain the scope of the prohibition on publication of materials that may inflict injury to religious sentiments vis-à-vis the *principle of freedom of expression under Israeli law. In a 1988 case the Supreme Court addressed the constitutionality of prohibiting the screening of the movie The Last Temptation of Christ based on concerns for the religious sentiments of the Christian community in Israel. The Supreme Court held that freedom of expression is one of the basic values in the Israeli legal system and is viewed as the essence of democracy. Freedom of expression, however, is not unlimited and should not harm the rights and freedoms of others or public order. The Court recognized that the movie was screened in many countries around the world, including countries with Christian populations. Moreover, there was no obligation to watch the movie; therefore no serious and severe injury to the feelings of those who did not watch it existed. In 2015, a request to prohibit distribution of the 2015 edition of the French satirical magazine Charlie Hebdo based on it allegedly being offensive to Muslims in Israel was rejected by the Haifa District Court. The Court decided that the title page, which showed a cartoon of a tearyeyed Muhammad holding a sign saying je suis Charlie ("I am Charlie") under the heading tout est pardonne' ("all is forgiven") did not constitute an offense to the religious feelings of Muslims in violation of section 173 of the Penal Law. Instead, the Court determined, the cartoon conveyed the protest of Muhammad against the murder of Charlie Hebdo's workers and two others, and the injury of many.*

Jordan

Jordan explicitly criminalizes blasphemy. Article 273 of Jordan's Penal Code of 1960 punishes with a term of imprisonment of one to three years any individual who insults the Prophet Mohammed. In addition, article 278 provides that anyone who publishes anything, whether it be printed, a manuscript, a picture, a drawing, or a symbol, that results in offending religious feelings or beliefs is *punishable by a term of imprisonment not exceeding three months or a fine not exceeding twenty dinars (about US$28). In a recent case decided in August 2016, Nahid Hattar was accused of blasphemy for sharing a satirical cartoon on his Facebook page. Hattar was detained for fifteen days on charges of insulting the Islamic religion. In September 2016, he was shot to death by Islamic extremists on the day of his trial.*

Kuwait
Kuwait has laws that have been used to punish individuals accused of blasphemy. Law 19 of 2012 on National Unity amended article 111 of the Penal Code to criminalize and impose harsher penalties for any publications or broadcasts, including via social media that could be considered offensive to religious sects or groups. The law punishes such crimes with a fine ranging from US$36,000 to $720,000 and a maximum of seven years in prison. In April 2016, a prominent female academic and human rights activist in Kuwait was charged with blasphemy under the law. Sheikha al-Jassem was summoned to the public prosecutor's office after legal complaints were filed against her over an interview she gave on TV about the Islamic religion. According to news reports, al-Jassem stated that the Constitution of Kuwait should be above the Quran and Islamic law (Shari'a).

Lebanon
Lebanese law criminalizes publicly cursing the name of God. The penalty for this offense is between one month and one year of imprisonment. In addition, anyone who publicly acts in contempt of the rites of any religion or encourages such acts is punishable by six months' to three years' imprisonment.

Libya
Libyan law criminalizes acts that publicly offend any of the religions that perform their rites in the open by imposing on the actor a penalty of up to

one year imprisonment or a fine of up to 50 Libyan dinars (about US$35).229 Such acts include the reenactment of a religious celebration or rite for the purpose of mockery or entertainment. Offenses against the Islamic religion and verbal statements not befitting the Divine Being, the Messenger of Islam, or the prophets are punished by up to two years' imprisonment.

Malta
Article 2 of the Maltese Constitution provides that the Roman Catholic Apostolic Religion is the official state religion of Malta. While it did not use the specific term "blasphemy," Malta had a blasphemy law until early 2016, contained in articles 163 and 164 of its Criminal Code, which prohibited the public vilification of the Roman Catholic Apostolic Religion. There were many prosecutions under these articles. Article 342 of the Criminal Code continues to provide that any person who commits an act that constitutes a public order offense under article 338 of the Criminal Code faces a minimum penalty of a fine of €11.65 (approximately US$12.50) and a maximum penalty of three months' imprisonment if the offense "consists in uttering blasphemous words or expressions."

Morocco
The newly enacted Press Law of 2016 refers to the crime of offending the religion of Islam. However, no provisions that define the elements of this crime or the penalties assigned to it were located. In addition, under Moroccan law anyone who entices a Muslim to abandon his Islamic belief or follow another religion by exploiting his weakness or need for assistance, or through the use of educational, health, or other institutions, is subject to a penalty of six months to three years' imprisonment and a fine of 200 to 500 Moroccan dirhams (about US$20 to $50). The same penalties apply to anyone who intentionally interferes with religious rites or celebrations where this

causes disturbances or affects the dignity of such religious acts. In August 2013, Moroccan authorities arrested Mohamed El Baladi, a Christian convert from Islam, for proselytizing two other Muslims. A week after his arrest, El Baladi was found guilty of attempting to incite at least one young Muslim to leave Islam and was sentenced to thirty months in prison, along with a fine of 1,500 dirhams (about US$182). After filing an appeal, the court of appeal acquitted El Baladi for lack of evidence.

Oman
Article 209 of Oman's Penal Code makes punishable with a term of imprisonment of between ten days and three years, or a fine of five to five hundred Omani Riyals (approximately US$13 to $1,300), any individual who (1) publicly blasphemes God or the Prophet Mohammed, (2) commits an affront to religions and faiths through the spoken or written word, or (3) breaches the peace of a lawful religious gathering.

Qatar
Article 256 of Qatar's Law No. 11 of 2004 incorporates punishment against individuals who are considered as being in contempt of God or Islam. It reads as follows:

Whoever commits the following acts shall be punished with imprisonment for a term not exceeding seven years:

1. Insulting Allah through writing, drawing, gesturing or in any other way or through any other means.

2. Offending, misinterpreting or violating the Holy Quran.

3. Offending the Islamic religion or any of its rites and dictates.

4. Cursing any of the divine religions according to the regulations of Islamic law.

5. Insulting any of the prophets through writing, drawing, gesturing or in any other way or through any other means.

6. *Sabotaging, breaking, damaging or violating sites or their contents if they are made to perform religious rites for one of the divine religions according to the regulations of Islamic law.*

Qatar also criminalizes proselytizing. Under article 257 of Law No. 11 of 2004, any individual who establishes an organization to proselytize may be punished with a term of imprisonment of up to seven years. In May 2013 a Nepali teacher who taught chemistry at Qatar Academy was jailed in Doha on felony charges for insulting Islam after allegedly comparing Muslims to terrorists in a verbal exchange with students—an allegation that the teacher denied.

Saudi Arabia

Islamic law (Shari'a) is the law of the land in Saudi Arabia. The country has no penal code. The main sources of Islamic law are the Quran (Muslims' holy book) and the hadith (ascribed sayings of the Prophet Mohamed). The Quran and Hadith do not explicitly mention any worldly punishment for blasphemy. Quranic verse 33:57 states that God will damn those individuals who annoy God or his prophet, but does not mention a specific punishment.

The Saudi legal system also encompasses royal decrees and fatwas issued by the Council of Senior Religious Scholars. Punishments for blasphemy involve imprisonment, fines, and lashing by whip, and may include death. In addition, questioning the fundamentals of Islam is considered an act of terrorism. Article 1 of the antiterrorism law issued in January 2014 defines a "terrorist act" as "the act of questioning the fundamentals of the Islamic religion on which this country is based." In December 2016, Ponnam Shankar, an Indian citizen, was arrested for allegedly offending Islamic sentiments by displaying the Hindu God Shiva on a wall. In November 2015, the Shari'a General Court of Abha (a city in the southwest region of Saudi

Arabia) found Ashraf Fayadh, a poet, guilty of blasphemy and apostasy and sentenced him to death. However, the death sentence was subsequently overturned, to be replaced with 800 lashes and imprisonment for eight years, in exchange for Fayadh publicly renouncing his poetry. He was charged with an array of blasphemy and apostasy-related offenses, including blaspheming "the divine self" and the Prophet Mohammad, spreading atheism and promoting it among the youth in public places, mocking the verses of God and the prophets, refuting the Quran, denying the day of resurrection, and objecting to "fate and divine decrees" cited in Sunnah (speeches and actions of the Prophet) and Quranic text.

Sudan

Under Sudanese law anyone who in any manner curses or insults in public any of the religions, their rituals, beliefs, or sacred sites, or incites a feeling of belittling their followers, is subject to a penalty of up to six months' imprisonment, a fine, or up to forty lashes. The law also criminalizes apostasy. In 2015, two Sudanese pastors, a Czech aid worker, and a Sudanese civil rights activist were arrested on the suspicion that they were trying to encourage Muslims to convert to Christianity and for publicly speaking out against the ill-treatment of Christians in Sudan. They were still in prison as of December 2016, a year after their arrest.

Syria

Syrian law criminalizes any acts committed publicly through writings, oral statements, or gestures that insult or encourage insulting religious rituals practiced in public. An offender is subject to a penalty of two months' to two years' imprisonment.

Tunisia

The Tunisian Constitution assigns to the state the obligation of protecting and preventing violations *of the sacred. Article 121(3) of the Penal Code makes it an offense to "distribute, offer for sale, publicly display, or possess, with the intent to distribute, sell, display for the purpose of propaganda, tracts, bulletins, and fliers, whether of foreign origin or not, that are liable to cause harm to the public order or public morals." Offenders are punishable with imprisonment for six months to five years and a fine of between 120 and 1,200 dinars (about US$53 to $528), and the offending materials are immediately confiscated. Furthermore, article 226(2) states that individuals who "openly violate good morals and public decency through gestures, speech, or trouble others in an obscene way shall be punished by a period of imprisonment of six months and a fine of 1,000 dinars [about US436]."*

In addition, the 2011 Press Law provides that anyone who intentionally and publicly undermines any of the authorized religious rites through writings, statements, or other means of communications shall be punished by a fine of 1,000 to 2,000 Tunisian dinars (about US$436 to $872). It also provides that anyone "calling for hatred between the races, religions, or members of the population by inciting to discrimination, using hostile means or violence, or publishing ideas based on racial discrimination shall be punished by a period of imprisonment between one and three years and a fine between 1,000 and 2,000 dinars."

In March 2012, Jabeur Mejri was sentenced to seven-and-a-half years in prison and ordered to pay a fine for posting images on Facebook deemed blasphemous against the Prophet of Islam. He was found guilty of "undermining public morals" and "attacking sacred values through actions." In 2014, Jabeur Mejri received a presidential pardon.

United Arab Emirates

Articles 312, 315, and 319 of the Penal Code of the United Arab Emirates (UAE) criminalize the act of religious blasphemy. Article 312 provides that an individual who insults the rituals or practices of Islam, the divine, and the recognized religions must be punished by imprisonment, a fine, or both. Article 315 stipulates that individuals insulting the rituals and practices of other religions must be punished by imprisonment, a fine, or both as long as those rituals and practices are protected by Islamic law. Finally, article 319 states that individuals who resist or defame the foundations or teachings of the Islamic religion or its essential doctrines, vilify Islam, preach religions other than Islam, or call for a different doctrine or thought are to be punished by a period of imprisonment not exceeding five years.

In July 2015, the UAE issued Law No. 2 of 2015 on banning the act of insulting religion and religious figures. Article 4 of the Law prohibits any act that would be considered as insulting the Divine, or one of his prophets or their wives or companions. It penalizes individuals committing those acts with a period of imprisonment of no less than seven years and a fine of between five hundred thousand Dyrhams (approximately US$136,124) and one million Dyrhams (approximately US$272,249).

In a case decided in May 2015, the Dubai Court of First Instance convicted an Indian national of blasphemy against Islam for posting a status update on Facebook cursing the Prophet and Islam after watching a news report about the war in Iraq.

West Bank
The law applicable in the West Bank criminalizes the publishing, through writings, pictures, drawings, or symbols, anything that insults the religious feelings or beliefs of other persons. Offenders are subject to a penalty of up to three months' imprisonment or a fine of up to 20 dinars (about US$28). The same penalty applies to any person who publicly and in the hearing of another person utters similar insulting words. A higher

penalty of one to three years' imprisonment applies to anyone who curses one of the recognized prophets.

In November 2010, Waleed Hasayin, a blogger, was detained by the Palestinian Authority in the West Bank after being accused of mocking Islam, the Quran, and the Prophet Mohammed in online postings under the username "God Almighty."

Yemen

Articles 194(1) and 195 of the Penal Code of Yemen sanction the act of blasphemy. Article 194 provides that "whoever publicly broadcasts (i.e., communicates) views including ridicule and contempt of religion, in its beliefs, practices, or teachings" is "punishable by imprisonment not exceeding three years, and a fine." Article 195 also states that the punishment for this offense must be imprisonment not exceeding five years or a fine if Islam is the religion or doctrine that is the subject of ridicule, contempt, or belittlement.

Source: The Law Library of Congress, Global Legal Research Center, January 2017

Countries like Algeria generally do not become involved in such disputes, while in countries such as Saudi Arabia and Iran, cases like blasphemy or apostasy are dealt with harshly and brutally. In Malaysia, the state laws in Kelantan and Terengganu make apostasy a crime punishable by death, while in some other states like Perak, Malacca, Sabah, and Pahang, apostasy by Muslims is viewed as a crime punishable only with jail terms. During Mahmoud Ahmadinejad's presidency, the Iranian regime has engaged in a systematic battle to track down and reconvert or execute those who have changed their religion from Islam (Marshall & Shea, 2011). According to the Islamic penal code, even cases of blasphemy and apostasy on the Internet or social media punishable by death (Gulf News, 2008).

Reports from the Telegraph (2008) have indicated that the Iranian clerical regime do not differentiate between children and adults when exercising the death penalty. For example, the regime hanged a boy named Hossein Soodmand in 1990 for apostasy, when he had converted from Islam to Christianity at the age of 13. Many adherents to the Baha'i faith were also targets of the Ayatollah's oppression and execution following his rise to power during the 1979 Islamic revolution.

Polygamy is permitted in Sharia law but restricted to simultaneous marriage with four lawful wives. However, an unlimited number of slave concubines may be added at that time. Divorce is usually straightforward for men and sometimes impossible for women, as men are not obliged to justify their actions or intentions. According to Sharia law, a woman may be seen only by her own husband or next of kin. Almost all the Middle Eastern countries are governed with dual legal systems, which comprise on one hand a Western-inspired civil code, and on the other, a peculiar status or family law, mainly built upon Sharia law. Such dualistic legal systems often oppose each other within the borders of the same county. When the parliament of the semi-autonomous Kurdistan Region in Iraq ratified its more secular and pro-western family law in 2012, antagonism between Kurdistan and the country's federal family law, based on Sharia law, became evident and widespread. According to Kurdish family law, polygyny is not accepted, and no man can legally register a second wife within Kurdistan's administrative borders. However, people have been known to travel to Baghdad or other non-Kurdish districts to register their wives and return.

Reports indicate that Iraqi federal family laws have caused further social conflict and disputes within the country's diverse ethno-religious groups:

> Regarding the high number of Yazidi women, who were raped by ISIS fighters, many of them got pregnant as a result, and were not allowed to abort the pregnancy due to Iraqi legislation that bans abortion, unless there are special health reasons. Razaw Ahmed and other lawyers had asked for exceptions to the abortion ban for the Yazidis, but had not been heard. (Landinfo, 2018)

The Iraqi Kurdish Regional government's legislation has become stricter in fighting female genital mutilation and violence against women and this model is now considered to be an anti-FGM model for other countries to follow (Rudaw, 2015).

In January of 2004, just a few months after Saddam's fall, the Iraqi interim government, supported by many Iraqi Islamist parties including the Islamic Supreme Council of Iraq launched Resolution 137, replaced more secular Iraqi laws with Sharia law. The current Iraqi family law is discriminatory towards women, particularly regarding divorce, inheritance, or child custody, and in the courts of law, a woman's testimony is in many cases worth half of that of a man. As a result, there have been many cases where men have openly murdered their female family members without being touched by the authorities. A teenage university girl in Basra, southern Iraq, was accused of falling in love with a British soldier and was murdered by her own male family members, who were never tried or charged for murder (Sarhan, & Davies, 2008). While the Shia school of jurisprudence permits short term marriage (Sigha) to be contracted for a specific time, other Islamic schools (mostly Sunnis) view such acts as prostitution. According to some reports (Katzman, 2018), "Iran is placed in Tier 3 (worst level) for failing to take significant action to prevent trafficking in persons. Iranian women, boys, and girls are trafficked for sexual exploitation in Iran as well as to Pakistan, the Persian Gulf, and Europe." The deep rifts between diverse Islamic schools regarding their laws is something which prevents these countries from reaching unified human rights regulations based on Islamic legislation.

According to many human rights observer groups, Iran is ranked high in the number of executions it performs. Since Rouhani took the office of president, these numbers have increased to over 1,500 cases between 2015 and 2016. In addition, stoning is still practiced as a form of capital punishment. Although Iran's judiciary apparatus issued a ban on stoning in 2002, Iranian officials later called that directive an advisory, thus putting stoning sentences at the discretion of individual judges and ensuring the practice's continuation. Figure 4.1 shows the ascending trend of executions within the Islamic republic of Iran.

At the dawn of the Islamic political system in Iran, Ayatollah Khomeini acted to the contrary of international human rights guidelines. When his appointed Prime Minister, Mehdi Bazargan, reportedly requested in 1979 that he be more careful with political executions for the sake of diplomatic relationships with the outside world; Ayatollah Khomeini responded that "those prisoners were not human and therefore not eligible for the human rights protection!" According to Amnesty International, in the summer of 1988, about 4,500 teenagers and leftwing groups were executed by the Iranian regime in addition to

Figure 4.1
Executions in the Islamic Republic of Iran: 2003 – 2013

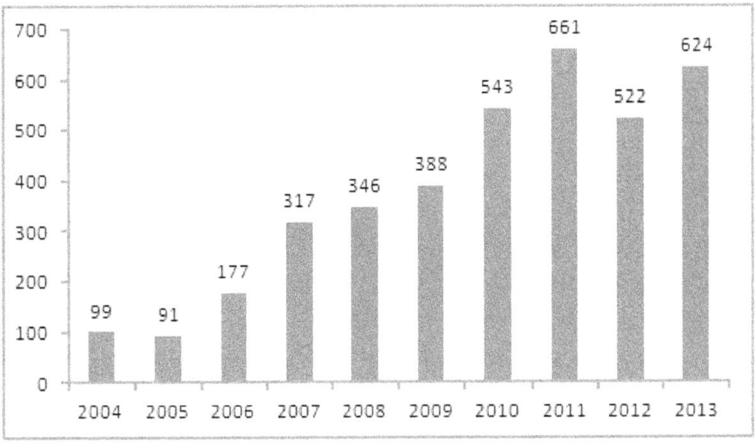

Year	Executions
2004	99
2005	91
2006	177
2007	317
2008	346
2009	388
2010	543
2011	661
2012	522
2013	624

Source: UN Human Rights Council, Report on Iran's Human Rights, 13 March 2014

the 20,000 people executed earlier in the decade. Iran has not held any officials involved in the summer 1988 executions accountable.

Iran is party to the International Covenant on Civil and Political Rights and the Convention on the Rights of the Child, and is obligated to discontinue executing minors. However, such executions continue at an alarming rate. Islamic countries such as Saudi Arabia, Iran, Pakistan, and Nigeria have incorporated traditional Islamic criminal jurisprudence such as Qisas and Hudud (laws mandated and fixed by God) into their legal system, making it incompatible with modern principles of human rights. Such retributive models of justice differentiate offences against God from crimes against man. Punishments range from public lashing to stoning to death, amputation of body parts (i.e. hands), and execution. With the exception of conservative states on the Arabian Peninsula, sharia-based criminal laws had been replaced to some extent in almost all Islamic countries during the 19th century by European legal models. However, the revival of Islamic movements in the late 20th century triggered the full reimplementation of Sharia law in many countries (Mayer, 2009).

In a recent public address, Sultan Hassanal Bolkiah, the dictator of the small South-East Asian nation Brunei, announced he would implement "stronger" Islamic teachings and stricter Islamic laws against LGBT communities, robbery, and defamation of the Islamic prophet: "I want to see Islamic teachings in this country grow stronger" (Tan, 2019).

Yvette Tan (2019) in a BBC report touches on some shifts within the country's legal system:

- Offences such as rape, adultery, sodomy, robbery, and insult or defamation of the Prophet Muhammad will carry the maximum penalty of death.
- Lesbian sex carries a different penalty of 40 strokes of the cane and/or a maximum of 10 years in jail.
- The punishment for theft is amputation.
- Those who "persuade, tell or encourage" Muslim children under the age of 18 "to accept the teachings of religions other than Islam" are liable to a fine or prison sentence.
- Individuals who have not reached puberty but are convicted of certain offences may be instead subjected to whipping.

Such aspirations are hypocritical, especially given that the same ruler is known to have transferred billions of dollars of the national wealth to purchasing luxurious hotels in the US and Europe, do not operate according to Islamic tradition or values. While such investments do not bring any tiny benefaction to the Islamic *Umma,* they create private amusement oases for the elites and Sheiks of Muslim countries.

Sharia law devotees occupy a paradoxical existence when conducting their daily lives inside and outside of Islamic countries, and such an existence clearly departs from any acceptable foundations of human rights. States that promote Sharia-centred Islamic human rights prevent their own minorities from practicing religious activities while the same time do not tolerate any resistance toward their religious expansion outside their own realm. A series of new million-dollar mosques have brought Islam out of its traditional territories into the public arenas of western societies. In 1991 for example, 46 Muslim countries spent over 17 million dollars on building a mosque and cultural center in Manhattan, New York. Similarly, the immense Turkish Şehitlik Mosque was constructed in the center of Berlin in 2005. Additionally, in September 2018, the Turkish President Recep Tayyip Erdogan spent 20 million euros to construct Germany's largest mosque in Cologne. Furthermore, the German Hanau *"Islamobil"* (Rashid, 2006) represents a mosque on wheels touring across Germany to inform people about Islam and invite citizens to the faith.

Friday evening street prayers on London's world-famous Berwick Street or in the Clichy-la-Garenne and Goutte d'Or districts of Paris, in the German cities of Munich or Frankfurt, in the French cities of Marseille and Nice, and in many other places in Europe are justified by Saudis, Turks, Iranians, and Pakistanis. However, were any discernible structures designed for practices different than majority Islam erected within their own realms, Muslim countries would put up a ruthless amount of resistance. While Muslim communities' practices may be watched closely in many European cities due to conflicts between Sharia and secular laws, security purposes, or right-wing politicians, Muslims still have the relative liberal-democratic freedom to openly perform their religious practices. Conversely, such opportunities are rarely afforded by non-Muslim minorities residing within Islamic countries. For example, a Sunni Muslim living in the majority Shiite city of Tehran is not as able to pray publicly as his or her counterpart in Paris or Berlin. In the same way, a Shiite Muslim living in Saudi Arabia or Pakistan will have trouble openly practicing their religious or cultural events.

The first steps toward social integration and away from hate speech against Shiite minorities in Saudi Arabia were taken by the Crown Prince in 2004, who allowed a greater Shiite presence in government institutions and lifted restrictions on Shiite religious rituals, thus allowing the construction of mosques or *hussainiyas*. The observance of Ashura was also permitted as part of such remarkable approvals. For decades, the pre-eminent Saudi Shiite political figure Sheikh Hassan al-Saffar along with many other Shiite leaders from Qatif and al-Hasa had been major sources of contention and political confrontation in Saudi Arabia. Al-Saffar renamed his Shiite Reform Movement the Organisation for the Islamic Revolution in the Arabian Peninsula (OIR, Munathamat al-Thawra al-Islamiyya fil Jazira al-Arabiyya) (al-Rasheed, 2011). In January 2016 the Iranian-backed Shiite clergy and devotee of velayet-e-faghih was executed by Saudi authorities along with 46 other people. In 2009, he had threatened the Saudi government, claiming that if Shia rights were not respected, the Eastern Province with its majority Shiite population would secede. He was reported to have been arrested and beaten by the Saudi secret police agency of the Presidency of State Security, also known as the Mabahith, which is known to be the official organization dealing with counterintelligence and national security in Saudi Arabia. A Middle East report on Saudi Arabia in 2005 states:

> While resisting calls from tribal warriors to suppress Shiites violently, the Kingdom from the outset pacified and marginalised them. Shiites remain under-represented in official positions, and students complain of open hostility from Sunni instructors. Jobs in the police and military are rare and promotion prospects there rarer still. While restrictions have loosened, Shiites continue to face obstacles to the free and open observance of their faith.[3]

The report continues: "Ominously, a rising number of Saudi Sunni jihadi militants have been drawn to Iraq, motivated by opposition to the U.S. but also to the Shiites' increased role."

When Mohammed bin Salman was appointed as Saudi Arabia's Crown Prince in August 2017, an ambitious and wide-ranging plan to bring economic and social reforms to the kingdom was unveiled. While he was announcing the lifting of the country's draconian ban on women driving, his intelligent office was arresting high-profile women's rights activists and clamping down on even minor forms of dissent. According to human rights organizations and the Freedom House reports, evidence indicated that that Crown Prince was personally behind the assassination of the exiled journalist Jamal Khashoggi in Istanbul in October 2018. A second mass execution of Saudi oppositional members was carried out under this freshly appointed Crown Prince, which ultimately ended 37 lives.[4] The executions were carried out by beheading, crucifixion, and public displays of some of the bodies as to act as deterrents for others.

Another instance of hypocrisy in the Sharia law lies in apostasy. While a conversion from Islam to another faith is considered apostasy and punishable by death, converting *to* Islam, even from other formally recognized monotheist religions such as Christianity or Judaism, is not viewed as a crime.

Shi'ism has proven itself a difficult concept for the sociologist of religion to grasp. Like the proverbial blind men trying to fathom the identity of the elephant they are touching, the social actors and clergies of the Iranian revolution also appear to be reaching completely different and in many cases contradictory conclusions. Ayatollah Nuri argued that the various freedoms given to the people by the constitution were antithetical to Islam, because "sovereignty belonged to God, the prophet, and the *Ulema*. The masses had no right to exercise sovereignty."[5] He further stated, as Khomeini would several decades later, that "God alone is the lawmaker in Islam" and His laws are to be "understood and disseminated by the learned clergy."

Like Ayatollah Nuri, Khomeini believed that modem government should closely resemble the theocratic Muslim communities of early Islam in which the only legitimate rulers were the clergy, who are assumed the mantle of leadership directly from Mohammed through the Imams. A strong leader is still needed because the people are, generally, "devout, simple-minded and intellectually docile. There is no need for elections and representative government, because the laws are prescribed by Islam and the clergy have emerged as the best guides and have reluctantly accepted the burden of government."[6] King Fahd also once said that: "Muslim peoples do not want or need Western democratic principles: they prefer *shura, majlis, ijma'* (consultation, tribal council, consensus) and so forth (BBC, 1992).

Ayatollah Khomeini was concerned with establishing a political system on the bases of Sharia law, which he referred to as hokumat-e islami. However, the actual outcome of his ideology was a perplexing political system in which clerical disputes and disagreements became immediately apparent. Although Khomeini strove toward "the rule of religion," the post-revolutionary Prime Minister Mehdi Bazargan notes that he crystallized his ideology as the rule of the clergy, "called it the rule of God (hakemiyat-e Allah)," and pursued his ideological goals by "rejecting the nation, nationality and rule of law."[7] Bazargan, who was himself an Islamic theologian, vehemently rejected the incorporation of Sharia law into the modern political system. "From a social and political point of view, the absolute power of Islamic jurisprudence (velayat-e motlagheh faghih) is nothing but authoritarianism and religious and political despotism, which erodes citizens' freedom, personality, and independence."[8]

In his book *The Impossible State,* Wael Hallaq, professor of Islamic Law at Columbia University, supports the notion that modern state politics and contemporary western sovereign political systems are incompatible with the Islamic tradition. He believes there are contradictions between "Islamic governance" and the "Western" modern state formation, since an Islamic State is based on God's sovereignty, with Sharia law as the fundamental Islamic moral code (Hallaq, 1995). Aside from liberal Islamic theologians, many Shiite traditional clergies have felt the need to reject the legitimacy of Sharia-based jurisprudence and Velayat-e Faghih, including the late Sheikh Morteza Ansari, Akhund Khorasani, and Mohammed Hossein Nayini.

Another dispute within the Islamic countries involves the variations and extent of Islamic jurisprudence and its impact on citizens' daily lives. Fred Halliday (1993) notes:

> within the Islamic world there is as much variation on this matter as there is uniformity. Between Turkey, Indonesia and Senegal, or between Tunisia, Yemen and Kuwait, there is an enormous variation in political, social and economic systems; Governments claiming to be Islamic range from tribal oligarchies and military dictatorships to clerical regimes and ethnic tyrannies. Any study of the obstacles to democracy in the Middle East will certainly have to take into account the histories of these countries and the way in which Islamic doctrine was used to justify despotic states in the past." (Halliday, 1993, pp.156-157).

The implementation of Sharia laws and Islamic regulations therefore occurs in totally different forms and intensities. For Ayatollah Khomeini and Pakistani clergies, pronouncements against the author of the Satanic Verses constitutes proper juridical grounds to order an execution fatwa, while for many other Islamic clergies, the issue simply counts as a matter of personal freedom.

Similarly, the Israeli-American Orthodox rabbi and ultranationalist politician Meir David HaKohen Kahane vehemently advocated that the Israeli government should adopt Jewish religious law and supported the outrageous exclusivity of Israel's democracy to its Jewish citizens. He also went further to propose that the Israeli government enforce fundamentalist and orthodox Jewish laws codified by Maimonides during the middle ages. However, he was assassinated in November 1990 by El Sayyid Nosair, an Egyptian-born American citizen trained by Islamic terror organizations in Pakistan. The truth is that democracy and human rights are the products of 20th century societies with little to no theological, clerical, or religious roots. It appears that to a large extent, religion, traditionalism, and dictatorships go hand in hand. Wherever traditional societies with fundamentalist religious and ideological frameworks rule an entire population, liberalism will be at peril and a real democracy and civil society will not be able to flourish.

Since the Houthis and their allies entered the city of Sana'a in September 2014 and began exercising control over the capital and other parts of northern Yemen in 2015, freedom of expression, association, and peaceful assembly in areas under their control have become further curtailed. Public critics and opponents including journalists, Human Rights Defenders, and members of the Baha'i community have been arbitrarily arrested and have in many cases disappeared. In June 2015, nine journalists, including those who worked for the al-Islah-affiliated online news outlet were detained in a single raid in Sana'a. By the end of 2015, Houthis closed at least 27 NGOs in the capital.

Cartoonist Atena Farghadani, an Iranian Human Rights Defender, was arrested in December 2014 and sentenced to almost 13 years imprisonment for drawing a satirical cartoon protesting a bill that would criminalize voluntary sterilization and restrict access to contraceptives and family planning services. After she shook hands with her male lawyer in 2015, she was charged with "illegitimate sexual relations short of adultery" and was forced to undergo a virginity test. However, she was released in May 2016 after her sentence was reduced to 18 months.

Iran's authoritarian power structure and its rigid ideology-rooted constitution have long failed to approach the full extent of human rights and social justice. The Iranian constitution and legal system is has perhaps the most evident examples of contradictions between theocracy and modern democracy. According to the Islamic constitution, people's guardianship belongs to the Islamic clergies (faghihs). Khomeini's concept of vilayat-e faqih (Guardianship of the Islamic Jurist) is said to applied to everyone in the absence of Mahdi (the twelfth Imam). Accordingly, the clergies are the only rightful political/governmental leaders because "God had commanded Islamic government" and "no one knew religion better than the *ulama*" (Islamic clergy) (Nasr, 2007):

> Before the Middle East can arrive at democracy and prosperity, it will have to settle these conflicts—those

between ethnic groups such as Kurds, Turks, Arabs, and Persians, and, more importantly, the broader one between Shias and Sunnis. Just as the settlement of religious conflicts marked Europe's passage to modernity, so the Middle East will have to achieve sectarian peace before it can begin living up to its potential. (International Crisis Group, 2005).

Since the establishment of the Wahhabism by Muhammad ibn Abd al-Wahhab in the eighteenth century as one of the fundamentalist Sunni views of Islam, anti-Shiite principles as outlined in Saudi Arabia and neighbouring areas have been retained into the twenty first century. According to this Islamic jurisprudence, Shiites are seen as infidels and *rafida*, those who transgress *Tawhid* (the principle of God's unity) and promote *Shirk* (polytheism). Many Sunni clerics accuse the Shiite Muslims of heresy or *Bid'ah* which is seen as an unforgivable crime and punishable by death. There are also *fatwas* issued by Sunni clerics (*Ulamas*) which designate Shiites as apostates and justify their killing (International Crisis Group, 2005).

Along with the concomitant empowerment of the country's Shiites, the 1979 Islamic revolution and its subsequent interventions in the Iraq wars and the rest of the Middle East immensely fuelled Sunni-Shiite hostilities and led to extreme forms of human rights violations. The number of the Shiite or Sunni foreign fighters involving in terrorist activities in the Middle Eastern countries including Iraq, Syria, Lebanon, Afghanistan, and Yemen are massive and steadily growing. Inside the Muslim countries correspondingly the authorities are paranoid that if their Shiite or Sunni minorities occupy key political or economic decision-making positions, it might be a threat to national security. The authorities in these countries allege their own minority citizens are allied with other countries in the region. Such claims might even have some historical bases, but even such involvement ought not justify the systematic discrimination and state oppression these groups face regularly. A recent report by Amnesty International indicates that most Middle Eastern countries have been extensively exercising the death penalty against their people, including children (see Box 4.2). The Iranian Islamic regime has maintained the death penalty for ambiguously phrased offences such as "spreading corruption on earth", "insulting the Prophet", "enmity against God", "threatening national security", or "insulting religious values".

In the four decades following the Islamic revolution, many religious minorities such as the Kurdish Yaresan are still not recognized under the Islamic Constitution, and have faced systematic discrimination in education, employment, and access to social and economic resources. In addition, many of them are persecuted for practising their faith. According to the Amnesty International 2017-18 report,

> Fair trial provisions of the 2015 Code of Criminal Procedure, including those guaranteeing access to a lawyer from the time of arrest and during investigations, were routinely flouted. The authorities continued to invoke Article 48 of the Code of Criminal Procedure to prevent those detained for political reasons from accessing lawyers of their own choosing. Lawyers were told they were not on the list approved by the Head of the Judiciary, even though no official list had been made public (Amnesty International, 2018).

Box 4.2: Amnesty International 2017-18 report on Death penalty cases in the Middle East

> Iran, Iraq and Saudi Arabia remained among the world's most prolific users of the death penalty, carrying out hundreds of executions between them, many after unfair trials. In Iran, Amnesty International was able to confirm the execution of four individuals who were under 18 at the time the crime was committed, but several executions of other juvenile offenders were postponed at the last minute because of public campaigning. The Iranian authorities continued to describe peaceful campaigning against the death penalty as "un-Islamic", and harassed and imprisoned anti-death penalty activists. In Saudi Arabia, courts continued to impose death sentences for drugs offences and for conduct that under international standards should not be criminalized, such as "sorcery" and "adultery". In Iraq, the death

penalty continued to be used as a tool of retribution in response to public outrage after attacks claimed by IS. Bahrain and Kuwait both resumed executions in January, the first since 2010 and 2013 respectively; the death sentences had been imposed for murder. Egypt, Jordan, Libya and the Hamas de facto administration in the Gaza Strip also carried out executions. Except for Israel and Oman, all other countries in the region continued a long-standing practice of imposing death sentences but not implementing them.

Source:
https://www.amnesty.org/download/Documents/POL1067002018ENLISH.PDF

The Cairo Declaration of Human Rights in Islam does not account for such violations against Muslim minorities within Islamic nations, and in addition, the fundamental universality of human rights has been disputed by some Islamic nations following the 1979 Iranian revolution. Since their ascension to power over the entire country in the 1980s, the Iranian clerics were criticized harshly regarding their national affairs and hostile policies toward minorities.

The imperative to maintain a militant stance is a factor in the continuing widespread abuse of human rights in Iran. Public executions, floggings and amputations are a relatively easy way for the government to demonstrate its uncompromising commitment to revolutionary Islamic values. Curtailing the use of such punishments could be interpreted as capitulation to pressure from the West, and could be exploited by the radical faction to advance its political cause at the expense of the moderates. (Amnesty International, 1990)

However, their laws have been designed to protect Islam and the status of the Islamic clergies instead of promoting civilians' rights. Such laws here are also male dominated in their very nature. Even the textual structures and the writing bodies of legal documents are male dominated: *he* and *his* occur frequently throughout all texts, while and almost no *she* or *her* can be found. While moderate Muslim feminists argue that the core of Islam lies on a gender-neural ideology, many trust that male dominated interpretations within the Islamic tradition have led to centuries of female oppression. In support of this latter position, Islamic theologians like Fakhruddin Razi (1149-1209), Imam Ibn al-Qayyim (1292-1350), Ibn Taymiyyah (1263-1328), and others refer to the Qur'an verse 2:282 (Surah Al-Baqarah), which plainly differentiates between the value of men's and women's testimonies:

> Believers! Whenever you contract a debt from one another for a known term, commit it to writing. Let a scribe write it down between you justly, and the scribe may not refuse to write it down according to what Allah has taught him; so let him write, and let the debtor dictate; and let him fear Allah, his Lord, and curtail no part of it. If the debtor be feebleminded, weak, or incapable of dictating, let his guardian dictate equitably, and call upon two of your men as witnesses; but if two men are not there, then let there be one man and two women as witnesses from among those acceptable to you so that if one of the two women should fail to remember, the other might remind her. Let not the witnesses refuse when they are summoned (to give evidence). Do not show slackness in writing down the transaction, whether small or large, along with the term of its payment. That is fairest in the sight of Allah; it is best for testimony and is more likely to exclude all doubts. If it be a matter of buying and selling on the spot, it is not blameworthy if you do not write it down; but do take witnesses when you settle commercial transactions with one another. And the scribe or the witness may be done no harm. It will be sinful if you do so. Beware of the wrath of Allah. He teaches you the Right Way and has full knowledge of everything.
> (Quran verse 2:282, Surah Al-Baqarah)

Scholars have been known to use this Qur'an verse as an evidence for women's testimonies being less valuable than men's. In addition, many Islamic theologians use this Qur'an verse to claim their discriminatory legal stance towards women and assert that women are more prone to error than men. Such misogynous and discriminatory stances against women can just as easily be seen within the works of more recent theologians. The Egyptian Islamic scholar Sayyid Qutb (1906-1966) saw women's psychological composition and maternal instincts as major obstacles against the kinds of objectivity necessary in order to be legitimate witness.

It is important to note that there are numerous authors and researchers who deny any Qur'anic bases of male domination or discriminatory stances against women. Some authors take a step further and trust that the Qur'anic interpretations and Islamic legal discourse mirror the worldviews and interests of specific male dominated social groups. "Believing Women in Islam" by Barlas (2002), "Beyond the Veil" by Mernissi (1975), and Leila Ahmed's (1992) "Women and Gender in Islam" expose the patriarchal interpretations of the Qur'an and Islamic scriptures and their claims to authority in order to propose other alternatives, which reinstate women's equal rights and centrality within Islamic countries. Many new generations of Islamic feminist groups—mostly female scholars, researchers, and activists—work toward initiating newer interpretations of the Qur'an and Islamic scriptures, which promulgate a women-centered exegesis and more female-dominated readings of those resources.

The Universal Islamic Declaration of Human Rights ratified by many Islamic countries in September 1991 is paradoxical and vague in many of its articles. The Declaration is based on the Islamic ideology, in which Allah has made the Islamic *Ummah*, (nation) the best of nations, and this somehow subordinates and discriminates other nations, which fall outside of the what the *Ummah* encompasses. Similarly, taqwa (piety) and amal al-saleha (good deeds) are seen as the foundation of humankind's superiority over others. Here, *Taqwa* refers to the "fear of Allah" and avoiding "*shirk* with Allah" (or the sin of practicing polytheism); something which causes discrimination or exclusion against other religions or minorities such as Hindus, who worship multiple deities.

On basis of such a view, Punjabi minorities in Muslim dominated countries like Afghanistan suffer all forms of atrocity and discrimination. Estimates of the Afghan Sikh community indicate a population of 200,000 people in 1940s, while current estimates put them at only around 300 families (Wyeth, 2018):

> During the Taliban's control Sikhs were required to publicly identify themselves with yellow armbands and mark their homes and businesses with yellow flags. The Sikh tradition of cremating their dead proved to be a significant source of tension with the regime due to the practice being forbidden in Islam. Often bodies would need to be transported to Pakistan for cremation ceremonies. (Wyeth, 2018)

The inconsistency within the laws and jurisdictions of Afghanistan has caused its non-Muslim communities, especially Sikhs, to be excluded from the state's preservation:

> Sikhs continue to face discrimination in the labour market and avoid sending their children to public schools due to bullying. Education in many cases is only available informally at gurdwaras. Sikhs have had to scale back celebrations of their religious festivals so as not to attract attention. Yet as a visibly recognisable group, they are subject to harassment and pressure to convert to Islam when in public. (Wyeth, 2018)

Some Iranian researchers and historians claim that brutal mass conversions and adoption of Shiite Islam in the 16th century Safavid Dynasty preserved Iran from perishing as a sovereign state. However, recorded historical events indeed prove the contrary. After the infamous and bloody forced conversions during the 16th century, Iranian empires lost control over millions of square kilometres of land, including Western Armenia and Kurdistan (1514), Bahrain (1521), Baghdad (1638), the Caucasus (1828), western Afghanistan (1857), Baluchistan (1872), and Turkmenistan (1894).

II. Compatibility of Islam and Democracy

Aside from secular academic writers, theorists and devotees of the Islamic political system such as Abu-ala Mawdudi and Seyyed Qotb were exceedingly concerned about the possible coexistence and compatibility of democratic values and the Islamic ideology. They see an immense contradiction between people's sovereignty in modern democratic systems and the Islamic theocracy based on the God's Sovereignty. The Islamic Divine Governance is founded Sharia law, while western democracies are based on regulations conceived of by human beings. For example, all papers presented at a 2005 Iranian regime's conference on Islamic religious democracy tried in vain to attest to the propriety and integrity of the "religious (Islamic) democracy" and the impairment and fragility modern western democracies (Khoramshahi, 2005).

There are scholars and intellectuals within the Middle Eastern Islamic nations who indicate the unfeasibility of a complete integration of Islamic traditions and modern democratic legislations and ways of life. They either request a clear separation between the traditional interpretations of religious prescripts and today's human life, or wish to prevent religion's involvement in modern Muslim society. Syrian contemporary political activist and intellectual, Louay Safi (2006), rejects any implementation of Sharia laws in the people's modern life in Muslim countries. He proposes that historical social conditions must be reflected upon while reviewing past implementations of such laws in historical Islamic cultures. In other words, one must be able to individually accept or reject a specific faith on foundation of individual opinion without being exposed to external pressure or coercion. (Safi, 2006).

Any claims that fundamental human rights and democratic values are embodied in the Islamic ideology and related laws (Khadduri, 1946; Ishaque 1974; Said, 1979) are at best Islamic authorities' idealisms and not genuine human entitlements. In an article, Jack Donnelly (1982) posits that such ideological and religious claims about human rights involve human dignity (if not male Muslim dignity in particular), which is the ultimate *goal* of human rights, but not human rights in of itself. He also views such claims to be a duty or responsibility of the Islamic ruler and society, but not an example of the true rights and entitlement of a human being.

> Without a doubt the social and political precepts of Islam reflect a strong concern for human good and human dignity, but although such concern is important in itself and would appear to be a prerequisite for human rights notions, it is in no way equivalent to a concern for, or a recognition of, human rights. (Donnelly, 1982).

Manoranjan Mohanty (2012) observes human rights to be "political affirmations of a desirable human condition articulated in course of struggle". He also trusts that human "rights should be delinked from duties as the two are important on their own and one should not be seen as a condition for the other." (Mohanty, 2012).

Sometimes elucidations or political standpoints in this respect are overly pessimistic, exaggerative, or even inimical, even though they may offer some semblance of truth. In a 2014 article that indirectly praises Islamic nations' authoritarianism, Andrew Green, former UK Ambassador to Syria and to Saudi Arabia claims that democracy does not work in the region, where the rule of law tends to be absent:

> Democracy is empathically not the solution for extremely complex societies and Western meddling only makes matters immeasurably worse. The fundamental reason for our failure is that democracy, as we understand it, simply doesn't work in Middle Eastern countries where family, tribe, sect and personal friendships trump the apparatus of the state. These are certainly not societies governed by the rule of law. On the contrary, they are better described as *favour for favour* societies. (Green, 2014)

For many Islamic scholars and especially feminist researchers, there are huge gaps between traditional Islamic family law and the values of more modern and democratic countries:

> "The legal systems under which women live in Muslim countries are mostly dual systems. They consist, on the one hand, of civil law, which is indebted to Western legal systems, and on the other hand, of family or personal status law, which is mainly built upon Sharia. The civil law as well as the constitutions of many Muslim states provide for equal rights between women and men. However, Islamic family law as variously manifested in Muslim nations poses obstacles to women's equality." (Offenhauer, 2005)

Box 4.3: 2019 Freedom House Report on Democracy and Freedom in the Middle East

MIDDLE EAST AND NORTH AFRICA: REPRESSION GROWS AS DEMOCRACIES STUMBLE

Authoritarian states across the Middle East and North Africa continued to suppress dissent during 2018, and even the few democracies in the region suffered from self-inflicted wounds. However, elections held in Iraq and Lebanon could stabilize those countries and open the way for modest progress.

Political repression worsened in Egypt, where President Abdel Fattah al-Sisi was re-elected with 97 percent of the vote after security forces arbitrarily detained potential challengers. In Saudi Arabia, after the government drew praise for easing its draconian ban on women driving, authorities arrested high-profile women's rights activists and clamped down on even mild forms of dissent. Evidence also mounted that Crown Prince Mohammed bin Salman had personally ordered the assassination of self-exiled critic and Washington Post columnist Jamal Khashoggi in Istanbul, dashing any remaining hopes that the young prince might emerge as a reformer.
The consolidation of democracy in Tunisia continued to sputter; as freedoms of assembly and association were imperiled by legislative changes and the leadership's failure to set up a Constitutional Court undermined judicial independence and the rule of law.

Nationalism escalated in Israel—the only other country in the region designated as Free—placing strain on its democracy. A new law allowed the interior minister to revoke the residency of Jerusalem-based Palestinians for, among other things, a "breach of loyalty" to Israel. Moreover, an addition to the country's Basic Law downgraded the status of the Arabic language and introduced the principle that only the Jewish people have the right to exercise self-determination in the country.

National elections in Iraq and Lebanon held some promise of further gains. Despite allegations of fraud and a controversial recount, Iraqis witnessed a peaceful transfer of power following competitive parliamentary polls. However, antigovernment protests in the southern city of Basra at year's end were met with a disproportionately violent response by security forces. In Lebanon, parliamentary elections took place for the first time since 2009, restoring a degree of legitimacy to the government after repeated postponements of the balloting.

Source: Freedomhouse.org (https://freedomhouse.org/report/freedom-world/freedom-world-2019/democracy-in-retreat)

Cyberattacks against many human rights advocates, lawyers, and political activists have become an undeniable threat in many countries of the Middle East. Nowadays, cyberspace and related technologies have functioned as both supportive and detrimental mechanisms toward citizens. For the authoritarian regimes of despotic governmental systems the presence of social and human rights activists are nothing but bêtes noires. The local authorities and the central government have fervently tried to implement filtering policies and new legislations limiting citizens' freedom and rights in the name of "preventing cybercrimes", "fighting terrorism" or "national security measures".

Just 50 years after the adoption of the Universal Declaration of Human Rights (UDHR) the UN General Assembly in 1998 reaffirmed the principles of freedom and justice by adopting the "Declaration on the Right and Responsibility of Individuals, Groups and Organs of Society to Promote and Protect Universally Recognized Human Rights and Fundamental Freedoms" – which is frequently abbreviated to "The Declaration on Human Rights Defenders" (HRD). According to this declaration, the activism of civic society actors which support human rights and related principles are duly recognized and the responsibility is placed on related states to protect the HRDs from any possible harm and threats. In line with the HRDs Declaration and other international standards, Amnesty International considers an HRD to be "someone who, individually or in association with others, acts to defend and/or promote human rights at the local, national, regional or international levels, without resorting to or advocating hatred, discrimination or violence." (Amnesty International, 2018).

Narges Mohammadi is an Iranian HRD, and was the vice president of the Centre for Human Rights Defenders in Iran before it was disbanded by the authorities. Iranian courts sentenced her to 22 years' imprisonment for her human rights work, including campaigning against the death penalty. In addition, Nasrin Sotoudeh, a lawyer and a tireless advocate of human rights who had defended many political prisoners was arrested in September 2010 on charges of spreading propaganda and collaborating to harm state security. While Sotoudeh has been frequently harassed and imprisoned for her activism, she has remained defiant both inside prison and out. Once again in 2018, she was imprisoned and the judge sentenced her to a total of 38 for varied reasons. On June 2019, Amirsalar Davoudi was sentenced to 30 years in prison and 111 lashes for his human rights work. He was accused of "insulting the Supreme Leader" and "spreading propaganda against the system" as well as publicizing violations through a channel set up on the Telegram mobile messaging app and giving media interviews.

In 2009, Iranian clergies executed many Kurdish political prisoners, including Ehsan Fattahian, despite an international campaign calling for his release. Ehsan was born in Kermanshah, the largest Kurdish city in Iran, and was executed by hanging for "enmity against God". During the same trial on May 2010, Farzad Kamangar, a young Kurdish schoolteacher, poet, and journalist was also executed. Kamangar's lawyer, Khalil Bahramian had announced that "nothing in Kamangar's judicial files and records demonstrates any links to the charges brought against him." (Center for Human Rights in Iran, 2008).

In many instances where ethnic or religious minorities in the Middle East would face execution, members of the ruling majority would instead be punished with lesser penalties for the same charges. Importantly, many Middle Eastern countries have shown the highest rates of execution in response to crime in the world. A 2017 Amnesty International report shows that 84 percent of the global executions were carried out in the four Islamic nations of Iran, Saudi Arabia, Iraq, and Pakistan, while more than half (51 percent) of them specifically occurred in Iran (Amnesty International, 2018) Here, Figure 4.2 shows that a majority of the human rights defenders detained in Iran are of the ethnic rights category.

**Figure 4.2
Human Rights Defenders Detained in Iran in
2014 by Category**

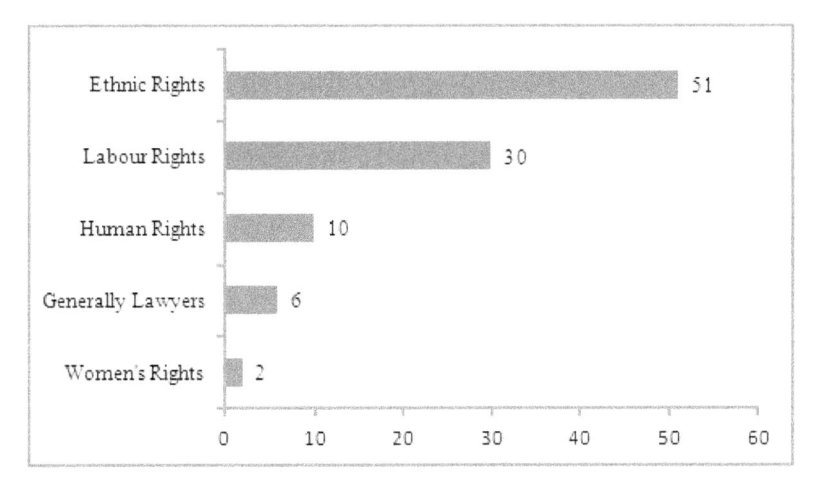

Category	Count
Ethnic Rights	51
Labour Rights	30
Human Rights	10
Generally Lawyers	6
Women's Rights	2

Source: UN Human Rights Council, Report on Iran, 13 March 2014

III. Human Rights Violation Against Indigenous Minorities: Kurds

After Assyrian and Chaldean ethnic groups, Kurds are likely the oldest residents of Mesopotamia and today's Middle East, while they also comprise the largest ethnic minority in the world without their own state. The historically evident linguistic, cultural, and religious characteristics of the Kurds prove them to be descendants of the Medes, who had settled in present-day Iran, Iraq, Turkey, and Syria during the second millennium BCE (Dyakonov, 1956). They created the Medic Empire, one of the first recognized empires in the region, which centuries later was united by Cyrus the Great into a single realm and heralded as the

Achaemenid Empire. As the native residents of Mesopotamia, the Kurds have been and are an essential thread in the ethno-cultural and political fabric of entire region. Famous Kurdish dynasties ruled over large geographical territories for centuries until the end of the First World War, when the collapse of the Ottoman Empire split the land into smaller hostile nation-states like, Iraq, Turkey, Syria, and Lebanon. The European powers' betrayal against the Kurdish nation, which culminated in the notorious Sykes-Picot agreement, served to pour gasoline on a smoldering fire and triggered successive atrocities and suppressions against the indigenous Kurds in each newly established country.

The snobby, power-thirsty parvenus who had suddenly gained political rule over a heterogeneous, multiethnic, and coercively put-together political entity now became the butchers of their own subjects. In each newly established nation-state, an intense and merciless policy of national homogenization, forced resettlements, and brutal assimilation was initiated, which in turn encouraged resistance among the targets. In differing intensities across Iran, Iraq, Turkey and Syria, the Kurdish natives of diverse religious backgrounds became the target of all forms of political aggression and state violence. Since the start of this harsh reality, the Kurdish nation established its underground resistance and protection units almost in all corners of its half a million square kilometre territory; from Afrin in northeastern Syria to Dersim and Amed in Turkey, all the way to the Barzan region in today's Iraqi Kurdistan and Mahabad or Kermashan in southwest Iranian Zagros mountains. From Ataturk to the British-backed Reza Shah in Iran and the brutal Baathist regimes of Saddam Hussein in Iraq and the Syrian Hafiz Assad regime, the despotic military elites took control over an entire nation and have since ruled ruthlessly with an iron fist.

In each of these countries, ethnic and religious minorities, and especially the Kurds, became the easiest target of oppression in form of assimilation, resettlement, ethnic cleansing, genocide, and exclusion. After almost a hundred years since the establishment of Turkey, Erdogan's repressive regime in 2019 along with Putin's support and a corrupt Trump administration unilaterally crossed its southern border. While this was ostensibly done in order to establish a 'safe zone' for his own citizens, he has committed a modern act of ethnic cleansing against Kurdish citizens. Erdogan's exercise of military power against the Kurdish forces in Syrian Kurdistan (also called *Rojava*, or Eastern Kurdistan) is for no reason but to manipulate the demography of the region and further destabilize of the Middle East. The Kurds in Syria have proven to be the most reliable allies in the fight against fundamentalist terrorist organizations supported by Turkey, Saudi Arabia, and Iran. Each of these governments have brandished their extreme hatred toward the Kurds and have rarely wished to settle such disputes peacefully.

Most recently, Turkish political elites have not attempted to hide their desire to support domestic and international ISIS fighters in combatting Kurdish and Syrian Democratic Forces (SDF) in northern Syria. A major issue with Erdogan's regime is that his government often seems overly eager to join forces with Islamist fundamentalist groups such as Jebhat-al-Nusra, Al-Qaida, and Salafis, while at the same time is hesitant to see any Kurdish oppositional group in Syria reach some sort of political agreement. Instead, this Turkish militarist regime views the Kurds as a national security threat and terrorist organization.

When the Trump administration pulled its forces from parts of Rojava in Syria on October 9th, 2019, many media outlets and international organizations justifiably claimed that the "US military is being stripped of its honor" or "Trump is backstabbing its own most trusted allies". The sudden removal of American troops gave the green light to the Turkish aggressors to start their brutal campaign against the innocent citizens of northern Syria. The invaders' targets were not only civilians including women, children, and the elderly, but also the members of Non-Governmental Organizations and non-militaristic institutions. Notably, Hevrin Khalaf, co-chair of the newly established and peaceful Syrian Future Party was executed recently by Turkish backed mercenary factions. The peaceful political party sought to draw membership from diverse ethnic and religious factions, and intended to build mutual relations between Turkey and Iraq. Its founding congress took place in Raqqa under the slogan to build a "democratic, pluralistic and decentralized Syria."[9] The Turkish army and its Syrian rebel proxies launched their coercive campaign (the so-called Operation Peace Spring) against the Kurds in Tal Abyad and Ras al Ayn, which claimed dozens of civilian's lives in just the first few days. In addition, Christian communities in northeast Syria also became the target of the Turkish attacks for the first time in over a century:

> The Syriac-Assyrians and Armenians of northeast Syria have been divided on their feelings towards the Kurdish-

led, U.S.-backed Syrian Democratic Council (SDC) that took control of the area after the defeat of ISIS. But they remain united against the prospect of a war between Turkey and the Kurds, which is now beginning to wreak havoc on their homeland. [historical records show that the] indigenous Christian ethnic groups used to be one-third of northeast Syria's population, but many left during the Arab nationalist regimes of the twentieth century. There are no reliable statistics today, but Ishak [an SDC diplomat of Syriac-Assyrian origin] estimates that there are only forty or fifty thousand Syriac-Assyrians left in the region."[10]

Since the establishment of the modern political state at the start of the 20th century, Kurdish leaders and activists in Iran have also been targets of all sorts of atrocities by both monarchist and Islamist regimes. Many leaders of oppositional groups within the Kurdish community had become easy targets for the regimes' coercive apparatus. The political atrocities of the Shah heralded tragically in the brutal execution (hanging) of the democratically elected Kurdish president and cabinet ministers of the Kurdistan Republic in Mahabad in 1947. Since then, Kurds have become the targets of assimilation, displacement, and extermination, and the Shah's policies towards establishing "one language, one nation", was nothing short of "culturicide" and "linguicide". Such discriminative policies were executed not only against Kurds, but also many other ethnic minorities in the country.

In less than three decades, the largest Kurdish and Azeri cities and regions in the country became a chilling success story of assimilation. The author of this volume remembers how his father in 1970s and 1980s was frequently taken into custody for the purposes of interrogation by the regime's security and intelligence forces just because he was in the possession of Kurdish-language literature. At the time, the publication of any texts in an ethnic language (even when apolitical) was seen as a political crime which carried with it long prison sentences. The Kurdish people were required to smuggle such publications from Iraqi Kurdistan, where Saddam's regime showed less paranoid sensitivity.

The Islamic revolution in Iran intensified the political oppression against not only the Kurds, but also against all non-Shiite ethnic and religious minorities. Tens of thousands of political activists and members of oppositional organizations, intellectuals, and former politicians were executed in cold blood.

Ayatollah Khomeini ordered a decree of Jihad against Kurdistan in 1981 and paved the way for the Kurdistan region of Iran to become militarized in the decades following his death, which initiated a wide range of incarcerations and massacres of civilians, community leaders, and intellectuals. Through the Ayatollah's despotic system of velayat-e faghih, hundreds of thousands of Kurdish citizens were slaughtered, imprisoned for life, or exiled, while their family members were forcefully silenced or even displaced from their hometowns.

Under the guise of socio-political or economic reform and development in the Middle East, ruling authorities have deceitfully continued and in many cases intensified their repressive policies towards their citizens. Both Iranians and Saudis have been fraudulently holding double standards and misleading the international community by only showcasing examples of change and reform. At the end of Iran-Iraq war in 1988, the Iranian president Rafsanjani was framed as an economic re-constructivist and political reformist, though the worst forms of human rights violations, oppression, and state sponsored terrorism were recorded both inside and outside the country during his term. While Rafsanjani was trying to attract western countries' investment and industrial knowledge in order to augment his development strategies, he had also sent his terror agents abroad to European countries to slaughter opposing leaders and political activists. Thousands of Iranian political prisoners were sent to mass killing machines during his term, and hundreds of elite political dissidents were murdered.

In 1989, Rafsanjani's intelligence agents masquerading as diplomats arranged a meeting with Dr. Abdurahman Ghasemlou, a university professor, political scientist, and leader of the Kurdish oppositional party (the Kurdistan Democratic Party of Iran, KDPI) in Vienna to discuss a reconciliation plan for the Kurds in the country. However, they brutally assassinated him along with two of his associates at the meeting place in Vienna. Because of a promised business agreement with the Iranian regime, the Austrian political leadership escorted the terrorists to the Schwechat airport and returned them to Tehran. This tragic story is documented in a book (Eskort nach Teheran) by the Austrian Green Party leader at the time, Peter Pilz. Pilz later noted that one of the murder witnesses (witness D) had claimed that the later Iranian President Ahmadinejad was also part of this terror campaign in Vienna.

Ghassemlou's successor, Dr. Sadegh Sharafkandi, a university professor and a well-educated scientist, was also the target of a brutal terror attack, this time in Berlin. Additionally, in August 1991, the president Rafsanjani's great-nephew, Zeynalabedine Sarhadi led a successful assassination campaign against the last pre-revolutionary Prime Minister of Iran, Dr. Shapour Bakhtiar in Paris. The Iranian regime since its establishment has committed thousands of assassinations and state-sponsored terror on its oppositional groups. Box 4.4 provides a list of the Iranian regime's assassinations of prominent oppositional leaders and activists during Rafsanjani's presidency.

Sayyed Assadollah Ladjevardi, the notorious Iranian conservative prosecutor and warden, used to call his preferred torture "Shir Kakao" (chocolate milk) time. As such, prisoners regularly referred to Lajavardi as the butcher of Evin prison. Imprisonments, torture, violence, and abusive acts for Middle Eastern state authorities as well as regular civilians are often described through euphemisms and sarcasm. For example, Iranian SAVAK authorities are known to refer to interrogation rooms as *preparation rooms*,[11] and torture was called "caressing" or "navazesh" in Farsi, while the Islamic authorities after the Iranian revolution in 1979 called it *guiding punishment* or Taazir (divine penalty). When a person lands in the state prison, vernacular Iranian culture refers to it as *aabkhonak Khordan*, or drinking cold and fresh water; a soothing and thirst calming fresh drink in a hot season.

A great danger to the foundation of civil society is public apathy toward torture, war crimes, and crimes against humanity. The situation becomes increasingly dangerous when a grassroots population gets deterred by their government's intimidation or constant indoctrination, and begin to close their eyes to hideous truths. Edwardo Galeano notes that "the first person killed by torture triggered a national scandal in Brazil in 1964. The tenth person to die of torture barely made the papers. Number fifty was accepted as 'normal'" (Mossallanejed, 2005).

Religiously sanctioned violence and torture might be spread in many societies and cultures around the globe but in the Middle East, it has become part of formal state business:

> In Iran, Saudi Arabia, Sudan, Nigeria, Pakistan, Mauritania, Bangladesh and some other countries the law permits flogging people who drink alcohol or do not observe the dress code of the government. Men and women, especially women are stoned to death for the crime of adul-

Box 4.4
The Islamic Republic of Iran's Assassinations of Prominent Political Dissidents

Date	City	Country	Target	Position	Killer
7 December 1979	Paris	France	Shahriar Shafiq	Head of the Iran Azad Group, nephew of the last Shah of Iran	Muslim Liberation Group
22 July 1980	Bethesda, Maryland	United States	Ali Akbar Tabatabaei	President of the Iran Freedom Foundation, former press attaché to the Iranian embassy	Dawud Salahuddin
7 February 1984	Paris	France	Gholam Ali Oveisi	former Chief Commander of the Imperial Iranian Armed Forces	Islamic Jihad Organization
19 May 1987	Vienna	Austria	Hamid Reza Chitgar	Representative of Labor Party of Iran	Suspected Iranian agents
July 13, 1989	Vienna	Austria	Abdul Rahman Ghassemlou	Head of the Democratic Party of Iranian Kurdistan	Suspected Iranian agents
			Abdullah Ghaderi Azar	Assistant to the Head of Democratic Party of Iranian Kurdistan	
1 April 1990	Nynäshamn	Sweden	Karim Mohammedzadeh	Iranian Kurdish dissident	Reza Taslimi
24 April 1990	Coppet	Switzerland	Kazem Rajavi	Representative of the National Council of Resistance of Iran. Former Ambassador of Iran to the UN	Suspected Iranian agents
6 September 1990	Västerås	Sweden	Efat Ghazi	Member of the Kurdistan Democratic Party of Iran	
12 July 1991	Tsukuba	Japan	Hitoshi Igarashi	Japanese translator of Salman Rushdie's novel *The Satanic Verses*.	Islamic Revolutionary Guard Corps
6 August 1991	Suresnes	France	Shapour Bakhtiar	Former Prime Minister of Iran. Head of the National Resistance Movement of Iran	Ali Vakili Rad
August 7 1992	Bonn	Germany	Fereydoun Farrokhzad	Iranian dissident	Suspected Iranian agents
September 17 1992	Berlin	Germany	Sadegh Sharafkandi	Head of the Democratic Party of Iranian Kurdistan	Mykonos restaurant assassinations
			Fattah Abdoli		
			Homayoun Ardalan	One of the leaders of the Democratic Party of Iranian Kurdistan	
			Nouri Dehkordi		
6 July 1996	Stockholm	Sweden	Kamran Hedayati	Iranian Kurdish dissident	Suspected Iranian agents
29 April 2017	Istanbul	Turkey	Saeed Karimian	Iranian television executive, owner of Dubai-based GEM TV	VAJA
17 July 2019	Erbil	Iraqi Kurdistan	Osman Köse	Turkish Diplomat	Turkish Kurd Assassins backed by VAJA

Source: Wikipedia.org https://en.wikipedia.org/wiki/List_of_Iranian_assassinations

---

tery. Here, governments turn ordinary people into torturers by inciting them to throw stones at the victims. They are told to bury men up to their bellies and women up to their breasts and start throwing stones; they are instructed to choose stones which are neither too small nor too large, in order to prolong the victims' agony. This type of torture is a part of the criminal code of some fundamentalist countries. (Mossallanejed, 2005)

Naive sarcastic rhetoric and diatribes sometimes become a form of abuse, prejudice, and discrimination against the "others" and minorities within politically integrated national entities. Speaking local languages or even wearing traditional clothes outside the home communities may also contribute to negative stereotypes attributed to the speaker. Such bigoted attitudes only intensify further during political disputes and ethno-cultural struggles. I remember how Iranian post-revolutionary events and enmity against indigenous people (including Kurds) had transformed into abusive and public exchanges. During the Kurdish-Iranian dispute and Ayatollah's Jihad against Kurdish people in the 1980s, my uncle was often ridiculed by non-Kurdish drivers, passengers, or shopkeepers when he was working as a regional and intercity passenger driver. Once, he described the contemptuous and dismissive language of a restaurant owner, who overtly asked his cook to prepare "two skews of autonomy"[12] when my uncle wanted to order two skews of kebab. The 20th-century prominent French sociologist, Pierre Bourdieu, coined the term "symbolic violence" to account for types of non-physical violence encountered in power differentials between social groups. The entire history of the Middle East overflows with waves of symbolic violence not only during times of war but also in peacetime.

According to the Kurdistan Human Rights Center, 446 people were executed in the prisons of the Islamic Republic of Iran in 2010 alone, of which 86 were Kurdish citizens. Out of 44 executions in 2016, 27 cases (over 61%) were Kurdish citizens. These reports show that some of the victims included lawyers who represented Kurdish political prisoners in revolutionary courts. For example, a recent report prepared by the United Nations Human Rights Commission's Special Rapporteur on the situation of human rights in Iran indicates that:

> in February 2019, Massood Shamsnejad, a professor and lawyer, was sentenced to six years in prison for propaganda against the State after he had represented several Iranian Kurdish political prisoners. In its comments, the Government noted that Mr. Shamsnejad had been charged with membership in hostile groups, with the purpose of disturbing the security of the country; and propagation activities in favor of the terrorist group. It also noted that the verdict upon appeal had been referred to the branch of the provincial Court of Appeal, pending a final decision. (United Nations, 2019)

Additionally, the report shows that the "Kurdish political prisoners charged with national security offences represent almost half of the total number of political prisoners in the Islamic Republic of Iran and constitute a disproportionately high number of those who received the death penalty and are executed." (United Nations, 2019).

In June 2007, Iranian authorities arrested Mr. Mohammad Sadiq Kaboudvand, a prominent Kurdish Human Rights advocate, journalist, and editor. According to the Center for Human Rights in Iran (2009), he was charged for

> acting against national security through the founding of the Human Rights Organization of Kurdistan (HROK), [...] widespread propaganda against the state by disseminating news, [...] opposing Islamic penal laws by publicizing punishments such as stoning and executions, [and ...] advocating on behalf of political prisoners. (Center for Human Rights in Iran, 2009).
>
> Through his efforts as editor of an independent weekly newspaper, *"Payam-e Mardom"* (people's massage) and establishing HROK, Kaboudvand promoted human rights and justice for Iranians and Kurdish citizens. Therefore, many international organizations such as Amnesty International regarded him as a prisoner of conscience. He was kept in solitary confinement multiple times—in one case for over five months—just to prevent him from influencing other prisoners. Although he and his son were suffering from serious illnesses, they were held without adequate medical care despite health professionals' warnings and advice. Kabudvand was eventually freed from prison on May 2017 after 10 years of being held captive.

Almost all Kurdish political prisoners are charged with national security offences, and according the UN Human Rights Commission's report, they represent almost half of the total number of political prisoners in the entire country. Similarly, they constitute a disproportionately high number of those who receive the death penalty and are executed (United Nations, 2019):

> In 2018, 828 Kurdish citizens were arrested, many of whom were sentenced to long years of imprisonment and were charged with crimes relating to civic activism and membership in Kurdish political parties. In the first six

months of 2019, 199 Kurdish citizens were arrested. A total of 17 of those prisoners were women, 115 were arrested for charges relating to membership in Kurdish political parties, 24 were charged in relation to their civil activities, 7 were arrested for organizing Nowruz celebrations, 22 were environmental activists, 7 were arrested for labour activities, 3 were charged for their religious belief and activities and 4 were charged for managing social networks such as Telegram. At present, 55 of the 199 Kurdish detainees were sentenced to up to 15 years in prison. At least 17 Kurdish prisoners were executed: 14 for murder and 3 for drug-related crimes. (United Nations, 2019)

On February 2018, the Kurdish political prisoner Ramin Hosein Panahi was executed by the order of the Islamic Revolutionary Court of the Republic of Iran. Another Kurdish political prisoner, Hedayat Abdollahi-Poor, was sentenced to death in the same year. One of the major Kurdish religious minorities of Iran are the approximate 2 million followers of Yaresan (Ahl-e Haq) faith, who are not accepted in the Islamic legislation. During the Islamic revolution, many of them were forced to convert to Islam while many others were imprisoned or executed for publicly practicing their faith. "The absence of constitutional and legal recognition for non-recognized minorities entails denials of fundamental human rights for their followers. Left outside the national legal framework, unrecognized minority religious groups such as Baha'is, Christian converts, Sufis, including the Gonabadi order, Yarsanis and the Sabean-Mandaeans, are the targets of discriminatory legislation and practices." (United Nations, 2019).

Box 4.5: UN Human Rights Commission's Special Rapporteur Recommendations on Iran

The Special Rapporteur Recommends that the Supreme Leader and Relevant Legislative Institutions:

(a) Amend article 13 of the Constitution to ensure that all religious minorities and those who do not hold any religious beliefs are recognized and able to fully enjoy the right to freedom of religion or belief;

(b) Amend all articles in the Islamic Penal Code that discriminate on the basis of religion or belief;

(c) Amend existing legislation to abolish the death penalty for crimes not meeting the "most serious crime" threshold according to international human rights law;

(d) Urgently amend legislation to prohibit the execution of persons who committed a *hudud* or *qisas* crime while under 18 years of age and who, accordingly, are children;

(e) Urgently amend the legislation to commute all existing sentences for child offenders on death row;

(f) Repeal the established *gozinesh* requirements and any other policies that condition access to employment on the basis of individual beliefs, in line with the Constitution.

The Special Rapporteur Recommends that the Government of the Islamic Republic of Iran:

(a) Permit the United Nations Special Rapporteur on the situation of human rights in the Islamic Republic of Iran to enter the country for monitoring visits;

(b) Ensure that all persons accused of any crime are afforded due process and fair trial guarantees, including access to a lawyer of their choosing during all stages of the judicial process and are provided with legal aid and access to interpreters during court proceedings;

(c) Ensure that human rights defenders, including women human rights defenders, and human rights lawyers and journalists are not threatened with or subjected to intimidation, harassment, arbitrary arrest, deprivation of liberty or other arbitrary sanction, and release all those detained in connection with their work;

(d) Immediately release all dual and foreign nationals arbitrarily detained in the Islamic Republic of Iran;

(e) Ensure that all individuals within its territory and subject to its jurisdiction are treated equally before the law without distinction of any kind such as race, sex, language, religion, sexual orientation and political or other opinion;

(f) In accordance with article 18 of the International Covenant on Civil and Political Rights, to which the Islamic Republic of Iran is a party, ensure that everyone has the right to freedom of thought, conscience and religion, including the freedom to have or to adopt a religion or belief of their choice, or not to have or adopt a religion, and the freedom, either individually or in community with others and in public or private, to manifest their religion or belief in worship, observance, practice and teaching;

(g) Refrain from targeting members of recognized and non-recognized religious minorities with national security-related charges and end the criminalization of the peaceful expression of faith;

(h) Cease the indiscriminate killings of border couriers and take measures to regularize their work;

(i) Allow places of worship for all religious minorities to be opened, including Sunni mosques and new churches throughout the country;

(j) Refrain from persecuting peaceful religious gatherings in private homes and other premises, refrain from convicting religious leaders and cease the monitoring of citizens on account of their religious identity;

(k) Allow all students of ethnic and recognized and non-recognized religious minorities full and equal access to State universities on the basis of academic merit;

(l) Ensure that minority languages are made available to children of ethnic minorities at the primary school level.

Source: UN Human Rights Commission, General Assembly, 18 July 2019

Endnotes

1. Quran: Surah At-Tawbah [9:28].
2. As according to the Oxford Dictionary of Islam.
3. The Shiite question in Saudi Arabia, Middle East Report N°45 – 19 September 2005: https://www.refworld.org/pdfid/43bd1ce24.pdf
4. European Saudi Organisation for Human Rights (ESOHR), https://www.webcitation.org/77sp6OpXQ?url=https://www.esohr.org/en/?p=2196)
5. AMJAD, supra note 17, at 38 (quoting S. Akhavi, religion and politics in contemporary Iran: Clergy-State relations in the Pahlavi period 26-35 (1980)).
6. Ayatollah Rouhollh Khoeyni, Islamic Government, Joint Publications.
7. Analysis of the velayat-e motlaghe faghih azadi movement of Iran, Tehran, 1987.
8. Analysis of the velayat-e motlaghe faghih azadi movement of Iran, Tehran, 1987.
9. RUDAW.net; https://www.rudaw.net/english/middleeast/syria/121020194
10. ibid.
11. Ezat Mossallanejed, (2005).
12. This was referred to the post-revolutionary Kurdish oppositions' request of autonomy, which received violent responses from Ayatollah Khomeini and led to his notorious Jihad Fatwa against Kurdish people.

References

Abou El Fadl, K. (2007). The Great theft: Wrestling Islam from the extremists. HarperOne.

Ahmed, L. (1992). Women and gender in Islam: Historical roots of a modern debate. New Haven: Yale University Press.

Allen, J. (2006). Rabble-rouser for peace: The authorized biography of Desmond Tutu. London: Rider.

Al-Rasheed, M. (2011). A History of Saudi Arabia. New York.

Amnesty International. (2018). Human Rights Defenders under threat – A shrinking space for civil society. London, UK.

Amnesty International, (1990). Iran: violations of Human Rights 1987-1990. Retrieved from https://www.amnesty.org/download/Documents/200000/mde130211990en.pdf

Amnesty International, (2018). Amnesty International Report 2017/18: the state of the world's Human Rights. London, UK: Peter Benenson House.

Amnesty International. (2018) Death Sentences and Executions in 2017. London, UK: Peter Benenson House.

Barlas, A. (2002). Believing women in Islam: Unreading patriarchal interpretations of the Qur'an. University of Texas Press: Austin.

BBC. (1992, March). Fahd's declarations on the establishment of a Consultative Council in Saudi Arabia. BBC Summary of World Broadcasts.

Center for Human Rights in Iran. (2008). Kurdish teacher facing execution based on "zero evidence". Retrieved from https://iranhumanrights.org/2008/03/kamangar-sentence/

Center for Human Rights in Iran. (2009). Mohammad Sadiq Kaboudvand. Retrieved from https://www.iranhumanrights.org/2009/01/mohammad-sadiq-kaboudvand/

Donnelly, J. (1982). Human rights and human dignity: An analytic critique of non-western conceptions of human rights. The American Political Science Review, 76(2), 303-316.

Dyakonov, I.M. (1956). Midian History: From ancient times to the end of the 4th century BCE. Moscow – Leningrad.

Elliott, A. (2006, March). In Kabul: a test for Shariah. New York Times.

Faranarzi, S. (2018). Iran's Sunnis resist extremism, but for how long? Atlantic Council, JSTOR.

GlobalSecurity, (n.d.). Hanafi Islam. Retrieved from https://www.globalsecurity.org/military/intro/islam-hanafi.htm

Green, A. (2014). Why Western democracy can never work in the Middle East. Retrieved from https://www.telegraph.co.uk/news/worldnews/middleeast/11037173/Why-Western-democracy-can-never-work-in-the-Middle-East.html

Gulf News. (2008, July). Iran considering death penalty for web-related crimes.

Hallaq, W.B. (1995). The impossible state: Islam, politics, and modernity's moral predicament. New York: Columbia University Press.

Halliday, F. (1993). Orientalism and its critics. British Journal of Middle Eastern Studies, 20(2) 145-163.

Ibrahim, H. (2006). The Blackwell Companion to Contemporary Islamic Thought. Blackwell Publishing.

International Crisis Group. (2005). The Shiites question in Saudi Arabia, Middle East. Report N°45 – 19 September 2005.

Katzman, K. (2018). Iran: politics, human rights, and U.S. policy specialists in Middle Eastern Affairs. Congressional Research Service.

Khoramshahi, M.B. (2005). Democracy on the scale of Islam: religious democracy. Tehran: ICRO.
Landinfo. (2018). Kurdistan Region of Iraq (KRI) Women and men in honor-related conflicts. The Danish Immigration Service.
Marshall, P. & Shea, N. (2011, October). Silenced: How apostasy and blasphemy codes are choking freedom worldwide. Oxford University Press.
Mayer, A.E. (2009). Law. Modern legal reform. In Esposito, J.L. (Ed.). The Oxford Encyclopedia of the Islamic World. Oxford: Oxford University Press.
Mernissi, F. (1975). Beyond the Veil: Male-female dynamics in a modern Muslim society. Bloomington, IN: University of Indiana Press.
Mohanty, M. (2012). Reconceptualising rights in creative society. Social Change, 42(1), 1-8.
Mossallanejed, E. (2005). Torture in the age of fear. Hamilton, Canada: Seraphim Editions.
Nasr, V. (2007). The Shia Revival: How conflicts within Islam will shape the future. W. W. Norton & Company.
Offenhauer, P. (2005). Women in Islamic Societies: A selected review of social scientific literature. Washington, D.C.: Library of Congress.
Omar, A.R. (2009). The Right to religious conversion: Between apostasy and proselytization. In Abu-Nimer, M. & Augsburger, D. (Eds.). Peace building by, between, and beyond Muslims and Evangelical Christians, (pp. 179–94). Lexington Books.
Rashid, A.A. (2006). Mosque on Wheels Takes Islam to the German Streets. Retrieved from https://www.dw.com/en/mosque-on-wheels-takes-islam-to-the-german-streets/a-2111438
Reality Check, (2018). Pakistan Christian: Which countries still have blasphemy laws? Retrieved from https://www.bbc.com/news/world-46046074
Roberts, H. (2014). Berber Government: The Kabyle Polity in Pre-colonial Algeria, I.B. Tauris & Co Ltd. NY.
Rudaw. (2015). Kurdish FGM campaign seen as global model.
Safi, L. (2006). Apostasy and Religious Freedom. Retrieved from: http://www.islamicity.org/2845/apostasy-and-religious-freedom/ (retrieved February 20th 2019)

Sarhan, A., & Davies, C. (2008, May). My daughter deserved to die for falling in love. The Guardian.

Tan, Y. (2019). Brunei implements stoning to death under anti-LGBT laws. Retrieved from https://www.bbc.com/news/world-asia-47769964

Telegraph, (2008, October). Hanged for being a Christian in Iran.

United Nations (2019). Situation of human rights in the Islamic Republic of Iran. Report of the Special Rapporteur on the situation of human rights in the Islamic Republic of Iran. Retrieved from https://undocs.org/en/A/74/188

Wyeth, G. (2018). A precarious state: the Sikh community in Afghanistan. Australian Institute of international Affairs. Retrieved from http://www.internationalaffairs.org.au/ustralianoutlook/precarious-state-the-sikh-community-in-afghanistan/

Chapter 5

Rudiments of Quality of Life Research For the Middle East & Sensitive Communities

I. Introduction

Quality of life (QOL) research and social reporting today belong to the most pragmatic research disciplines in social sciences and sociology and are fundamental mechanisms in much broader contexts of social indicator systems. This may have been one of the main contributing factors that have identified such academic capacities as "social engineering". Today, QOL research within its short existence has developed itself from a simple material inspection of a country's living conditions to a combination of multidimensional, post-material, and subjective analyses of peoples' lives, which incorporates social and spatial justice, equity, and human rights. While the number of field analyses in the subjective study of the quality of life has firmly increased in industrialized countries, most developing countries still hesitate to participate in such research. Importantly however, the theories and models of QOL research and subjective well-being analyses have generally improved and multiplied.

Some researchers attempt to use simplified and limited versions of the research for assessing QOL, such as in case- or condition-related models and domain-oriented or health related quality of life (HRQOL) models. However, many employ more sophisticated and elaborate models, which evaluate quality in diverse domains of life and measure the overall/universal subjective QOL and well-being in a society. However, incorporating an immense set of diverse variables—which may not correlate closely with QOL—into the research process does not yield valuable or comprehensible academic results. Apart from how we obtain a portrait of overall well-being using either Top-Down or Bottom-Up models, it is crucial that post-materialistic and psychosomatic QOL indicators can be incorporated in an acceptable, reliable, and scientifically valid research model. As argued in this chapter, an ideal type of analysis includes a comprehensive and combinatorial model of an overall subjective QOL that accounts for important domains and incorporates all objective and subjective indicators. Here, pioneers of such models are mentioned as to offer fruitful discussions of field analyses and further contribute to QOL research. Recent catastrophes involving war, violence, and forced migration in the Middle East require a more comprehensive and human-based QOL approach, in which human dignity, human rights, and elements of social justice are a primary focus.

While this chapter presents a general overview of the theoretical and conceptual attributes and the historical and scientific spectacles of QOL research, it also discusses how the barriers and difficulties of research associated with sensitive societies may be untangled and overcome. Furthermore, this chapter acts as a guide that explains how to introduce cutting-edge scientific models to developing countries. Finally, this chapter discusses how developing countries that face budgetary or disciplinary obstacles to implementing modern academic approaches could extend their capacity for subjective and objective QOL analyses in economical and efficient ways.

II. Definitions, Conceptualization and Theories of Social Indicators of Quality of Life

A social indicator is a parameter, factor, or element that can bear a statistical value, degree, or level. It is quantifiable, meaning that it can have a numerical value assigned to it. In other words, a social indicator is any evidence or statistic that enables us to evaluate all or parts of human life, its trends, and positions. When we talk about Age as an indicator, we refer to a numeric value which indicates that how many years a person has been living.

Of equal importance, social indicators enable us to assess where we stand in relation to specific aspects of life. Tony

Atkinson and his colleagues in their book "*Social indicators: the EU and Social Inclusion*" note that "social indicators are important tools for evaluating a country's level of social development and for assessing the impact of policy." (Atkinson, Cantillon, Marlier, & Nolan, 2003). Social indicators encompass the same logic in mathematics and theoretically involve an infinite number of variables. For example, the indicator "education" denotes an individual's literacy level and can be grouped into categories such as *no education, primary education only, middle school*, or *secondary education*. This variable again could be further categorized according to gender, age, geography, urban/rural settlement, etc. This same procedure could be applied to other indicators including health, mortality, marital status, dwelling, employment, leisure time, or family size. Social indicators can be distinguished by their measurability (directly/indirectly measurable), desirability (positive or negative), or degree of visibility (objective or subjective).

There is no doubt that the main goals of social indicators, as is discussed in this chapter's historical background of the discipline, are to either measure social change or to evaluate citizens' life conditions and standard of living. Some scientists believe that social indicators should exist on an individual level as opposed to being aggregated. Similarly, they must also be oriented towards societal goals and measure the outputs of any program or policy, not the input (Noll, 1999). A substantial problem here is that by only considering the direct effects and outputs of parameters, we will be required to be overly selective, meaning that many important indicators will likely not be accounted for. By only considering outputs, we would inappropriately eliminate indicators like the number of high schools, teachers, medical doctors, or policemen, which not only indicate some standard's level, but also directly or indirectly affect quality of life. While such parameters may not overtly impact QOL measures, there is no doubt that they should be considered in the long list of social indicators. Any parameter or indicator which interprets a nation's social situation in any way should be considered a significant social indicator. Similarly, any variables that have a comprehensive, direct, or positive effect on an individual should be considered a QOL indicator.

While many objective and material elements are significant and influential in QOL research, most QOL scientists today agree that subjective indicators like happiness, satisfaction, and psychosomatic cognition must also be included, which in a nonbiased academic survey, should lead to a more comprehensive QOL analysis. Indeed, such a combinatory model was developed by Wolfgang Zapf in 1984, whereby the cross-tabulation of objective and subjective indicators gives four types of QOL conditions (Zapf, 1984), as in Table 5.1 below:

Table 5.1
Executions in the Islamic Republic of Iran: 2003 – 2013

Objective Well-being	Subjective Well-Being	
	Positive	Negative
Good	Well-being	Dissonance
Bad	Adaptation	Deprivation

Source: Source: Zapf (1984)

1) **Well-being**: combination of good objective and positive subjective indicators.
2) **Dissonance**: combination of good objective and negative subjective indicators.
3) **Adaptation**: combination of bad objective and positive subjective indicators.
4) **Deprivation**: combination of both bad objective and negative subjective indicators.

Such a conceptualization within QOL research is thus far the most sophisticated model in existence, though I argue that it is essential that personal and societal indicators of sustainable development are included in the process of analysis. While a research project that only considers personal objective and subjective elements can assess an individual's or society's QOL across a specific time frame, it will not be able to evaluate the sustainability of such qualities in relation to environmental elements or the society's development as a whole. In addition, any measures of a person's happiness and satisfaction must account for their society's level of sustainability. Here, sustainability refers to environmental preservation, human rights, democracy, generational accountability, human dignity, and good governance.

In coming sections and especially under "Modern developments and approaches in Quality of life research," we are going to further discuss different models of QOL research and modern theories which have been frequently applied in this field.

III. Historical Background of Social Indicators Movement

Although classical as well as modern philosophers have to some extent pointed out social and economic factors affecting the human life and society, social indicator systems are essentially a product of the modern capitalistic world. Before becoming an important discipline in the modern social sciences, concerned governments or governmental agencies struggled to find solutions for their internal calamities or prevent socio-economic troubles. Social indicators were discussed during President Hoover's administration in 1929, when he ordered sociologist W.F. Ogburn and others to undertake a national survey on social trends in the United States. In an announcement on October 11th 1932, the president declared that the reason for his order was that "it should serve to help all of us to see where social stresses are occurring and where major efforts should be undertaken to deal with them constructively" (Mitchell, 1933).

It can be argued that the catalyst that instigated social indicator research was the decade-long severe worldwide "Great Depression," which started in 1929. Furthermore, immediately following the Second World War, many developed countries, welfare states, and global organizations like the United Nations became interested in finding the best means of implementing service programs while also measuring the effects of their investments on their citizens' lives. The Second World War's catastrophic impact on nations' socio-economic structures hastened such research into an era which today is known as the social indicators movement. To make evaluations that used effective, practical, and sophisticated parameters, the collaboration of scholars, practitioners, government agencies, and policy makers was required. However, while local governments and the international community were of no doubt instrumental in providing missing information, the lack of reliable data was still a main concern.

As perhaps the first academic attempt at building a system of social indicators, Raymond Bauer conducted a study on the social and human effects of NASA's projects conducted under the American Academy of Arts for NASA in 1960s. Not only was he a pioneer of the field, but he also coined the term *social indicators*. Subsequently, one of the early works of United Nations Research Institute for Social Development (UNRISD) titled "Social indicators of development," analyzed social variables that were affecting economic development models. In his report prepared under UNRISD, Drewnowski (1966) outlined the concept of a social policy that quantifiably analyzes the social elements of development. However, he and many other affiliated or independent scientists tried in vain to construct a single unified international index which showed the wide range of living conditions across diverse countries. While the success of such an approach is debatable, these early researchers did continue on to pioneer tremendous works which emerged later in studies of social indicators. In his report titled "Level of Living," Drewnowski and Scott (1966) assessed peoples' living conditions based on socio-economic indicators such as health, housing, security, education, and income. Finally, in 1989, the UN Department of International Economic and Social Affairs published the "*Handbook of Social Indicators*" as a guide for researchers at national, regional, and international levels concerned with the selection and compilation of social indicators regarding the standard of living and related social and economic conditions (UN, New York, 1989).

In 1970, European countries under the Organization for Economic Co-operation and Development (OECD) also created a program of work on social indicators which, in recent decades, has been undertaking its reports in a more pragmatic way. In 1986, the OECD published a compendium of social indicators, and in 2001, started an extensive report entitled "Society at a Glance: OECD Social Indicators" which was elaborated on by the OECD Directorate for Employment, Labor, and Social Affairs. This ongoing project investigates how well OECD countries are progressing and how effective their actions in promoting social progress are.

Importantly, the 2009 edition of the report included a wide range of information on social affairs and indicators. For the first time, their report contained information on diminutive indicators including youth behavior, bullying, and adult height

(OECD, 2009). Outside the United States and European Union, UN-affiliated organizations like, WHO, UNDP, and UNICEF and international organizations like the World Bank or IMF have also developed systems of social indicators for their own purposes.

Since their establishment, these organizations have attempted to collect a worldwide set of factors which are mainly provided by the respective countries. In the recent decades, a handful of developing countries have also tried to gather information on social indicators and some have even developed special units in charge of collecting and evaluating suitable social indicators to be used in their national and regional programs and planning. The urgency of addressing these countries' development challenges and fighting poverty and citizens' vulnerabilities has forced many of these countries to institute their own units which deliver appropriate social data within a reliable system of social indicators.

A recent attempt initiated by an African communications entrepreneur at building a more homogenous index of social indicators for African countries is known as the "Ibrahim Index". Although the index was originally intended to measure and monitor African governments' accountability, it also covers an extensive set of diverse parameters which demonstrate to some degree these countries' living conditions. Aside from rapidly changing factors related to the continent's political landscapes, the Ibrahim Index has employed 84 different indicators organized into four comprehensive categories: Human Development, Safety & Rule of Law, Participation and Human Rights, and Sustainable Development.

The World Values Study (WVS) Group started in the 1980s with the goal of analyzing a wide spectrum of socio-economic and political parameters to understand the changes in global attitudes that affect people's QOL. In 1994, this project covered indicators from over 70 percent of the world's population in countries with varying stages of development from all five continents.

Apart from international statistical centers and some meager governmental social research units, there is no significant mechanism of social indication in most developing countries. Most social indicator models that have been implemented in these countries do not venture beyond demographic censuses or some housing and labor statistics. As a result, social indicators analyses have not found a suitable purpose in governmental or public spheres, though some projects are treated as scientific endeavors strictly within academia.

While the study of social indicator systems at first glance seems to be a discipline that primarily collects statistics on social or societal characteristics and elements, QOL research and social reporting and monitoring function as two significant pillars of its pragmatism; both have enabled scientists and politicians alike to evaluate or monitor conditions, tendencies, and changes of a nation's social parameters. Successful QOL research and social reporting within the context of social indicators have given some scholars the confidence to discuss social engineering and experimental sociology. While such a claim may at first seem exaggerative, it does not make a mountain out of a molehill. The reality is that as modern disciplines in the study of social indicators, social engineering and experimental sociology have proven able to assist a wide range of clients from academia to those in the economy, politics, and decision-making. Micro and macro studies in developed countries and multi-national organizations including the UN, OECD and EU have used both models as solid and reliable foundations for analyses and planning. The following sections analyze the field's background in philosophical terms followed by a discussion of the origins and historical backgrounds of QOL research as a modern field of social indicators systems and social sciences.

IV. Doxography and Philosophical Origins of Quality of Life Studies

Debates on the nature of peoples' lives may have started simultaneously with classical contemplations in philosophy. Fundamental metaphysical questions about existence, reason, the value of human life, and the way it should all be applied to the real world has relentlessly been part of philosophers' ambitions. Democritus assumed the focal reason of the human's life was a hedonistic one. In their book, *The Greeks on Pleasure,* Goasling, Charles, and Taylor (2002) portray the ways through which classical philosophers such Democritus, Socrates, Protagoras, Aristotle, and others regarded human life. A fundamental aspect of Democritus's ethical theory is the maximum attainment of pleasure as a state of well-being (Goasling, Charles, & Taylor, 2002), where pleasure is the greatest purpose in human life and ultimately the supreme good. Accordingly, the evaluation of good and bad in one's behavior depends on how they tend to help or hinder achieving maximum pleasure. However, Democritus drew an important distinction between life enjoyment and satisfaction, in that true satisfaction lies not in one's possessions or external luxuries, but in having peace of mind and a good spirit.

Aristippus (435-356 BCE), a student of Socrates and the founder of the Cyrenaic school of philosophy, is another hedonist philosopher who not only preached the goal of life as pleasure but lived a luxurious life himself. Unlike Democritus, the pleasure he was referring to was more inclined toward sensual gratification, such as sleeping with courtesans and enjoying fine food and old wines. Epicurus (341-270 BCE) also instructed that pleasure and happiness were the purposes of life. However, he instead interpreted happiness as a tranquil life characterized by peace, freedom from fear, and the absence of pain and by living a self-sufficient life surrounded by friends. Epicurus' version of life satisfaction and pleasure differs widely from other hedonist thinkers to the extent that one should have a more virtuous and temperate life. He honored the joy of simple pleasures and emphasized avoiding excessive bodily desires such as sex or overindulgence.

While thinking about people's lives nearly three millennia in the past comprises a significant logical leap from today's capacity for research and science, such statements show how our philosophical ancestors viewed and advocated desirable lives. Regardless of whether these scholars' views are approved or disapproved of by other philosophers, they have made an undeniable contribution to the subject matter of people's living conditions. However, these contributions are all doxographic, and at best serve to add detail to the QOL discipline. The above scholars and many others provide a general guide to evaluating people's life satisfaction and level of happiness based to some on the extent to which cerebral or material enjoyments are assured. As such, the only means here to measure the level of human satisfaction is to trace how one has enjoyed their life in spiritual or materialistic terms. None of the traditional philosophers developed a model through which the net worth of pleasure and pain or people's happiness levels could be examined.

In more recent times, perhaps the first philosopher to design such a measurement model was Jeremy Bentham (1748–1832). In a utilitarian way, he tried to help authorities and policy makers calculate the degree of pain or pleasure in a person's action. His famous algorithm, known as the felicific (or utility) calculus, correlated moral statements (goodness or badness and rightness or wrongness) with the level and extent of pain or pleasure with which an action may incur. In his book *An Introduction to the Principles of Morals and Legislation* (Bentham, 1789) he argues that the rightness of an action is determined by its utility, the amount of the pleasure it has produced, or the extent to which it has prevented pain. The only rational aim of human action is to produce the maximum amount of pleasure enjoyed by society and to avoid pain as much as possible. To measure the amount of the pleasure or pain in a human action, he deems that we should first consider the intensity, duration, certainty or uncertainty, propinquity, fecundity, and purity of that pleasure or pain. The fecundity of a pleasure or pain may be determined by the chance that the pleasure or pain will be followed by pleasures or pains of the same kind. The purity of a pleasure or pain may be determined by the chance that the pleasure or pain will not be followed by pleasures or pains of the opposite kind (Bentham, 1789).

Although Bentham's approach appears to be an important step toward designing an appropriate model of measurement within studies of QOL, it is still far from modern scientific reality and is apprehensible regarding its philosophical reasoning. One of the most current criticisms of his theory may be its inconsistency in relation to different people's standing on value and the amount of happiness and suffering that is possible in a given scenario. If a driver loses control of a vehicle and kills 5 strangers for example, his personal suffering might still be less than it would have been were he to have instead killed his own mother. In sum, Bentham's model remains a far cry from what is now commonly accepted as empirical research.

V. Modern Developments and Approaches in Quality of Life Research

In the last four decades, QOL research has flourished as a modern field in social sciences, while its roots go back to the social indicators system. Initially, the purpose of the social indicators movement was to assess the quality of citizens' lives while also evaluating the efficacy of government programs on society and people's lives. From a mere gathering of preliminary indicators, QOL research has developed into an expansive and encompassing collection of indicators that are at times unrelated to one another. Because of this, an important issue exists that requires addressing: Incorporating immense sets of diverse data which may not directly correlate with QOL into an analysis may lead to confusion and not yield any valuable or comprehensible results. However considering only a few factors in a QOL evaluation, risks oversimplifying the data and producing an unreliable analysis.

Sometimes economists or politicians attempt to showcase their country's standard of living and level of development by solely focusing on GDP values. While such an attempt may indicate a country's general economic standing, it cannot demonstrate a population's quality of life. Today, many approaches use social and human indicators to appropriately supplement GDP or other pure and simple economic factors. Poverty reduction, satisfaction of basic human needs, and increases in people's levels of satisfaction with different aspects of their lives in general are steps which have become the main concerns of academia and policy-making apparatuses in this field. Modern societies in both developing and developed countries have valid and reasonable concerns about improving or sustaining individuals' QOL and well-being. Such strides beyond monetary indicators in evaluating QOL lead to a broader conceptualization of the discipline and stronger paths of analysis. In contrast and objection to the GDP and other material/economic indicators, the concept of a Gross National Happiness (GNH) index defines an indicator of QOL and social development. This term was coined in 1972 by the king of Bhutan and has since been used as a mechanism for evaluating the efficacy of governments' and related agencies' policies and programs. Originating in Buddhist values, this concept is part of a more practical analysis of well-being, happiness, and QOL, and counts as a guiding factor in all governmental activities and planning. The principle factors within GNH focus on people and how they interact with their environment: physical, mental and spiritual health; social and community vitality; living standards; cultural vitality; and good governance and ecological vitality. In a similar approach, the US government has introduced an Environmental Impact Statement (EIS) under the national Environmental Policy Act (EPA) to control certain actions and programs in accordance with environmental guidelines and responsible maintenance of the quality of human environments.

In recent years, a new trend in humanitarian science, namely positive psychology, analyzes the reasons and origins of individuals' happiness and satisfaction. Similarly, while traditional psychology mainly focuses on negative aspects of human life such as depression, hopelessness, pessimism, mental illness, or aggression, positive psychology aims to identify the components of human experience that make life worth living. Indicators related to respecting women's, children's, and human rights, social and spatial justice, economic inclusion, and human dignity have become key in any evaluation of well-being and QOL. In similar research, Joar Vitterso demonstrates that Emotional Stability (ES) makes up approximately 34% of the variance in subjective wellbeing (Vitterso, 2001).

Health Related Quality of Life (HRQOL) research has begun diversifying itself into many sub-disciplines, such as children or adult HRQOL or the QOL of mentally or physically disabled populations. HRQOL has also flourished due to medical advances and policies which minimize medical expenditures while protecting vulnerable community members and improving their QOL. In 2004, researchers at the University of Botswana presented a research project on the "Quality of life for persons living with HIV/AIDS in southern Africa," in which they showed how age, education, or income along with variables related to the severity of the illness such as the time spent in bed or number of hospitalizations have affected the QOL of people living with HIV/AIDS (Phaladze et al., 2004).

There are many models and indexes which have been developed in recent years to measure the quality of life of medical patients, like the Functional Living Index-Cancer (FLIC) which evaluates lung cancer patients' QOL. These disease specific QOL research models target a specific population in order to both understand their circumstances and how they fit within the tapestry of larger society. While such research mechanisms are useful to many medical institutions and service providers in supporting those in need, these models are rarely empirically supported and do not fully demonstrate subjective wellbeing or overall QOL.

When performing QOL analyses, researcher may use other factors like political elements to evaluate a population's QOL. At the Institute for Social and Economic Research at the Rhodes University, Valerie Moller attempted to demonstrate through several studies how democracy and political developments in South Africa are interrelated with subjective well-being, QOL, and life satisfaction among South Africans (Moller, 1998).

Still, others focus on the intricate relationships between traffic/transportation systems and QOL. Having led many projects in this field, Ralf Risser demonstrated how increases in the volume of motorized individual traffic (MIV) negatively affect peoples' QOL. He has proposed a suggestions catalog on how to control and reduce the traffic problems, which would directly contribute to increases in the quality of people's lives (Risser et al., 1990). Such approaches may at times sound controversial, as a higher number of vehicles in a society can also indicate a higher QOL.

It is important to note that, ultimately, the above endeavors simply scrutinize QOL in a shallow and constrained fashion. Because of a selective and marginal use of indicators in existing analyses, measures of QOL are in many ways still fragmented at best. As an applied field of social sciences, QOL research spans a wide range of disciplines including sociology, economics, psychology, political science, and environmental studies. A population's QOL assessment may only become significant when a wider scope of indicators is incorporated into the process, especially when the subject is about the overall or universal quality of life. Furthermore, QOL research distinguishes between objective and subjective QOL and how it changes across different domains and aspects of life. It its young history, the QOL field has developed from simple one-dimensional and materialistic analyses into a multi-dimensional, durable, sustainable, and comprehensive approach that includes subjective indicators. Although material aspects in a person's life are important, a society's socio-economic policies and programs also play an enormous part in determining QOL and can lead to more specific analyses of life satisfaction, happiness, and wellbeing.

There are countless works published in the last few decades that propose models, theories, and hypothesis involved in QOL research. According to tabulation from the economics database Econ-Lit, while only 4 papers on life satisfaction and happiness were published between 1991 and 1995, this number reached over 100 articles between 2001 and 2005. If we consider a wider range of related themes in the QOL research and social indicators analyses, this article growth over time would likely be exponential.

Kammann and his colleagues in 1983 tried to analyze the role of happiness in well-being (Kammann, Farry, & Herbison,

1984). In 1974, Alex C. Michalos founded his journal "Social indicators research: An international and interdisciplinary journal for Quality of Life Measurement," and has since then contributed enormously to the field. In 1985 he developed his Multiple Discrepancies Theory (MDT) model to measure the QOL. In this model, he tried to present a new approach in assessing the level of Happiness (H) and Satisfaction (S) among 700 university undergraduates, and had assumed that the (H) and (S) were functions of perceived gaps between what one had and what one wanted. One of the forerunners of the social indicators movement and QOL research today is undoubtedly Heinz-Herbert Noll, the director of the Social Indicators department of the Center for Survey Research and Methodology (ZUMA) in Germany. In his extensive book on social reporting and social indicators, he examines social reporting approaches and social-state monitoring in the context of social indicators systems and shows their different perspectives. In addition, the second part of his work discusses institutions of the welfare state and personal welfare, while the last part focuses on the family and living conditions (Flora & Noll, 1999).

Additionally, Paul Abramson and Roland Inglehart indicate a worldwide trend whereby societies are beginning to shift away from material concerns of well-being toward a post-materialistic system of values which focuses on development of more humane societies, greater democratization, and freedom (Abramson & Inglehart, 2009). When taking this into account then, much of the Middle East, which suffers from enduring autocratic systems and widespread repression and human rights abuses, appears to be moving backward in terms of how its citizens are treated.

Any number of desired factors or indicators can be integrated into a QOL research model, and the factors that are chosen will often vary depending on the relevant culture or country; an element which may be of a high importance in one culture may not be of any interest in another. In addition, a single group's priorities will readily change over a given period of time. For example, technological advances like the speed of an Internet connection or a new communication device may be particularly salient for people in modern societies, but irrelevant for many poor countries in the Global South. However, it ought not be forgotten that the selected factors or indicators must be directly or indirectly measurable. Thankfully, there are many successful scales and models in the social sciences which easily render varied indicators into quantifiable data. If non-measurable indicators are used too frequently, we risk jeopardizing the scientific accuracy and reliability of a research project, making it speculative at best.

In recent times, there are two main approaches have been recognized over others in this field. The Top-Down-Model, for example, measures the global/overall subjective QOL to provide an assessment of important domains. Conversely, the Bottom-Up-Model assumes that a subjective QOL measurement is only made possible by first assessing its different elements or social domains, such as quality of employment, income, health, dwelling, education, or environment. Although both models have been successful in analyzing a population's QOL, an arguably wise approach would be to make use of some combination of the two. The only notable consideration here is that incorporating a large number of mostly meager indicators into the model would make obtaining a scientific result a long and exhausting process. The software package LISREL (Linear Structural Relationships) enables the statistical modelling of linear relationship among variables, which would be a constructive way of analyzing which indicators best explain subjective QOL. Here, it should be noted that a study at the University of Vienna supports the "Bottom-Up-Model," which presumes that different domains in life determine the subjective QOL (Kienberger, 1997).

As indicated in Figure 5.1, findings of another study on the QOL of Kurdish and Non-Kurdish urban populations in Iran indicate how the four main life domains like Lebenserfüllung (fulfillment of material needs), Arbeitsqualität (job quality), Wohnungsgröße (size of residence), and Wohnraumdichte (housing density) fundamentally affect the individuals' subjective QOL and together account for over 50 percent of the variance in QOL scores (Rahmani, 1999).

QOL research in most of the Middle East has not fared any better than social indicators research and has hardly been able to function as a standalone discipline. Here, most small-scale research projects have either focused on specific groups, which are typical in HRQOL analyses, or have incorporated some objective indicators which cannot explain the population's overall QOL. In 1998, a study on Kurdish and Iranian urban settlements led by the University of Vienna (Rahmani, 1999) attempted for the first time to assess the QOL of urban migrants

Figure 5.1

Relationship Between Subjective Quality of Life and Some Important Impact Factors (Social Domains) in the Urban Population of Iran, 1999

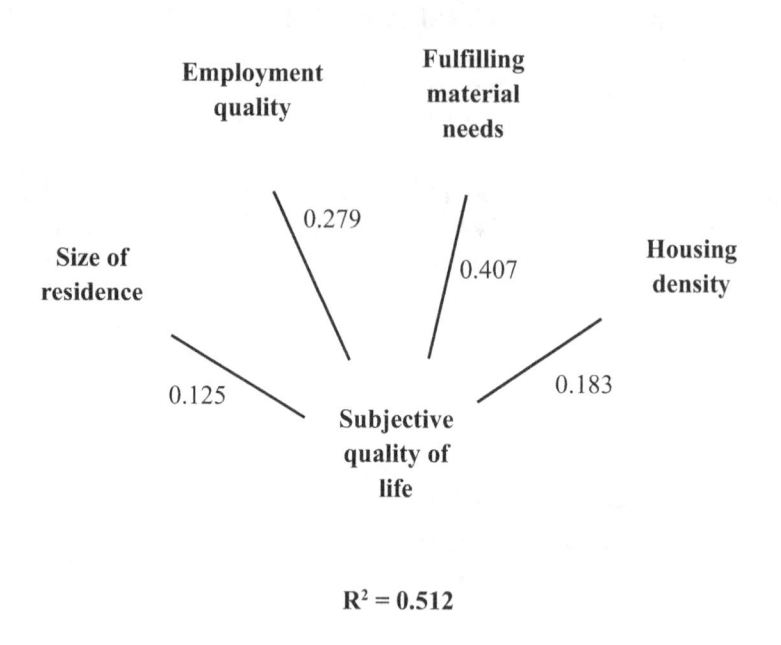

```
     Employment        Fulfilling
      quality          material
                        needs

                 0.279
  Size of                          Housing
  residence            0.407       density

          0.125               0.183
               Subjective
               quality of
                  life


              R² = 0.512
```

Source: Fereydoon Rahmani, University of Vienna, 1999.

---

in Kurdistan and the agglomeration of Tehran. Despite the limitations of such a sensitive, religious, and state-controlled society, the small-scale project managed to reach out to an acceptable sample size. Their results indicate that Kurdish citizens' overall QOL was markedly lower than non-Kurdish citizens in Tehran. The following year, close to 40 percent of Iranians showed a very low subjective QOL, while only 10 percent reported very high QOL. In other words, about 90 percent of the Iranian population experiences a very low to an average QOL, which is horrendous. Additionally, the disparity between the underprivileged Kurdish urban regions and the Agglomeration of Tehran is enormous. While only 2 percent of those in Kurdish regions reported having the highest subjective QOL, the proportion was higher than 6 percent in Tehran. Similarly, the number of those reporting an average quality of life in Tehran was also higher, at 64.2 percent. Out of a total of 272 interviews in this year, 11 people scored in the extreme lowest level of subjective QOL, all of whom were from the Kurdish urban region. A comparison with similar findings from two different research projects for rural Austrian (Schulz et al., 1985) and Viennese (Schulz, Rahmani, et al., 1998) populations show a higher quality of life for all Austrians and much higher quality of life for Vienna's population (see Figure 5.2).

The comparisons of subjective QOL between the female populations of all aforementioned areas indicate significant discrepancies. Almost 35 percent of females report a high subjective QOL in Vienna, while in the Kurdish region it is about 19 percent and in the agglomeration of Tehran only a meager 7 percent. These data (*as shown in Table 2*) indicate that one third of females living in Iranian Kurdish cities experience a very low subjective quality of life while a similar index shows a lower rate of 16 percent for Vienna and 22 percent for the agglomeration of Tehran.

Figure 5.2
Subjective Quality of Life in Different Regions (%)

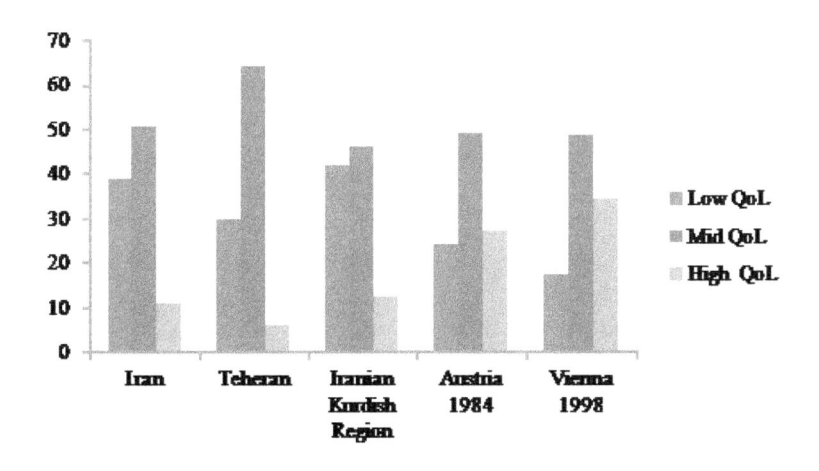

Source: Fereydoon Rahmani, University of Vienna, 1999.

Table 5.2
Subjective Quality of Life in Iranian and Austrian population by gender (%)

	Tehran Agglomeration			Kurdish Urban Region			Austria 1984			Vienna 1998		
	M	F	Total	M	F	Total	M	F	Total	M	F	Total
Low	35.0	22.2	29.9	49.5	33.3	41.7	21	28	24.1	18.3	16.3	17.1
Average	60.0	70.4	64.2	44.8	47.5	46.1	52	46	48.9	48.1	48.9	48.8
High	5.0	7.4	6.0	5.7	19.2	12.3	27	26	27.0	33.7	34.8	34.2

Source: Worlfgang Schultz & Fereydoon Rahmani, 1999.

VI. Limitations of Quality of Life Research in the Middle East and Sensitive Societies

It is no secret that a salient issue in scientific research in many developing countries would revolves around funding allocations and financial problems. However, the intention here is not to discuss the bugetary issues of countries' research programms, but instead outline the socio-cultural, political, and religious restrictions in QOL analyses and identify ways of resolving and addressing these issues without negatively affecting their reliability or validity. In the many closed and undemocratic countries of the Global South, it is often difficult for a scientist or researcher to independently implement a study. In such countries, any research project is controlled by the government or related agencies, and requires initial approval from the authorities. We have witnessed many cases where a research project has been revoked or cancelled in the planning stages or barred from publication if it lacked the government's restrictions and regulations. In other situations, many authorized research findings may become subject to self-censorship, turned into an ineffective iterim/departmental report, even become abandoned or illegalized.

As has always been the case with social research projects, endeavors such as QOL analyses or building a social indicators system in a given country mainly involve human beings and socio-cultural or political interactions between people and society. Any reliable standards for subjective QOL analyses must thus be socio-culturally and politically sensitive. Countless research findings have shown that in measuring subjective QOL, many variables and factors are involved that affect life conditions, people's happiness levels, and degrees of satisfaction differently. These also differ according to the region's culture or political system, or even level of development.

An important factor when analyzing elements relevant to subjective QOL measures, especially in developing or non-democratic countries, is the level of people's satisfaction with the political system or their degree of political participation. In free and democratic societies, questions like "How satisfied are you with the political system in your country?" or "How lucky are you to live in such a political condition?" are straightforward and easy to ask. However, touching on such elements in non-democratic systems is usually problematic and challenging, if not dangerous. Yet, if we avoid such questions and instead indirectly measure political satsfaction in a specific domain, we ought to still be able to piece together effective parts of the population's subjective QOL. One way to curtail this problem is to create general questions without directly pointing at any indicators. For example, "How satisfied are you with your life in this country, generally?". Another way could be to transform questions related to political factors into ones that are oriented around one's participation in decision making processes, such as "How happy are you with your participation in important decisions of your living area, town or country?" In extreme cases, researchers have measured participation in social affairs to indirectly view the effects of political circumstances on a person's life. These could be merged into a more generalized cluster of questions in which "participation in important decisions of the community" would be listed as only one of the items in the questionnaire's design. Such models could look like the following:

How satisfied are you in your life with regards to the following parameters:
(1= Very satisfied, 2= satisfied, 3=average, 4=unsatisfied, 5=very unsatisfied)

1. Quality of environmental programs in the area you live in?
2. Infrasturctures and quality of buildings in your city?

3. Quality of parks, green and recreational spaces in your city?
4. Quality of public and governmental services?
5. Participation in important socio-political or community descisions?

Such sensitive inquiries may thus be concealed within a wider range of questions. Additionally, the questions are designed to give the impression that they focus on smaller geographical areas such as a city, town, or neighbourhood, while in reality the answer could relate to the entire political system of the country. One may argue that since authoritarian regimes do not give their citizens the full right to participate in political affairs, there is no need to inquire about the people's political participation. However, we should not forget that a reliable analysis of people's QOL—especially subjective QOL—in dictatorial regimes that does not include satisfaction levels related to political factors would not be viable. For example, some studies conducted in Latin America indicate a consistent negative relationship between enforced compulsory voting and happiness (Weitz-Shapiro & Winters, 2008).

Some researchers may argue that civilians' levels of political participation]are a result of life satisfaction or happiness, and not the cause. In other words, happier and more satisfied people are more likely to vote and participate in their country's political processes. The answer to such an argument may depend on the type of political system in which subjective QOL is measured. In an authoritarian system for example, any political participation or voting systems are symbolic at best, and people's opinions and role in the political decision making process are very marginal, meaning that talking about such combinations is pointless. This theory may garnish support in countries which experience a democratic process and not restrict political participation.

Beside political limitations in social research projects, we may encounter cultural, societal and religious restrictions as well. The complexity of executing a research project, especially with subjective QOL analyses or other fields in social sciences, is typically two-fold. While many restrictions may be strictly imposed by the government's interferences and controls, others may be enforced by ordinary members of society. In a restricted religious society with overwhelming governmental control, inquiring about people's religious activities—such as investigating the time and frequency of visits to a place of worship—would often prove overly challenging. A successfully conducted student research project on the lifestyles and leisure activities of Iranian youths in 1988 underwent not only self-censorship but also cencorship at the publicatuion stage by the publisher and state magazine (Rahmani et. al., 1988). In this research project, teenagers in the region of Tehran were asked to answer a set of questions about how they spent their leisure time and some of the questions, for example, were related to visiting the places of worship and the frequency of their weekly visits. Although this research yielded controversial findings like low numbers of youths "visiting the mosques and other worship places" in Tehran and a higher rates of "watching western movies and listening to artists like Michael Jackson" (which could help the government understand this vulnurable generation), the results were subjected to censorship.

Such projects have certainly aroused interviewees' fear and distrust during the data gathering stage. Providing answers to such sensitive issues would almost certainly provoke anxiety or tension, especially when an imposing and watchful government is in power. By making the inquiries less direct, more detailed and confidential answers in such situations can be obtained. In the case of the questionnaire model proposed above, the question could be redirected as to ask the "frequency of visiting religous and cultural places" instead of the more direct "How often you visit a mosque on weekly basis?" Sometimes however, cultural and societal restrictions are more of an obstruction than governmental controls, and while this can happen in any culture or society, this resistance will tend to manifest more vigorously in traditional societies. Social demographers have often been faced with difficulties when trying to collect data on contraceptive methods for analyzing family planning models and policies in different cultures and communities. Speculatively in this example, gender correspondence between interviewer and interviewees would positively help in collecting more reliable answers.

Sometimes normalizing the tone and tendency of an inquiry helps investigators obtain responses that are more reliable and representative of the situation. One of the questions which was asked in an analysis of Austrians' quality of life in 1998 involved informants' level of satisfaction with their sexual relationships, which was ultimately completed in a hassle-free and reliable way. When the same inquiry was performed in a pre-test involving Iranian and Kurdish participants in both Austria and in Iran, it encountered more missing values, especially for female respondents. What this means, is that in tradtional cultures like Iran, inquiring about sex–particularly with regard to females— would broach a taboo area of life, as "having sex" normally means "being married" in such cultures and the law does not approve of such occurrences outside of marriage. In such cases, many researchers have synchronized scores involving sexual and marital relationships into one index to minimize the hassle and secure more reliable data. In this case, instead of directly asking "How satisfied are you with your sexual life?" the question was changed to "How satisfied are you with marital-sexual life?" (Rahmani, 1999).

One other restriction in the analysis of subjective well-being could be a general dependence on the mood and memory of individuals being interviewed (Kahneman & Krueger, 2006). Since these elements are strongly determined and affected by the socio-political conditions of the related country, they would indirectly influence the statistical results. Though such problems are not only found in developing countries, peoples' mood and feelings are likely to be affected differently (and more negatively) than in in developed countries because of more volatile socio-political circumstances. The only way to overcome such restrictions and eliminate or minimize these negative effects is to conduct the interviews at different times instead of gathering the questionnaire data in just one or two days of the year. This part of the research project could be spread over an entire season, or samples could be selected at different national occasions and ceremonial events in which people are experiencing different mental and emotional conditions.

VII. Suggestions for Implementing QOL Research in the Middle East and Developing Societies

We understand that QOL research, along with other techniques in sociology and social sciences, manifests within the applied and pragmatic sector of social research. Without becoming involved in the long-lasting traditional arguments positivism and anti-positivism devotees have fallen victim to, QOL analysis and social reporting are undeniable and evident practices in any sociological analysis or social study. By helping decision makers and government agencies properly mold their policies and programs, the applied findings from modern advancements in this field will help to improve people's objective and subjective QOL and will be vital for developing or under-developed societies as well as industrialized countries. Although we might find some institutions in developing countries like national statistics bureaus which may provide a narrow outline of social indicators, a specialized QOL analysis division is rarely found. Even within social science departments of such countries, the study of social indicators and the QOL field still have not taken root.

    A cost effective and efficient means toward building such a system will likely involve assigning a section in existing social science departments for this purpose. A feasible and constructive platform where social scientists and statisticians come together would likely need to first exist within the confines of academia. Since the competency and extent of QOL studies would depend firstly on the academic capability of its instructors and secondly on the institution's financial capacity, it would be more feasible at this time for some graduate or post-graduate social science classrooms to be turned into practical research units. With this, an academic institution would be able to lead the way toward establishing a sovereign social indicators and QOL research center. Employing modern methods and theories, implementing new workable models of field analysis, and involving enthusiastic graduate student groups in comprehensive field research units would be the best approach starting such a journey. A beginning of this kind would encourage further expansion and future developments in the discipline, which would in turn supply the authorities and policy makers of such countries with appropriate data and academic findings. A main concern, however, might be how familiar the students are with the basics of the field research, or in other words, the extent to which they are equipped with the methods and theories of social science research. If most of the participating students are not versed in the essentials of applied field research, a proximity or conjunction with other sociological and social science departments would help prepare and guide such students for this initial propose.

    Such a strategy is of a threefold benefit to these countries. Firstly, it will distinguish the university and affiliated department as a training center for researchers, as the mandate of a progressive academic institution is to carry out research. Graduate programs in QOL analysis and related field research practices are thus fundamental in this regard. Secondly, this strategy will feed decision makers and government agencies directly or indirectly with scientific inputs and findings which can count the backbone of social policy and planning. Finally, it will transform the social science department into a control center, whereby analyses of citizens' QOL become interactive points of contact between academia and society. By the continuous application of such research models and ideas, a mosaic of the subjective and objective national QOL, along with the quality of social domains, would be outlined in a short period of time, which would not only augment a comparative national analysis between different regions but also support a temporal examination of peoples' QOL.

Since one of the pillars of QOL research involves reaching out to as many community members as possible, directly involving community members in the research process would only serve to strengthen the project. This idea incorporates a new form of scholarship into developing countries' academic settings, which encourages dialogue and co-operation between community members, students, and university institutions. In such a collaboration, academia would develop questions to assess the QOL-related needs of the community, which in turn would lead to a dynamic and interactive research model. Such a research model could combine classroom learning with the necessary social action, realism, and scientific authenticity to empower the community and students to address their own needs and agendas, help them to design their own future, and improve their overall QOL. Experiences in more industrialized societies have indicated that community involvement in academic research has led to a deeper understanding of the pertinent social conditions and related problems, and would emphasize the rise of knowledge and skills necessary to prepare studernts for strong civic engagement. Furthermore, such a participatory approach in social research would help the instructors and researchers examine their research project and check the efficiency of their actions. Therefore, at each stage of the research process, including design, questionnaire preparation, sampling, data gathering, and interpretation, they will be able to refer back to various members of the community with whom they have worked. The motto of the Centre for Community Based Research in Canada is "creating a better future for communities through research" and doing research *with* people instead of *on* people. Established in 1982, this small research center has performed over 320 studies and believes that "by demonstrating value and modeling the change we wish to see, we empower communities to take the first step towards social change".

VIII. Conclusion

Any debates on social indicators and peoples' quality of life could easily go back two millennia, and like any other scientific discipline, find its roots in the philosophical jargon of Ancient Greece. But as a factual science devoted to measuring situations, trends, or changes in populations' living conditions and QOL, it may be the youngest discipline in the social sciences and sociological milieu. The first known initiatives that focused on the study of social indicators arose following the Second World War, when nations began focusing on rebuilding their countries' infrastructure and measuring the human effects and consequences of their policies, finacial aids, and investments. This led to a need to establish a system of gathering necessary indicators and parameters that could be used to assess human situations and related changes in society. Many governmental agencies and academic circles have started a movement which later came to be known as the social indicators movement. In the course of such actions, new tools for analyzing and measuring social indicators as well as people's living condtions were introduced. Today, almost all western/industrialized countries in Europe and North America have built several models of social indicator systems, and occasionally publish detailed data on their findings. Some international organizations like the OECD or different UN-affiliated organizations gather many different kinds of social indicators from across the globe.

QOL research and social reporting have been tools and mechanisms in the rapidly-growing social indicator discipline which have helped those in science and politics better understand essential factors affecting peoples' lives in different industrialized societies. As a result, social indicators could be defined as important tools for evaluating a country's level of social development and for assessing the impact of a new or existing policy. Any parameter which shows and/or helps indicate a nation's societal circumstances should be considered significant. Furthermore, if parameters of this kind have a comprehensive and direct or positive effect on an individual, they should also be considered a QOL indicator. Although objective/material elements can affect people's QOL in some ways, the majority of researchers in this area now agree that subjective indicators like happiness, satisfaction, or cognition along with social justice, human rights, and human dignity must be integrated with objective indicators in an unbiased and academic approach to studying QOL. While we could simply consider a country's GDP level to be an indication of people's living conditions and QOL, this would prove to be too much of an oversimplification. There are numerous resarch models which account for additional factors in QOL evaluations, such as health related approaches (HRQOL), Gross National Happiness (GNH), and Environmental Impact Statements (EIS), or Motorized Individual Traffic (MIV) scores, which each partially account for QOL. As condition-related, disease-specific QOL models such as the Functional Living Index-Cancer model target a specific portion of the overall population, their findings shed light on vulnerable parts of communities with respect to specific conditions. However, it is important to incorporate a wider scope of indicators when assessing a population's QOL, especially when the analysis focuses on a population's overall or universal QOL. Furthermore, studies in this area should clearly distinguish between objective and subjective QOL and understand that factors underpinning QOL will differ for different domains, times, and aspects in life.

A researcher may try to assess a society's overall subjective QOL by using the Top-Down-Model, which first measures the overall subjective QOL in order to ascertain what the most important contributing factors may be. In contrast, the Bottom-Up-Model assumes that a measurement of overall subjective QOL is ideally obtained by first assessing its different contributing factors, and then combining the values to get a total score. From this, modern studies on subjective QOL analyses have demonstrated that a combination of both models could best illustrate the circumstances of QOL in a society. Finally Rahmani and Schulz (1999) have showed how the fulfillment of material needs, job quality, the size of one's residence, and housing density fundamentally affect the subjective QOL in both Kurdish and Non-Kurdish urban populations of Iran.

Although social indicators systems and QOL research as fundamental practices in social sciences have not found their proper place in the Middle East and developing countries, they are of vital importance for such countries. Related research in this region could start in a small sociology or social sciences department, and by involving graduate or post-graduate students, classrooms could become dynamic QOL research units. Such a strategy would benefit these countries, as it would distinguish the affiliated departments as training centres for researchers in the field, feed decision makers directly or indirectly with scientific inputs and findings, and provide a means for integrated and collaborative research between the classroom and community to take place.

References

Abramson, P. R., & Inglehart, R. F. (2009). *Value change in global perspective.* University of Michigan Press.

Atkinson,T., Cantillon, B., Marlier, E., & Nolan, B. (2003). *Social indicators: the EU and social inclusion.* Oxford, New York: Oxford University Press.

Bentham, J. (1789). *An introduction to the principles of morals and legislation.* Oxford University Press.

Cyril, J., Gosling, B., Charles, C., & Taylor, W. (2002). *The Greeks on pleasure.* Oxford NY: Clarendon Press.

Flora, P., & Noll, H. H. (Eds.). (1999). *Sozialberichterstattung und Sozialstaatsbeobachtung: individuelle Wohlfahrt und wohlfahrtsstaatliche Institutionen im Spiegel empirischer Analysen* (Vol. 20). Campus Verlag.

Kammann, R., Farry, M., & Herbison, P. (1984). The analysis and measurement of happiness as a sense of well-being. *Social Indicators Research, 15*(2), 91-115.

Kienberger, M. (1997). *Determinanten subjektiver Lebensqualität: Test von messmodellen und subgruppenanalyse nach soziodemographischen variablen.* Vienna: Institut für Soziologie.

Mitchell, W.C. (1933). *Recent social trends in the United States: Report of the President's research committee on social trends, volume: 1.* New York: McGraw-Hill.

Moller, V. (1998). Quality of Life in south Africa: Post-apartheid trends. *Social Indicators Research, 43,* 27-68.

Noll, H.H. (1999). Social indicators and social reporting: the international experience. Canadian Council on Social Development. *Symposium on Measuring Well-being and Social Indicators,* Ottawa.

Noll, H.H. (1999). *Sozialberichterstattung und sozialstaatsbeobachtung: individuelle wolfahrt und wohlfahrtsstaatliche institutionen im spiegel empiricher analysen.*

Noll, H.H. (2002). *Changing structures of inequality: A comparative perspective.* McGill-Queens University Press.

Noll, H.H. (2002). Towards a European System of social indicators: theoretical framework and system architecture. In *Social Indicators Research*.
Noll, H.H. (2003). Subjective well-being in the European Union during the 1990s. In *Social Indicators Research*.
Noll, H.H. (2004). Social indicators and quality of life research: Background, achievements and current trends. In Genov, N. (ed.), *Advances in sociological knowledge over half a century*. Verlag für Sozialwissenschaften.
Phaladze, N.A., et al. (2004). *Quality of life for persons living with HIV/AIDS in Southern Africa*. Bangkok: International Conference on AIDS.
Rahmani, F. (1999). *Urbanizierung und Lebensqualitaet im Iran* [PhD Dissertation]. Vienna: Institute for Sociology.
Rahmani, F. et. al., (1988). *Pankism va shebe-pankism dar Iran*. Tehran: ETELAAT Newspaper.
Risser, R,. et al. (1990). *Strassenverkehr und Lebensqualität*. Vienna: Literas Verlag.
Schulz, W., et al. (1985). *Lebensqualität in Österreich*. Vienna: Fakultät der Universität Wien.
Schulz, W., Rahmani, F., et al. (1998). *Ästhetik, territoriale Bindung und Lebensqualität in sechs Wiener Wohngebieten*. Vienna: Institut für Soziologie.
Vitterso, J. (2001). Personality traits and subjective well-being: Emotional stability, not extraversion, is probably the important predictor. *Personality and Individual Differences, 31*(6), 903-914.
Weitz-Shapiro, R. & Winters, M.S. (2008). *Political participation and quality of life*. Banco Interamericano de Desarrollo.
Zapf, W.(1984). *Individuelle wohlfahrt, lebensbedingungen und wahrgenommene lebensqualität*. Frankfurt/Main: Campus Verlag.

Literature

Abdel-Malek, A. (1962). Égypte, société militaire. Éditions du Seuil.
Abou El Fadl, K. (2007). The Great theft: Wrestling Islam from the extremists. HarperOne.
Abrahamian, E. (1982). Iran between two revolutions. Princeton University Press.
Abramson, P. R., & Inglehart, R. F. (2009). Value change in global perspective. University of Michigan Press.
Adamiat, F. (n.d). Fekre Azadi. Tehran: Taban Publications.
Ahmad, J.A.I. (1983). Occidentosis: a plague from the west. Contemporary Islamic Thought Persian Series, Mizan Press.
Ahmed, L. (1992). Women and gender in Islam: Historical roots of a modern debate. New Haven: Yale University Press.
Al-Attas, S.M.N. (1978). Islam and Secularism. Kuala Lumpur: Art Printing Works.
Algar, H. (2012). Freemasonry in the Qajar period, by online Encyclopedia Iranica. Retrieved from http://www.iranicaonline.org/articles/freemasonry-ii-in-the-qajar-period
Allen, J. (2006). Rabble-rouser for peace: The authorized biography of Desmond Tutu. London: Rider.
Al-Rasheed, M. (2011). A History of Saudi Arabia. New York.
Amanat, A. (2017). Iran: A Modern History. US: Yale University Press.
Amanat, A. (2009). Apocalyptic Islam and Iranian Shi'ism. London: I. B. Tauris.
Amnesty International. (2018). Human Rights Defenders under threat – A shrinking space for civil society. London, UK.
Amnesty International, (1990). Iran: violations of Human Rights 1987-1990. Retrieved from https://www.amnesty.org/download/Documents/200000/mde130211990en.pdf
Amnesty International, (2018). Amnesty International Report 2017/18: the state of the world's Human Rights. London, UK: Peter Benenson House.
Amnesty International. (2018) Death Sentences and Executions in 2017. London, UK: Peter Benenson House.
Anglim, S. et al. (2013). Fighting techniques of the ancient world 3000 BCE-500 CE. Amber Books.
Anvar, K. (1983). Memories, the great opportunity lost: a narrative of Tudeh Party's organization. Tehran: Hafteh Publications.
Arendt, H. (1970). On violence. Harcourt Publishing Company.

Arendt, H. (1976). The Origins of Totalitarianism. US. A Harvest Book Harcourt Inc.

Atkinson,T., Cantillon, B., Marlier, E., & Nolan, B. (2003). Social indicators: the EU and social inclusion. Oxford, New York: Oxford University Press.

Badr, A. (2006). Arabic Research and Publications. Beirut: Baba Sartre.

Bashiriyeh, H. (2011). The state and revolution in Iran: 1962-1982. New York: Routledge Library Editions.

Bakier, A.H. (2006). Lessons from al-Qaeda's attack on the Khobar compound. Terrorism Monitor, 4(6). Retrieved from https://jamestown.org/program/lessons-from-al-qaedas-attack-on-the-khobar-compound/

Balakian, G. (2010). Armenian Golgotha: a memoir of the Armenian genocide, 1915-1918.

Barlas, A. (2002). Believing women in Islam: Unreading patriarchal interpretations of the Qur'an. University of Texas Press: Austin.

Barraclough, S. (2001) Satellite television in Iran: Prohibition, imitation and reform. Middle Eastern Studies, 37(3), 25-48.

BBC. (1992, March). Fahd's declarations on the establishment of a Consultative Council in Saudi Arabia. BBC Summary of World Broadcasts.

Belge, C. & Karakoç, E. (2015). Minorities in the Middle East: Ethnicity, religion, and support for authoritarianism. Political Research Quarterly, 1-13.

Bellin, E. (2004). The robustness of authoritarianism in the Middle East: Exceptionalism in comparative perspective. Comparative Politics, 36(2),139-157.

Benjamin, D. & Simon, S. (2000). The new face of terrorism. The New York Times.

Bentham, J. (1789). An introduction to the principles of morals and legislation. Oxford University Press.

Bergen, P. & Pandey, S. (2006). The Madrassa scapegoat. The Washington Quarterly, 29(2).

Bishop, I.L.B. (1891). Journeys in Persia and Kurdistan. UK, London.

Bligh, A. The Jordanian army: between domestic and external challenges. In Rubin & Keaney (Eds.), Armed Forces in the Middle East (p.150). London: Frank Cass.

Bosworth, C.E. (1999). The History of al-Tabari, The Sasanids, the Byzantines, the Lakhmids, and Yemen, Volume V. The State University of New York Press.

Çelebi, E. (1991). The intimate life of an Ottoman statesman: Melek Ahmed Pasha (1588–1662). SUNY Press, (pp. 169-171).

Center for Human Rights in Iran. (2008). Kurdish teacher facing execution based on "zero evidence". Retrieved from https://iranhumanrights.org/2008/03/kamangar-sentence/

Center for Human Rights in Iran. (2009). Mohammad Sadiq Kaboudvand. Retrieved from https://www.iranhumanrights.org/2009/01/mohammad-sadiq-kaboudvand/

Colaguori, C. (2012). Agon culture: Competition, conflict and the problem of domination. de Sitter Publications.

Cyril, J., Gosling, B., Charles, C., & Taylor, W. (2002). The Greeks on pleasure. Oxford NY: Clarendon Press.

Davidson, N. (n.d.). In perspective: Tom Nairn. Retrieved from https://pureportal.strath.ac.uk/files-asset/4660428/In_perspective.pdf

Di-Capua, Y. (2012). Arab existentialism: An invisible chapter in the intellectual history of decolonization. American Historical Review, Oxford. Retrieved from http://blogs.law.columbia.edu/nietzsche1313/files/2016/06/DiCapua-Arab-existentialism.pdf

DiGiacomo, G. (ed.). (2016). Human Rights: Current Issues and Controversies. Toronto: University Of Toronto Press.

Donnelly, J. (1982). Human rights and human dignity: An analytic critique of non-western conceptions of human rights. The American Political Science Review, 76(2), 303-316.

Duggan, C. (2007). The force of destiny: a history of Italy since 1796. New York: Houghton Mifflin.

Dyakonov, I.M. (1956). Midian History: From ancient times to the end of the 4th century BCE. Moscow – Leningrad.

Elliott, A. (2006, March). In Kabul: a test for Shariah. New York Times.

Esfandiari, G. (2018). Nothing comes between Iranians and their satellite dishes — not even the police. Radio liberty. Retrieved from https://www.rferl.org/a/persian_letters_satellite_dishes_iran_police/24514665.html

Fani, R. (2012).Observation of the region's upheavals after Islamic Revolution: new waves of Islamism in the region. Retrieved from http://www.iichs.ir/Upload/Image/139410/Orginal/6bd50744_3371_4635_8c89_62d6c573d260.pdf

Faramarzi, S. (2018). Iran's Sunnis resist extremism, but for how long? Atlantic Council, JSTOR.

Fard, H.K. (n.d.). Scandal in Switzerland: Imperial court documents on drug trafficking of Amir Hooshang Dolu Ghajar. Retrieved from http://www.rezafani.com/index.php?/site/comments/regionalchangesafterrevolution/

Field, M. (1977). Middle East Annual Report. London.

Flora, P., & Noll, H. H. (Eds.). (1999). Sozialberichterstattung und Sozialstaatsbeobachtung: individuelle Wohlfahrt und wohlfahrtsstaatliche Institutionen im Spiegel empirischer Analysen (Vol. 20). Campus Verlag.

Fox, J. (1998). The effects of religion on domestic conflicts. Terrorism and Political Violence, 10(4), 43-63.

Gates, S., Hegre, H., Nyg, M., & Strand, H. (2010). Consequences of armed conflict in the Middle East and North Africa region. University of Oslo: Norwegian University of Science & Technology.

Gaub, F. (2014). Arab military spending: behind the figures. European Union Institute for Security Studies.

Gerges, F. (1997). The superpowers in the Middle East: Regional and international politics, 1955-67. Boulder: Westview Press.

Georgy, M. (2019). Exclusive: Iran-backed militias deployed snipers in Iraq protests. Retrieved from https://ca.reuters.com/article/topNews/idCAKBN1WW0B1-OCATP

Ginsborg, P. (2014). Family politics: domestic life, devastation and survival, 1900-1950. Yale University Press.

GlobalSecurity, (n.d.). Hanafi Islam. Retrieved from https://www.globalsecurity.org/military/intro/islam-hanafi.htm

Golkar, S. (2015). Captive society: The Basij militia and social control in Iran. Washington, D.C., Woodrow Wilson Center Press.

Grabar, O., Said, E.W., & Lewis, B. (1982). Orientalism: an exchange. New York Review of Books, 29(13).

Green, A. (2014). Why Western democracy can never work in the Middle East. Retrieved from https://www.telegraph.co.uk/news/worldnews/middleeast/11037173/Why-Western-democracy-can-never-work-in-the-Middle-East.html

Gulf News. (2008, July). Iran considering death penalty for web-related crimes.

Gurr, T. R. (1993). Minorities at risk: A global view of ethnopolitical conflicts. Washington, DC: United States Institute of Peace.

Haider, H. (2017). The persecution of Christians in the Middle East. University of Birmingham.

Hallaq, W.B. (1995). The impossible state: Islam, politics, and modernity's moral predicament. New York: Columbia University Press.

Halliday, F. (1993). Orientalism and its critics. British Journal of Middle Eastern Studies, 20(2) 145-163.

Halliday, F. (1997). The Middle East and the great powers. In Sayigh, Y., & Shlaim, A. (Eds.), The Cold War in the Middle East. Oxford: Clarendon Press.

Hedayat, S. (2013). The Blind Owl. Hedayat Foundation.
Henderson, B. (2011). Yemeni rooftop snipers fire at random at anti-regime protesters. The Telegraph. Retrieved from https://www.telegraph.co.uk/news/worldnews/middleeast/yemen/8774911/Yemeni-rooftop-snipers-fire-at-random-at-anti-regime-protesters.html
Horkheimer, M. (1992). Traditionelle und kritische theorie: fünf aufsätze fischer-taschenbuch-verlag. Pennsylvania State University.
Horton, G. (2005). Dying alive, a legal assessment of human rights violations in Burma. Divine Master Print CO., LTD
Human Right Watch. (2019). Syria: Events of 2018. Retrieved from https://www.hrw.org/world-report/2019/country-chapters/syria
Hutchinson, (1961). M. R. Pahlavi, mission for my country.
Ibrahim, H. (2006). The Blackwell Companion to Contemporary Islamic Thought. Blackwell Publishing.
Inman, P. (2011). Mubarak family fortune could reach $70bn, says expert. The Guardian. Retrieved from https://www.theguardian.com/world/2011/feb/04/hosni-mubarak-family-fortune
International Crisis Group. (2005). The Shiites question in Saudi Arabia, Middle East. Report N°45 – 19 September 2005.
Kammann, R., Farry, M., & Herbison, P. (1984). The analysis and measurement of happiness as a sense of well-being. Social Indicators Research, 15(2), 91-115.
Kamshad, H. (1966). Modern Persian prose literature. Cambridge: At the University Press.
Kaplan, R.D. (1994). The coming anarchy. the Atlantic Monthly
Kaplan, R.D. (1996). The ends of the earth: a journey at the dawn of the 21st century. New York: Random House.
Kara, Siddharth. (2017). Modern Slavery: A Global Perspective. New York: Colombia University Press.
Kasravi, A. (1999). History of the Iranian Constitutional Revolution. Amir Kabir Publications, Tehran.
Katouzian, H. (2003). Iranian history and politics: the dialectic of state and society. Routlege Cruzon, London
Katulis, B., deLeon, R. & Craig, J. (2015). The plight of Christians in the Middle East: supporting religious freedom, pluralism, and tolerance during a time of turmoil. Washington, DC: Center for American Progress.
Katzman, K. (2018). Iran: politics, human rights, and U.S. policy specialists in Middle Eastern Affairs. Congressional Research Service.
Keddie, N. R. (2007). Women in the Middle East. Princeton University Press.

Keddie, N.R. & Richard, Y. (2006). Modern Iran: roots and results of revolution. New Haven & London: Yale University Press.
Kermani, N.A.I. (1982). Tarikh-e Bidari-e iranian [history of Iran's awakening]. Tehran, Agah Publications.
Khoramshahi, M.B. (2005). Democracy on the scale of Islam: religious democracy. Tehran: ICRO.
Kianouri, N. (1982). Tudeh Party of Iran and the issues of our revolutionary homeland. Publication of Tudeh Party.
Kienberger, M. (1997). Determinanten subjektiver Lebensqualität: Test von messmodellen und subgruppenanalyse nach soziodemographischen variablen. Vienna: Institut für Soziologie.
Kiernan, B. (2007). Blood and soil: a world history of genocide and extermination from Sparta to Darfur. New Haven: Yale University Press.
Kinzer, S. (2003). All the Shah's men: An American coup and the roots of Middle East terror. New Jersey: John Wiley and Sons.
Klemm, V. (2000). Different notions of commitment (iltizam) and committed literature (al-adabal-multazim) in the literary circles of the Mashriq. Middle Eastern Literatures 3(1), 51–62.
Kürşad, T. (2011). Language and religion: Different salience for different aspects of identity. International Journal of Business and Social Science, 2(8).
Landinfo. (2018). Kurdistan Region of Iraq (KRI) Women and men in honor-related conflicts. The Danish Immigration Service.
Lemkin, R. (2005). Axis rule in occupied Europe: laws of occupation, analysis of government, proposals for redress. Washington: Carnegie Endowment for International Peace.
Levene, M. (1998). Creating a modern "zone of genocide": The impact of nation- and state-formation on Eastern Anatolia, 1878–1923. Holocaust and Genocide Studies, 12(3), 393-433.
Levene, M. (2005). Genocide in the age of the nation state, volume. 2: The rise of the west and the coming of genocide. London: I.B. Tauris and Co. Ltd.
Levene, M. (2014). The crisis of genocide, volume 1: devastation. The European rimlands 1912-1938. Oxford: Oxford University Press.
Lewis, B. (1982). The question of orientalism. New York review of books.
Lewis, B. (2002). The assassins: A radical sect in Islam. Oxford University Press.

Mark, J. J. (2009, September 02). War in ancient times. Ancient History Encyclopedia. Retrieved from https://www.ancient.eu/war/

Marshall, P. & Shea, N. (2011, October). Silenced: How apostasy and blasphemy codes are choking freedom worldwide. Oxford University Press.

Mayer, A.E. (2009). Law. Modern legal reform. In Esposito, J.L. (Ed.). The Oxford Encyclopedia of the Islamic World. Oxford: Oxford University Press.

Mernissi, F. (1975). Beyond the Veil: Male-female dynamics in a modern Muslim society. Bloomington, IN: University of Indiana Press.

McGlinchey, S. (2012). Arming the Shah: U.S. arms policies towards Iran, 1950-1979. [Dissertation]. Cardiff University Press.

Miklos, J.C. (1983). The Iranian Revolution and modernization: Waystations to anarchy. Washington, D.C. The National Defense University Press.

Miller, J. (1985). The embattled Arab intellectual. Retrieved from https://www.nytimes.com/1985/06/09/magazine/the-embattled-arab-intellectual.html

Mish, F. C. (1985). Akkad. Webster's Ninth New Collegiate Dictionary. Springfield, MA, Merriam-Webster.

Mitchell, W.C. (1933). Recent social trends in the United States: Report of the President's research committee on social trends, volume: 1. New York: McGraw-Hill.

Mlodoch, K. (2014). The Limits of Trauma Discourse: Women Anfal Survivors in Kurdistan-Iraq. Zentrum Moderner Orient, Klaus Schwarz Verlag Berlin.

Mohanty, M. (2012). Reconceptualising rights in creative society. Social Change, 42(1), 1-8.

Moller, V. (1998). Quality of Life in south Africa: Post-apartheid trends. Social Indicators Research, 43, 27-68.

Mossallanejed, E. (2005). Torture in the age of fear. Hamilton, Canada: Seraphim Editions.

Nasr, V. (2007). The Shia Revival: How conflicts within Islam will shape the future. W. W. Norton & Company.

Noll, H.H. (1999). Social indicators and social reporting: the international experience. Canadian Council on Social Development. Symposium on Measuring Well-being and Social Indicators, Ottawa.

Noll, H.H. (1999). Sozialberichterstattung und sozialstaatsbeobachtung: individuelle wolfahrt und wohlfahrtsstaatliche institutionen im spiegel empiricher analysen.

Noll, H.H. (2002). Changing structures of inequality: A comparative perspective. McGill-Queens University Press.

Noll, H.H. (2002). Towards a European System of social indicators: theoretical framework and system architecture. In Social Indicators Research.

Noll, H.H. (2003). Subjective well-being in the European Union during the 1990s. In Social Indicators Research.

Noll, H.H. (2004). Social indicators and quality of life research: Background, achievements and current trends. In Genov, N. (ed.), Advances in sociological knowledge over half a century. Verlag für Sozialwissenschaften.

Obiedat, A. Z. (2019). Identity contradictions in Islamic awakening: harmonising intellectual spheres of identity. Asian Journal of Middle Eastern and Islamic Studies, (13)3.

Offenhauer, P. (2005). Women in Islamic Societies: A selected review of social scientific literature. Washington, D.C.: Library of Congress.

Omar, A.R. (2009). The Right to religious conversion: Between apostasy and proselytization. In Abu-Nimer, M. & Augsburger, D. (Eds.). Peace building by, between, and beyond Muslims and Evangelical Christians, (pp. 179–94). Lexington Books.

Orwell, G. (2013). Nineteen Eighty-Four. London: Arcturus Publishing Limited.

Palmer, R. R. (1941). Twelve who ruled: the committee of public safety, during the terror. The American Historical Review, 47(3), 589–591.

Phaladze, N.A., et al. (2004). Quality of life for persons living with HIV/AIDS in Southern Africa. Bangkok: International Conference on AIDS.

Rahmani, F. (1999). Urbanizierung und Lebensqualitaet im Iran [PhD Dissertation]. Vienna: Institute for Sociology.

Rahmani, F. et. al., (1988). Pankism va shebe-pankism dar Iran. Tehran: ETELAAT Newspaper.

Raphael, D. (Ed.). (2016). Social; Determinents of Health, Canadian Perspectives. Toronto, Canadian Scholar's press Inc.

Risser, R,. et al. (1990). Strassenverkehr und Lebensqualität. Vienna: Literas Verlag.

Rain, I. (1974). Mirza Molkom Khan, zendegi wa koshesh-haie siasi-ou [Life and political struggles of Miraza Malkolm Khan]. Tehran: Safialishah Publications.

Rain, I. (1987). Faramushkhanah va faramasuniri dar Iran. Tehran: Amir Kabir Publications.

Rashid, A.A. (2006). Mosque on Wheels Takes Islam to the German Streets. Retrieved from https://www.dw.com/en/mosque-on-wheels-takes-islam-to-the-german-streets/a-2111438

Reality Check, (2018). Pakistan Christian: Which countries still have blasphemy laws? Retrieved from https://www.bbc.com/news/world-46046074
Roberts, H. (2014). Berber Government: The Kabyle Polity in Pre-colonial Algeria, I.B. Tauris & Co Ltd. NY.
Rudaw. (2015). Kurdish FGM campaign seen as global model.
Rubin, B.M. (2002). The tragedy of the Middle East. New York: Cambridge university Press.
R. W. Ferrier (Ed., 1996). A journey to Persia: Jean Chardin's portrait of a seventeenth-century empire. I.B. Tauris.
Safi, L. (2006). Apostasy and Religious Freedom. Retrieved from: http://www.islamicity.org/2845/apostasy-and-religious-freedom/ (retrieved February 20th 2019)
Said, E.W. (2003) Orientalism. Penguin Books.
Samakar, A. (2006). Man yek shooreshi hastam [I am a rebel]. Sherkat-e Ketab-e Los Angeles.
Saman, S. (2019). Stalemate in Victory Bridge]. Retrieved from https://saeedsaman.wordpress.com
Saravi, M., & Taghi, F.B.M. (1992). Tarikh-e Mohamadi (Ahsan Altawarikh). Amirkabir Publications.
Sarhan, A., & Davies, C. (2008, May). My daughter deserved to die for falling in love. The Guardian.
Schmidinger, T. (n.d). Der Mazdakismus im Iran. Widerstand gegen eine Theokratie.
Schulz, W., et al. (1985). Lebensqualität in Österreich. Vienna: Fakultät der Universität Wien.
Schulz, W., Rahmani, F., et al. (1998). Ästhetik, territoriale Bindung und Lebensqualität in sechs Wiener Wohngebieten. Vienna: Institut für Soziologie.
Shafizadeh, J. (2000). Poshte-h pardehaye enghlab [behind the curtains of the revolution]. Nima Verlag, Germany.
Shilani, H. (2019). Mass grave in southern Iraq believed to contain remains of Kurdish Anfal victims. Retrieved from https://www.kurdistan24.net/en/news/cfc66670-b1f2-4415-9c40-ccc296e5d519
Stanton, G.H. (2012). Countries at risk report – 2012, the international alliance to end genocide. Washington, D.C.: Genocide Watch.
Stiglitz, J.E. (2003). Globalization and its discontents. New York: W. W. Norton,
Tabrizi, T., & Rahim, A. (1968). Masālek ol-moḥsenīn [The ways of the charitable]. Tehran: Sherkat-i Sahami.
Tan, Y. (2019). Brunei implements stoning to death under anti-LGBT laws. Retrieved from https://www.bbc.com/news/world-asia-47769964

Telegraph, (2008, October). Hanged for being a Christian in Iran.

Tétreault, M.A. (1983). The organization of arab petroleum exporting countries: history, policies, and prospects. Pennsylvania State University.

Thual, F., & Basser, K. (1997). Francois Thual: Geopolitique du Chiisme. France: Khavaran publishers.

Tian, N., Fleurant, A., Kuimova, A., Wezeman, P.D., & Wezeman, S.T. (2018) Trends in world military expenditure. Retrieved from https://www.sipri.org/sites/default/files/2018-05/sipri_fs_1805_milex_2017.pdf Ibid

Transparency International. (2018). The officers' republic: the Egyptian military and the abuse of power. UK.

United Nation, (n.d.). Convention on the prevention and punishment of the crime of genocide. Retrieved from https://www.ohchr.org/en/professionalinterest/pages/crimeofgenocide.aspx

United Nations (2019). Situation of human rights in the Islamic Republic of Iran. Report of the Special Rapporteur on the situation of human rights in the Islamic Republic of Iran. Retrieved from https://undocs.org/en/A/74/188

Vitterso, J. (2001). Personality traits and subjective well-being: Emotional stability, not extraversion, is probably the important predictor. Personality and Individual Differences, 31(6), 903-914.

Weitz-Shapiro, R. & Winters, M.S. (2008). Political participation and quality of life. Banco Interamericano de Desarrollo.

World Bank, (2016). The cost of war & peace in the Middle East. Retrieved from http://www.worldbank.org/en/news/feature/2016/02/03/by-the-numbers-the-cost-of-war-and-peace-in-mena

Wyeth, G. (2018). A precarious state: the Sikh community in Afghanistan. Australian Institute of international Affairs. Retrieved from http://www.internationalaffairs.org.au/australianoutlook/precarious-state-the-sikh-community-in-afghanistan/

Zapf, W. (1984). Individuelle wohlfahrt, lebensbedingungen und wahrgenommene lebensqualität. Frankfurt/Main: Campus Verlag.

Zisser, E. (2001). The Syrian army on the domestic and external fronts. In Rubin & Keaney (Eds.), Armed Forces in the Middle East (pp. 118-22). London: Frank Cass.